The Politics of the Olympic Games

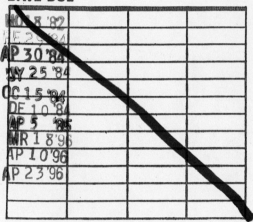

The Politics
of the
Olympic
Games

With an Epilogue, 1976-1980

Richard Espy

UNIVERSITY of CALIFORNIA PRESS
Berkeley Los Angeles London

To My Parents

University of California Press
Berkeley and Los Angeles

University of California Press, Ltd.
London, England

Printed in the United States of America

1 2 3 4 5 6 7 8 9

Contents

Preface

THE MODERN OLYMPIC GAMES symbolize the struggle between man's ideals and the reality within which he must live. Begun in 1896, they revived a system of sport competition in ancient Greek and Roman times which had been carried out every four years over a period of 1,000 years. An idealistic French nobleman, Baron de Coubertin, sought to adapt the concept of the ancient Olympic Games to modern conditions, providing an opportunity to revive and instill in the youth of the world through physical exercise and competition the "virtues" of fair play and soundness of mind and body. De Coubertin's ideal was to reestablish among men, as the basis for world peace and understanding, those virtues which in his eyes had been lost or were rapidly dying out. The modern Games, however, have been utilized not so much for international fair play, peace, and understanding as for national self-interest, survival, and pride. In reality, the world comprises numerous competing groups—be they nation-states, business enterprises, or other organizational entities—and their attendant ideologies, each of which for the purposes of self-preservation and expansion vies for the attention and resources of the world. The Olympic ideal has not been held equally by all concerned. At best a long-range objective, it has receded behind the demands of expediency and self-preservation. The Olympic Games have demonstrated the long struggle of an ideal to become reality.

When Baron de Coubertin revived the Olympic Games in 1896 after a gap of nearly 1,500 years (the last ancient Games were held in A.D. 394), his motives were at once practical and noble. The Baron was first and foremost a Frenchman and only secondarily a world citizen. His major objective was to bolster the lagging fortunes of the French nation by developing strong character and vitality in the youth of France through the spirit of competition and athletic participation. At the same time, the Baron believed the tensions and animosities existing among the peoples of the world could be lessened through the spirit of athletic competition. He envisioned a world of nations participating peacefully but competitively on the playing field rather than meeting violently on the battle ground.

This twofold quality of the modern Olympic Games has remained intrinsic. While Olympic officials have espoused the creed of universal participation for the betterment of mankind, the nations of the world have interpreted participation in the Games as an opportunity to express national identification. The ideal concept of the Games has not been rejected; it has merely been translated into practical terms.

In this light the Olympics take on the characteristics of any other international organization or forum for international participation. As a focus of analysis, it is apparent the Olympics mirror the international structure among nations. The world's two most powerful nation-states, the United States and the Soviet Union, have won the greatest number of medals. (They are not necessarily strongest in proportion to their populations. Avery Brundage, president of the International Olympic Committee from 1952 to 1972, noted that smaller countries sometimes excel in terms of the proportion of medals to total population. See the *New York Times,* 14 February 1960.) At the same time, the rise of the new nation-states following World War II, particularly in Africa, is evident in the national composition of the modern Olympic Games. Differences in national socioeconomic systems are reflected in the Olympic Games. In the Soviet Union and the nation-states of Eastern Europe, the pattern of social and economic relations is carried out by and for the state; thus the state is the financier. Among nations where the market mechanism prevails, such as the United States, state financing is held to a minimum. In each case the pattern of Olympic financing is handled in a similar fashion.

In addition to these obvious manifestations of the international structure among nation-states, a rise in international and transnational organizations can be noted as a consequence of nationalism and nation-states. This aspect of international relations is reflected in the Olympic structure itself, which consists of the International Olympic Committee and the various national Olympic committees. In addition there are international sport federations with attendant national bodies, and sports bodies created by nations or groups whose overseeing power becomes part of this network of associations. An important example is the Supreme Council for Sports in Africa.

The commercial aspect of the Games cannot be ignored. In 1896 this aspect was absent, at least in terms of today's standards, but since World War II the role of commerce in the Olympic Games has mirrored the role of commerce in international relations. The rise of multinational corporations to a position of economic and political strength is vividly exhibited in the modern Games in the development of television rights, commercial products and advertising, corporate contributions to national and organizing committees, and financial rewards for hosting the Games.

The Olympic Games, when viewed both as microcosm of and as actor in international relations, provides a unique opportunity to examine at one time the numerous forces on the international scene. Such a focus comprehends the many competing forces as one integrated whole, permitting a coherent analysis of broad systemic changes through time.

The Games play an interacting role, representing the international structure while remaining a part of that structure. In view of this reality, this study examines the role of the Olympic Games as an influential factor on the international scene and weighs future directions which the Olympic movement might consider in order to remain a forum for international participation.

Attention is centered on the period 1944 to 1976, concentrating primarily on four issues: (1) the evolution of the German question throughout the period, (2) the evolution of the question of Chinese participation in the Olympics throughout the period, (3) the question of South African and Rhodesian participation in the latter phase of this period, and (4) the role of sport federations, international organizations, and business interests in the Olympics throughout the period.

The time period 1944 to 1976 permits identification and analysis of the systemic changes in international relations which followed World War II and provides some perspective on possible future trends. The four major issues effectively illustrate the dynamics of interaction among the various political entities on the international scene. The German and Chinese questions document the evolution of relations between East and West. The South African/Rhodesian question and the roles of international organizations, of business interests, and of sport federations point up the forces for change in orientation, outlook, and allegiance on the world political scene.

Part one of this study includes a brief discussion of the role of sport in international relations, interpreting the Olympics not only as an international sporting event but, more important, as a forum for international participation. A conceptual basis is presented for analysis of the systemic changes in international relations, presenting the Olympics as forum and actor amid the forces and trends that shape the international scene.

Part two involves historical progression and analysis, examining the major issues in the Olympics from 1944 to 1976 as they relate to world events and trends. The period 1944 to 1976 is divided into three subperiods: 1944-1956, 1956-1968, and 1968-1976. All three reflect observable trends in world politics distinct from the others. The first subperiod, 1944-1956, establishes the basic framework of the post-World War II era, dominating world politics with the East-West cold war estrangement. The next subperiod, 1956-1968, while still reflecting the East-West conflict, marks the emergence of alternative forces on the world scene which flower during the 1968-1976 subperiod, altering relationships between East and West.

In terms of the Olympics, each subperiod is divided into four-year Olympiads, each begun by an Olympic Games. Political events at each Olympic Games result from the preceding four-year period, or Olympiad. For example, the XIV Olympiad (1948-1952) is associated with the 1948 Olympic Games, but the political events at the 1948 Olympic Games result from the preceding period or the XIII Olympiad (1944-1948). Hence, for the purposes of this study, the 1948 Olympic Games are combined with the XIII Olympiad rather than with the XIV Olympiad. Subsequent Olympiads and Olympic Games are handled in the same fashion.

By delineating and separating time periods in terms of Olympic events as they correspond to world events, this structure provides a means of examining systemic trends through time, isolating these trends by focusing on specific events and changes throughout successive time periods.

The primary source for this study has been the Avery Brundage

Papers at the University of Illinois, Champaign-Urbana. The collection provides the most definitive material available to date on post-World War II Olympic activities. The Brundage Papers illuminate what has long been an enigma on the international scene—the activities of the Olympic and international sport organizations. They are an excellent resource for explaining and understanding the politics of the Olympic Games.

Because this is first and foremost a political study dealing with sport and sport organizations, it does not purport to glorify or delineate heroic athletic feats. Only those athletic events are included that relate to this overall theme or that specifically symbolize a political trend or event. Similarly, political events at the Games that may have been particularly heinous or noteworthy are considered only insofar as they relate to this overall theme or manifest political trends and events on the international scene.

I am indebted to a number of people who gave time, advice, and encouragement in the writing of this book. Special thanks go to Maynard Brichford, archives librarian at the University of Illinois, for his help, guidance, and hospitality. I am particularly grateful to Fred Warner Neal at Claremont Graduate School for his open mind when I suggested the topic, and for his subsequent criticism, advice, and encouragement. Jack Sullivan and Albert Schwartz of Pitzer College helped enormously with their criticism of the manuscript. Two of my colleagues at Claremont Graduate School—Dean Curry and Jack Janes—were particularly helpful, supplying editorial and conceptual criticism. I owe a special debt of gratitude to Joan Edgar, reference librarian at Honnold Library of the Claremont Colleges, for her unceasing enthusiasm and help. I thank the officials and staff of the United States Olympic Committee for answering my many questions and for making materials available. Finally, many thanks to my wife, Monica, for her editorial assistance and especially for her moral support.

Richard Espy

Abbreviations

IOC	International Olympic Committee
NOC	National Olympic Committee
IF	International Federation
OC	Organizing Committee; Olympic Committee
OG	Olympic Games
SCSA	Supreme Council for Sport in Africa
SANOC	South African National Olympic Committee
USOC	United States Olympic Committee
EC or EB	Executive Commission or Executive Board
UN	United Nations
ICSPE	International Council for Sport and Physical Education
UNESCO	United Nations Educational, Scientific, and Cultural Organization
GANEFO	Games of the New Emerging Forces
OAU	Organization of African Unity
GAIF	General Assembly of International Federations
PGA	Permanent General Assembly (of national Olympic committees)
IAAF	International Amateur Athletic Federation
FINA	Federation Internationale de Natation Amateur
FIBA	Federation Internationale de Basketball Amateur
FIFA	Federation Internationale de Football Association
FIS	Federation Internationale de Ski
NATO	North Atlantic Treaty Organization
OAS	Organization of American States
LAFTA	Latin American Free Trade Association
EEC	European Economic Community (the Common Market)

PART I

SPORT AND POLITICS

1

The Role and Importance of Sport in International Relations

IN 1969, AFTER A SERIES of home-and-home soccer matches between El Salvador and Honduras in the qualifying rounds for the World Cup, El Salvador broke off diplomatic and economic relations with Honduras. The series had ended in a tie—one win for each country —but after each contest, riotous behavior by the citizens in each country had inflamed an already explosive national confrontation. Subsequently, after a playoff in Mexico City which Honduras lost, 4-3, war broke out between the two Central American states.[1]

The idea that two countries would break diplomatic relations and go to war over a soccer match—admittedly over other provocations as well—would seem ludicrous. Obviously passions run high during a sporting event; the competition between the two sides ensures this. But for nation-states to carry the outcome of the sporting event beyond the playing field indicates high seriousness.

Sport is frequently a tool of diplomacy. By sending delegations of athletes abroad, states can establish a first basis for diplomatic relations or can more effectively maintain such relations. Correspondingly, the cancellation of a proposed sport visit to another nation can be used by a state as a means of voicing displeasure with that specific government or with its policies. As a prime example, the 1971 visit of a table-tennis delegation from the United States to the People's Republic of China preceded and set the stage for the opening of long-severed diplomatic relations between the two countries. Similarly, sport can be used by one state as a "softening-up" device to obtain certain concessions from another. By conveniently losing a match, thereby flattering another state, an atmosphere beneficial to the attainment of trade concessions, for example, is considerably improved. In early 1977 the United States, in an effort to normalize relations with Cuba, sent a basketball team composed of players from South Dakota, whose quality was considerably less than the best the United States had to offer. Much to the delight of the Cubans, the United States team lost. The Soviet Union, in order to maintain good relations with neighbors such as Turkey, which lag behind the USSR in athletic achievement, encourages regional rather than national contests. It pits its weaker teams against neighbors such as Turkey so as not to demoralize or shame them completely.[2]

All states use sport as a diplomatic tool, some in an obvious fashion. The USSR makes no bones about the fact. *Pravda* in 1958 stated:

An important factor in our foreign policy is the international relations of our sportsmen. A successful trip by the sportsmen of the USSR of the people's democratic countries is an excellent vehicle of propaganda in capitalist countries. The success of our sportsmen abroad helps in the work of our foreign diplomatic missions and of our trade delegations.[3]

To illustrate quantitatively, as of 1975 the USSR maintained sporting relations with 87 countries and in that year nearly 20,000 Soviet sportsmen participated in competitions abroad.[4] The Soviet Union is not alone. The United States maintains considerable sporting ties and, as would be expected of larger states, can afford to finance large commitments.

The effectiveness of sport as a foreign policy tool derives from its essential neutrality. It is basically a cultural exchange, but unlike a traveling art exhibition, for example, sport exhibits the state's relative sense of political and economic strength through its prowess as a competitor on the playing field. Thus, generically, the competition in sport parallels the competition in political or other arenas, but because of sport's essential neutrality, the competition does not necessarily entail correlative political significance. The political import of sport is only what is imputed, so it can be used for a variety of foreign policy purposes without necessarily entailing overt political significance. Sport can provide a malleable foreign policy tool indicating various shades of political significance depending on the intent, and perceived intent, of the parties concerned.

The role and importance of sport in international relations is not limited to its use in foreign policy. Other actors on the international scene attach great importance to sport, especially to the Olympic Games. The Olympic Games demonstrate this phenomenon through the number of people who watch and participate, the increase in media attention over the years, the passions aroused worldwide on behalf of the competitors and, most convincing, through the controversies created within the Olympics which reflect trends in international relations over time.

An excellent example of this is the debate over amateurism versus professionalism, controversial since the inception of the modern Games in 1896. From the outset the Games were for amateurs only, for lovers of sport who participated solely for that reason.[5] Anyone who had at any time received remuneration for athletic activity was considered ineligible for the Games. Implicit in this rule was the idea of purity of spirit and mind, uncorrupted by material considerations, which served as a guidepost for youth to extend themselves beyond their own material lives, striving for something more important in life for themselves and for society.[6]

When the modern Games were established, sport was considered to be primarily an extraneous pastime. An athlete could participate at the top levels solely for the love of sport. Sport was gaining credence, however, in economic, political, and even academic circles as something exploitable for certain desired results. Business and economic circles saw potential monetary benefits. Politicians saw a means of reinforcing national identity. Academicians saw physical education as a valuable tool for the inculcation of normative values. All these forces were operative in the revival of the Olympic Games and have played an increasing role in the Games, as well as in sport in general. For these reasons the Olympic Games have taken on increasing importance to various concerns. As a result, participation in the Olympics is no longer just a pastime. It is a serious proposition for the athletes and for those others involved, be they nation-states, business organizations, the media, or the spectators.

Looking first at the athletes, it is a truism that in order to compete effectively with the best people, much time and effort is required. Gone are the days when a man could set his cigar beside the track, run a couple of laps and even set a record, then pick up his cigar again as if nothing had happened.[7] In addition to the time and effort involved, both the training and the competition entail a great deal of expense. Today it is difficult for the individual to make it alone without support in the form of subsidation. According to Olympic criteria, if an athlete is to be classified as an amateur, subsidation and even the amount of time devoted to one's sport are, strictly speaking, contrary to those criteria. The athlete is considered a professional even though no direct remuneration for services rendered is implied in the professional sense. In order to compete effectively, however, an athlete cannot afford *not* to be professional to a degree which applies to any top-flight athlete. This problem is not limited to the Olympic Games; it is only more visible there.

Another issue concerns who gives support and in what fashion. This problem is further complicated by international politics. With the participation of the Soviet Union in the Helsinki Games in 1952 after an absence of forty years, the question of "state amateurism" arose. Many in the West, notably in the United States, felt that the Soviet and East European athletes were not true amateurs because they were completely supported by their governments. The Soviet Union and East European governments vigorously objected to this interpretation, stating that their athletes were employed in other pursuits, military or academic, and in any case received no remuneration for their sport competition and victories. Moreover, they argued, the athletes should not be expected to change their way of life to meet the Olympic rules.[8] Avery Brundage, president of the International Olympic Committee from 1952 to 1972, scoffed at the American objections and pointed out that most American athletes were actually supported by universities solely for their athletic ability, a system that, according to Brundage, was essentially no different from state support.[9]

Beyond such cold war polemics is the issue of amateurism versus professionalism with regard to commercial interests. This reached a celebrated point in winter sport, notably in Alpine skiing. Athletes were receiving (under the table) money and openly advertised skiing paraphernalia at victory ceremonies.[10] Since World War II, the sporting goods market has grown immensely and professional sport has proliferated.[11] College sport, particularly at the larger universities, is an important part of the budget and a large income producer. This lucrative aspect of sport raises questions about the amateur status of the participants. Such economic interests forcibly alter the codes of sport organizations, and, more important, indicate the expanding role of sport in society.

Other factors to be considered are the roles of the media, the spectators, and the nation-states. With each successive Olympiad since 1960, the media, primarily television, has paid increasing sums to telecast the Games. The cost of the American rights to the 1976 Summer Games in Montreal, for instance, was $25 million; but ABC Sports spent $40 million to telecast them. The extra $15 million was used mainly for production costs. For the American rights to televise the 1980 Summer Games, NBC Sports has agreed to pay the Moscow Organizing Committee $85 million for the two-week spectacle.[12] These are phenomenal sums of money but the media is willing to pay the price because public interest in the Olympic Games and in sport in general is profitable, both in monetary terms and in terms of prestige and its ancillary benefits to future broadcasting events and programs.

The prestige factor affects the interest and purpose of nation-states in terms of participation in the Games. For example, a state will go to great effort to stand out at the Olympics. In the 1968 Mexico City Games, the American Jim Ryun was favored in the 1500 meter run, one of the major track events. His principal adversary was Kip Keino of Kenya. The Kenyans felt that Keino had a real chance to win if they could tire Ryun out and surprise him. To this end they asked Ben Jipcho, the other Kenyan entered in the race, to be the "rabbit" who would set a fast pace and thus sacrifice himself. The object was to make Ryun commit himself early in the race, draining his reserve energy. Keino was to lay back as in a normal race, reserving his own energy, making his move before Ryun could know what had happened and do anything about it. All worked according to plan. Ryun, though he made a gallant finish, could place no better than second. Keino, and Kenya, got the gold medal and the accompanying prestige.[13]

Prestige is inherent in any major international or national sporting event, because great importance is attributed to the competition by the athletes, the governments, and the spectators. For the spectators it is highly significant to have the team win or the nation triumph, to feel vicarious identification with the individual athletes and their successes and failures. In the 1976 Games when Mac Wilkins, the American world-record-holding discus thrower and eventual Olympic champion, embraced the second-place East German for a particularly good throw instead of his own third-place teammate, the American press and public were aghast, condemning Wilkin's act as nearly treasonous.

While the Olympics express such issues as amateurism versus professionalism, they also manifest more pervasive and widespread conditions in society. The amateurism versus professionalism issue at its basic level concerns only the athletes. The pressures on them, however, are so great and the interests involved so extensive that the issue actually involves much more.

The significance of the phenomenon of sport is not inherent but manifests itself in the uses to which it is put in society. Sport symbolizes the international environment and is also a pragmatic tool of that environment. Its manifold uses serve a variety of interests in international relations, a usefulness that can only increase as the effects of sport become more widely recognized and understood.

2

The World Political Structure

WITHIN THE WORLD political structure numerous forces compete for the attention and resources of the world. The Olympic system is but one of many actors. At the same time, the Olympic Games and the Olympic system reflect the world political structure by virtue of the attention which the other actors direct toward the Games and because of the Olympic system itself.

The Olympic Games are structured in terms of nation-states: the athlete is a representative of a nation-state; the national Olympic committees are organized by nation-state boundaries; international sport federations are composed of national federations that are organized by nation-state boundaries; the International Olympic Committee (IOC) is the umbrella organization for the other sport organizations within the context of the Olympic Games and other Olympic-sanctioned events; and IOC members themselves are considered as ambassadors to nation-state areas. Within this context the nation-state is the primary actor in the Games, albeit acting through the sport organizations. Theoretically the sport organizations of the Olympic system are private and semiautonomous, as are other transnational actors on the world stage. Since the Olympic sport organizations are structured similarly to nation-states, the Olympic system itself manifests traits and actions characteristic of international organizations. Peripheral to but also acting upon the Olympic system are such influences as the media, business, and international and regional organizations. By looking either at the Olympic structure or at the influences upon the Olympic system, three basic forces can be seen at work on the world scene: nationalism, internationalism, and transnationalism.

[*9*]

The unique structure of the Games and the Olympic system closely replicates the various actors on the international scene and also the organizational trends. Through an evolutionary process, also exhibited in the Olympic system, the nationalistic forces appear to be evolving toward more centralized organizational units. Simply put, the pattern is from a feudal (or, in certain cases, tribal) structure, to a national (nation-state) structure, to an international or transnational structure. The nation-state is still the primary actor on the international stage, but the organization of world civilization is evolving toward an altered and less significant role for the nation-state. This analysis does not imply the replacement of the nation-state by a world government. Rather, it implies a global organizational structure approaching a more balanced system of interaction among the various participants.

Some writers on international affairs have concentrated on the nation-state almost to the exclusion of other actors. They have suggested theoretical frameworks to explain the international system which ignore the other actors and their significant roles.[1] Other writers have predicted prematurely the demise of the nation-state, only to recant.[2] The fundamental misconception, on both sides of the issue, involves undue reliance on a few actors for the sake of a parsimonious theory. One cannot rely exclusively on one system of relations in one area, such as the European theater, nor rely on one set of actors, such as the nation-state, and fully explain a world system of relations. As Singer has noted, too much time has been spent on too few actors, with the intent of explanation without first an adequate description of the situation.[3] Basic to these inadequate descriptions of the world political structure is an exaggerated sense of the present. Without historical perspective, the present becomes all important in historical time.

BIPOLARITY AND A WORLD STRUCTURE

Out of the ruins of World War II, some scholars of international relations have derived a false sense of perspective. Many writers have believed that fundamental changes (for example, in state relations and weapons technology) were modifying the world political structure. Viewed in the light of prior history, the fundamental changes actually represented a process of evolutionary dynamics.

One perceived change was from a so-called balance of power framework among nation-states to a bipolar relationship.[4] The latter reputedly resulted from the postwar emergence of two nation-states, the United States and the Soviet Union, as the most powerful in the world. Under the prewar balance of power framework, power had been distributed among several states, each with alliance structures between themselves and weaker states. In the bipolar framework there were essentially two poles of power, each with its camp of nation-state followers.

In each framework the concentration of power was viewed as European-centered, particularly in the balance of power framework and to a lesser degree in the bipolar framework, in which power had expanded somewhat to the North American continent and Asia. The rest of the nations were seen as pawns in the hands of the Great Powers for alliance or exploitation purposes. In the balance of power framework the pawns were the colonial networks; in the bipolar framework the pawns were the European states and the new nation-states emerging from colonial status.

During this process numerous other nation-states with divergent interests were created. This fact points up the fallaciousness in suggesting that any areacentric or bipolar conceptual scheme might comprehensively explain a world system of relations. Fundamentally, the evolution of a concept and a process is involved in the change from a colonial empire system of relations to a vast autonomous system[5] through the emergence of numerous nation-states around the world. The sheer increase in the number of nation-states indicates a broadening of the concept of a nation-state. At the same time it represents an expansion in the alternative sources of power among and through nation-states. The basic issue, essential to any conceptual scheme, is whether the scheme is universally and equally applicable to all major forums of analysis. For example, a bipolar scheme applied to the United Nations, where the constitutional structure provides for numerous powers, does not correspond to the same scheme applied to the question of German unification, which is essentially an East-West confrontation.[6] Bipolar confrontations may exist in both forums, but not necessarily in equal measure.

A bipolar or areacentric conceptual scheme—having as its basis, and many times as its sole actor, the nation-state—is not universally applicable and does not acknowledge numerous other necessary participants. This does not rule out the nation-state, if construed to mean nationalism, as the driving force in world politics. Nationalism is and has been the creative force from which other actors and forces on the world scene have arisen. It represents an evolutionary process wherein abstract conceptual forces, rather than actors or organizational units, are the basis for a constantly evolving world political structure. In this respect a bipolar or nation-state construct is but a part of a much larger process.

NATIONALISM, THE NATION-STATE, AND THE WORLD

In order to describe the role of the nation-state in world affairs, I will consider nationalism as the conceptual basis on which the nation-state exists, and the dynamics of nationalism through time. Nationalism is the concept of man's political loyalty being owed to the nation, the nation defined as a "complex of social interactions (a network or networks), which now has, has had in the past, or aspires to have in the future, a state associated with it."[7] The nation is essentially a "cognitive mobilization"[8] around features experienced in common by certain peoples. Such features might include language, race, and religion—cultural or politico-economic characteristics. These characteristics—a cultural nationalism—describe one phase in the nationalizing process, for that process is basically the nationalization of the state with the end product being the nation-state. For a nation to evolve there must first be the idea of a state, or the actual entity of a state, around which a people can identify and which they can accept. The state then becomes a part of the people, actually, or conceptually, or both. The state is the legitimating bond for the transfer of political loyalty from a local allegiance to one of larger significance. In the words of Hegel, a group or a conglomeration of groups can only become a nation once it has submitted to the state and once the community and the state have "come to the end of the imperial phase of their relations."[9]

As population increases and as technology progresses, the networks of interaction become more complex, placing further demands on the state as governing apparatus. The increasing complexity of the networks tightens the patterns of interaction between the groups, enhancing shared characteristics. Meanwhile, in the middle of these networks, the state is attempting to cope with the increasing complexity of governing the whole structure. A democratization process is required, providing a more sophisticated form of governing structure which at least appears less imperial and more cooperative. That process provides the cohesive bond through which the networks of shared characteristics, cognitively mobilized, are cemented into a nation. By way of historical example, the unification of Germany in the middle of the nineteenth century was the product of increased network complexity, which enhanced the shared characteristics—such as language—then subsumed or bonded together by the Prussian state. France did not really become a nation until the state had been democratized by means of the French Revolution.

If one were to look at the conglomeration of nation-states in the world today, one would find evidence to support the idea that a nation is the product of the nationalization of a state—nationalism being the expression of that process. Few nations today are culturally homogeneous. Language, religion, and other characteristics are generally mixed, as with the Swiss and their numerous languages, or with the Soviet Union and its conglomeration of different races, languages, and ethnic groups, or with the African nations and their numerous tribes and languages.[10] Common to all is the state, which serves as the political bond for the network of relationships between the groups, enhancing those shared characteristics which have been cognitively mobilized through the patterns of interaction.

This is not to suggest that nation-states are fixed and complete. The history of nationalism has gone through many phases and has not been a consistent worldwide movement over time. Whereas it first began in Europe, it is by no means finished there; and its effects in Europe have not been the same in all areas at all times. The French Revolution brought about the final consolidation of the French state, and did so before the consolidation of the German and Italian states. The Pan-Slavic and Pan-German movements have carried over into the middle of the twentieth century; in fact, Cultural Slavism (the identification of culturally distinct Slavic peoples) is still a moving force in Yugoslavia. Elsewhere in the world, the decline of colonial networks following World War II has engendered nationalistic aspirations and the consolidation of nation-states.

Numerous sources of cultural nationalism still prevail in Europe and elsewhere (e.g., the revolt of the Basques in Spain, the Bretons in France, the French-Canadians in Canada, the Ibos in Nigeria, and the Ukranians in the Soviet Union) and many are sources of tremendous instability. But they point up some basic principles and forces at work in the structure and relations of the nation-state. Nationalism as a force is still very much alive, if not stronger than ever, but its structural and characteristic differences around the world have produced different patterns of relations. In Europe, where the concept has existed longest, the environment is most conducive to relations beyond the nation-state, to an advanced integration system. Sources of latent nationalism, however, have stymied that integrative process.[11]

Alternatively, sources of nationalism, in the sense of sovereignty in association with ideological orientations, have created opposing power relationships in response to threats to the sovereignty of these nation-states. As a result, following World War II, a bipolar East-West estrangement occurred between the Soviet Union and the United States and their respective camps, which continues today. The physical size, industrial capability, and military strength of the two nation-states are of such peerless magnitude that competition between the two has forced confrontation on numerous fronts around the world. Many writers have, as noted, viewed the postwar global structure in terms of this competition.

The sources of nationalism, as heterogeneous as they are, have created alternative power centers in other forums. Chinese nationalism has led to an estrangement with the Soviet Union, despite their supposed common political doctrine. The new emerging forces[12]—the Third World—have been relatively successful in aligning in international forums such as the United Nations[13] in order to make their presence felt. At the same time their nationalistic fervor has kept them apart as nation-states. Also, in response to the unequal power relations in the world (industrial capability, military strength), they have developed a kind of separate regional cultural nationalism regarding race and their common underdeveloped economic status.

The heterogeneous effects of nationalism have also created a force beyond nationalism—in a word, internationalism. In its literal sense, internationalism describes a system of relations between nations. Examples include the former League of Nations, the United

Nations, the European Economic Community, and the Organization of African Unity. Like nationalism, internationalism implies a political loyalty, but this time to something beyond the nation-state, to a link between states. The systems of internationalism, however, have not achieved the broader loyalty of the world community. In organizations such as the United Nations the primary loyalty of a member nation-state is to itself, and the organization is used as a forum for enhancing the interests of that member state.

Although the interests of member states are primary in most integration organizations, and although most states deal circumspectly within the organizations, their participation in itself indicates that some aspect of social control is not entirely fulfilled by the sovereign powers of a single state. The Latin American Andean Pact is a good case in point. This grouping of nation-states was created to provide guarantees of economic development for the members; their unification was to permit regional control and to coordinate activities. No one state would infringe on another and, in dealings with powers outside the region, they could present a united front in the interests of each individual unit.[14]

In a similar vein, the United Nations was conceived on the premise that international peace should not be entrusted to agreements between a few states; it was created to provide a forum for the peaceful settlement of disputes. Together the states were to combat such sources of international conflict as poverty, inequality, human degradation, and disease.[15]

The most far-reaching of any integration plan, at that level of internationalism, has been the European Economic Community (EEC). Evolving from the European Coal and Steel Community, the EEC now regulates various practices and spheres of activity which previously had been reserved to the separate member nation-states.[16] The original purpose was to create such a high degree of interdependence between states as to eliminate the threat of another European war.[17] More recently, the function of the EEC has been to maximize its bargaining position, economically and politically, by presenting a united face to the rest of the world, opposing a bipolar situation or any other forces with a counterforce of considerable strength.[18]

After World War II, the Western European nations were so devastated that, separately, they could not support or defend themselves. By accepting aid from the United States and by aligning together in a centralized organizational structure, they were able to become strong once again. Circumstances had forced them together, presenting the opportunity to act upon the realization that nationalism had nearly destroyed their civilization. This realization demonstrated that within nationalism itself lay the seeds for the foundation of an organizational construct going beyond the nation-state.

Operating at another level, the forces of transnationalism are represented by nongovernmental actors working beyond their national boundaries. Prime examples include multinational business firms, the Red Cross, and the Olympic movement. These forces, like those of internationalism, have worked coterminously with nationalism. As a result of the heterogeneous nature of nationalism they have been stronger in certain areas and at certain times.

Prior to World War II the higher level of development in Europe and its more established state structure facilitated the creation of numerous transnational actors such as the International Olympic Committee, making the Olympics an essentially European phenomenon. Following World War II, however, with the rise of more nation-states, and with the increasing degree of interaction among the nation-states and peoples of the world, the Olympics took on a more worldwide or transnational character. In the same vein, prior to World War II, multinational business was only a budding phenomenon, either associated with the colonial network of a country or, if primarily an extractive concern, associated closely with the home governments. After the war, increases in technological development, the decline of colonial networks, and changing conditions in home countries, such as costs of labor, forced many firms to seek not just extractive outlets but also manufacturing outlets in other nation-states.[19] By virtue of their size and the changed international conditions, these concerns became more autonomous from their home states, operating as substantial transnational actors.

Heterogeneous nationalism has been the agent responsible for the rise of international and transnational movements in the twentieth century, and the expansion of nationalism worldwide has fostered the parallel expansion of international and transnational organizations. From 1815 to 1900 the number of international or intergovernmental organizations went from 1 to 30; from 1900 to 1960 the total rose to 192. Most significant, from 1940 to 1960 the number of international organizations nearly doubled from 82 to 192. This corresponded to the tremendous increase in the nation-state system following World War II.[20] Similarly, the number of transnational organizations rose following World War II from 1,012 in 1945 to 1,899 in 1968. From 1850 to 1900 the rise was from 1 to 50. From 1900 to 1905, it went from 50 to 150, but by 1915 it had dropped down to 50. The number again rose steadily to approximately 150 by 1925, but by 1940 had again dropped to 50. After that the number rose rapidly.[21]

An evolving concept of the nation, manifested especially in the period following World War II, has caused a parallel evolution in the idea of internationalism, producing simultaneous transnational effects. On the one hand, nationalism, in conjunction with other factors, has created conflict and competition between nation-states, manifesting itself in various forums in terms of power relationships (i.e., as bipolar or East-West conflict or as North-South confrontation) involving the developed versus the underdeveloped countries. On the other hand, that same nationalism, by virtue of its heterogeneous effect worldwide over time, has produced an atmosphere that supports the concept and the implementation of internationalism, albeit with a nationalistic orientation. This is evidenced by such world organizations as the United Nations, or by regional setups such as the Organization of African Unity and the Organization of American States.

Through combinations of circumstance—such as the degree of interaction or the level of development of nation-states, and the divergent nature of nationalism around the world—transnational effects have been produced which interact with the forces of nationalism and internationalism.

In summary, the nation-state has remained the primary actor in delineating areas and peoples of the world. The divergent effects of nationalism over time, however, have created conditions for coterminous actors to emerge, to interact, and to create an evolving world network of relationships. A more equitable structure of power has thus developed among the various actors on the world stage, dependent of course on the forums and issues involved.

In this process the Olympic Games system is both actor and stage. The Olympic sport organizations are transnational actors. Their structure and characteristics, defined in terms of nation-states, manifest the three trends of nationalism, internationalism, and transnationalism. In this respect the Olympic Games system is also a stage upon which world political forces are displayed in competition. While the evolutionary forces contend in the Games system, the Olympic sport organizations must also contend as actors on the world scene, simultaneously presenting an arena of competition for the display of world political forces.

PART II

THE INTERNATIONAL RELATIONS OF THE OLYMPICS

3

1944-1956

THE MODERN OLYMPICS were founded in the late nineteenth century and reflected ideas essentially characteristic of the rich and the nobility of the Western world. This was understandable, since the founders of the Olympics were all of the wealthy class. But the world within which the Olympics were forced to operate was less characteristic of the idealistic virtues of a French nobleman than of a world where virtue was not universally practiced but was more often determined by circumstance and fashioned to prevailing conditions. That world was the twentieth century, an era of evolutionary and cataclysmic changes throughout the world on a vast scale.

In the first half of the twentieth century the world witnessed two world wars and a worldwide depression. While the Olympics have survived these catastrophes, the world in the second half of the twentieth century has been one whose political structure has been profoundly affected by the cataclysmic events of the first half. The Olympic movement, composed of most amateur sport organizations in the world, has harked back to its nineteenth-century origins for the answers to twentieth-century problems. This has created the essential quandary of the Olympic Games as a nineteenth-century phenomenon operating in the context of the twentieth century, as an ideal struggling to become reality.

On May 8, 1945, Germany surrendered to the Allies. On August 6 of the same year, the first atomic bomb was dropped on the city of Hiroshima, Japan; within a month the Japanese laid down their arms. World War II was over and, as in a game of musical chairs, the actors on the world stage scurried to create anew their respective roles.

The world had just witnessed the most devastating holocaust ever perpetrated against mankind. Close to forty million people are believed to have perished in the disaster.[1] The Soviet Union alone is estimated to have lost at least twenty million of its inhabitants.[2] Europe, for so long the center of world power, had been decimated.

The war had inexorably altered the prewar world relationships. The debilitated economies and industrial capacities of the European colonial powers precluded reassertion of control over their colonial possessions. Spurred on by the inflamed nationalism of the colonial inhabitants, the majority of the colonies were not long in gaining independence. What territorial gains the Third Reich had made during its short existence were entirely wiped out; Germany itself was no longer sovereign, but was divided into spheres of control by the Allied Powers, comprising the United States, Britain, France, and the Soviet Union. The Japanese Empire, built up so assiduously since 1895, was no more; like Germany, Japan was occupied by the Allies, with primary control in the hands of the United States.

Among all Allied Powers at the end of the war, the Soviet Union and the United States stood preeminent. Though the USSR had suffered tremendous human and material losses, it possessed a formidable army with which it quickly consolidated its position both at home and in Eastern Europe. The United States, physically unscathed by the war, emerged "with a tremendously enlarged industrial capacity, new prestige, and greater resources for action."[3]

The European continent was split into two basic spheres of influence: Eastern Europe, dominated by the Soviet Union, and Western Europe, dependent upon the United States both economically and militarily. Most of Africa and Southeast Asia were still under colonial rule, albeit tenuously. Japan was no longer a factor, and China was in the throes of a civil war. South America was still a remote continent subservient to the United States. In consequence of the war, the Allies ultimately joined forces to form the United Nations. Designed to expand the duties of the former League of Nations, the United Nations was expected to cope more effectively with disputes between states, to prevent further debacles on the level of World War II, and to create a forum for maintaining world peace.

In an atmosphere of world ruin and wreckage, the International

Olympic Committee began the process of reviving the Olympic Games. Just as it had affected other prewar international organizations, World War II had crimped the activities of the committee and had forced it to suspend operations for the duration of the war. The International Olympic Committee, however, had successfully weathered the storm and was now ready to revive the spirit of Olympism[4] throughout the world.

XIII OLYMPIAD (1944-1948) AND THE 1948 OLYMPIC GAMES

Following the conclusion of armed hostilities, the International Olympic Committee (hereinafter referred to as the IOC) quickly resumed its work. From August 21 to 24, 1945, the executive commission[5] of the IOC met in London, ostensibly to decide the sites for the 1948 Olympic Games. The cities of Baltimore, Los Angeles, Minneapolis, Philadelphia, Lausanne, and London had submitted bids for the Summer Games, and Lake Placid and Saint-Moritz had done so for the Winter Games. The United States cities were favored by the committee because of the great enthusiasm for the Olympics in that country, but for practical reasons (distance and expense involved in transport), they were ruled out. London, on the other hand, had been picked before the war to hold the canceled 1944 Games. Since construction had already begun before the war in preparation for the Games, it would only be a matter of completing the facilities. In turn, because Lausanne (the home of the IOC) was not picked as the site for the Summer Games, the committee compensated the Swiss by choosing Saint-Moritz as the site for the Winter Games.[6]

From the outset the choice of London was controversial. London had been devastated by German bombs and the economy of Britain was near collapse. The country had gone from a prewar-creditor to a postwar-debtor nation; there was insufficient production of capital to maintain the heavy overseas commitments of the empire and there were insufficient reserves to meet worldwide sterling demands.[7] Food, housing, and transportation were in short supply; in light of the government's imposed austerity program, critics of the Games questioned the wisdom of conducting such an extravagant spectacle under such adverse conditions. An editorial from the *London Evening Standard* read:

A people which has had its housing program and its food import cut, and which is preparing for a winter battle of survival, may be forgiven for thinking that a full year of expensive preparation for the reception of an army of foreign athletes verges on the border of the excessive.[8]

Not only was the choice of London criticized because of strained economic conditions but such a display of nationalistic rivalry so soon after the war was seen as colossal insanity.[9] On the other side of the issue, supporters of the Games and of London as the site of the contests argued that the world was in urgent need of the amity and understanding the Games would promote. As Benjamin Welles, a *New York Times* correspondent, pointed out:

For the British people, weary from two World Wars in thirty years and separated by only twenty-one miles of channel from a Europe split and tense with international strife, the sight of young men and women from the Balkans, from Scandinavia, from Western Europe and from the Middle East, from the Moslem world, from the British Empire and from the Western Hemisphere ... generally competing side by side, will have a tonic effect.[10]

Welles's statement (made in July 1948), like those of others already cited, shows how the London Olympic Games controversy underscored postwar conditions that exceeded the scope of a sporting event. Not only Britain but all of Europe and the Far East were in strained economic circumstances. Beyond the economic situation, matters were complicated by the political condition of the postwar world as a product of military occupation.

The military campaigns of the war had set the course of the developing political strife in the postwar world. At the end of the war the Soviet Army occupied most of Eastern Europe and constructed governments in those countries which were friendly to the Soviet Union, despite objections by the Western Allies to the Soviet methods.[11] Germany had been divided into zones according to prearranged plans of the Allies, but by July 1948 the Western Allies— the United States, Britain, and France—had merged their zones in Germany, pitting them against the Soviet East German zone (Berlin was de facto divided similarly). A currency reform undertaken by the Western Allies in Berlin without Soviet approval was, as the Soviet Union saw it, the "final straw." The Soviets instituted a blockade of Berlin, hoping to push the Western Allies completely out of the Soviet zone of Germany. Stalin is supposed to have said,

"The West will make Western Germany their own, and we shall turn Eastern Germany into our own state."[12] The Western Allies, however, met the blockade with an airlift for the Western sectors of Berlin. This proved successful not only in countering the blockade but in spawning the establishment of a West German state and eventually the North Atlantic Treaty Organization (NATO).

In the interim the European Recovery Program (the Marshall Plan) had gone into effect (denounced by the Soviets as a sellout to "American Monopolists"),[13] primarily to stimulate the speedy recovery of Europe, but also to avoid the possibility of communist takeovers because of the near economic collapse of Western Europe. The Soviets in turn instituted a plan of their own for Eastern Europe. Because of its poor economic position, Britain was unable to stabilize the situations in Greece and Turkey and requested United States aid. This was granted under the terms of the Truman Doctrine. Designed in 1947 to bail out the British in Greece and Turkey, the doctrine was a general treatise on American policy in "assisting all peoples to prevent forcible capture of their governments by minority parties."[14] At issue in the eyes of the United States, was not just the survival of Greece and Turkey, but of America itself.[15] To American policymakers the threat of communism, especially of Soviet expansion, threatened to "undermine the foundations of international peace and hence the security of the United States."[16] The Truman Doctrine became the quintessential policy of containment,[17] setting a precedent for American foreign policy which later administrations could not ignore and which inevitably determined much of later policy as well as of subsequent international events.

On other fronts political lines were being drawn whose patterns would show up in the Olympic Games. In the Far East, Korea was split in half, the North controlled by the Soviet Union and the South by the United States. By July of 1948 the Chinese civil war was almost over, with a Communist Chinese victory in sight. The process of decolonization in Southeast Asia and the Middle East was proceeding apace. The French were embroiled in a battle for control of Vietnam. Indonesia was in the process of getting its independence from the Netherlands. India had gained independence from Britain only to split along religious lines into two rival states —Moslem Pakistan and Hindu India—with disputed territories in between. The overriding issue in the Middle East was Palestine; its subsequent partition, producing the declaration of the State of Israel, provoked a perennial state of war between Israel and the surrounding Arab countries.

The IOC, between the time of the site selection and the Games themselves, had to deal with manifold issues. One issue was the participation of the Soviet Union in the Olympic movement. The Russians had not participated in the Olympic Games since 1912, displaying little interest from that time until World War II. Their competition had been confined mainly to their own country and to the internal development of sport. Following the revolution they set up in 1921, in direct competition with the Olympic movement, a "Red Sport International" that achieved little international success.[18]

In the West little was known of the sport movement in the Soviet Union. Most estimates were mere speculation. The Soviet alliance with the Allies in World War II, however, and Russia's postwar emergence as a world power spawned Western interest in possible Soviet participation in international sport. At the same time, the Soviet Union became interested in taking part in the world of international sport as it had already done in the political and military fields.

Olympic officials considered with trepidation the possibility of Soviet participation in the Olympic movement and in international sport. They had only a vague knowledge of the sport movement in the Soviet Union and they expressed concern over whether the Soviet sport organizations would conform to Olympic rules. But their basic fear was of possible Soviet expansion into and manipulation of the Olympic movement for its own purposes. This reflected the same general fear the West maintained regarding the Soviet Union. In the Olympics, of course, Russian manipulation and direct flouting of Olympic regulations would quickly and effectively undermine an essentially Western institution.

In reviewing past correspondence among Olympic officials, fear of the Soviets is evident. Following the war and the resumption of international sporting events, the Soviets immediately made overtures to participate in those sporting events and to join the international sport federations. By October 1946 the Russians had already participated in numerous international sporting events. Meanwhile, speculation increased in Western circles concerning the conduct of sport in the Soviet Union. For instance, in a letter from

Vice-President Avery Brundage of the IOC to President Sigfrid Edström, Brundage noted an article in the *Soviet News* which stated that the USSR was developing specialist athletes. Brundage assumed they were trained specifically for breaking records. Alarmed at such a prospect he wrote:

So far as I know, the USSR has not joined any of the International Federations. This situation is charged with dynamite and it is quite apparent that our meeting with the Federations in Lausanne were [sic] not too soon. If we are to prevent the machinery of international sport from breaking up and the high standards of amateur sport from collapsing, we will have to watch things very carefully and stop all deviations from our regulations.[19]

In anticipation of a Soviet bid to enter the Olympic movement, Olympic officials did all they could to find out about sport in the Soviet Union. Edström wrote to Brundage describing what he had found:

A newspaper in Switzerland now states that sport like everything else in Russia is organized by the State. There are no clubs like in our countries. It is a committee appointed by the State that runs everything with government money. The leader for the committee is consequently a paid man. His name is Nicolai Romanoff, and he rules 600 stadiums, 14,000 other sport grounds, 6,000 ski jump places and 45,000 volleyball play places.

All athletes that compete in foreign countries are specifically trained at the expense of the State and they are taught to compete in a fighting spirit.

Amateurism is not at all understood. Athletes who beat a world's record gets [sic] paid for it, etc.

Now, what shall we do? Our young athletes all over Europe are crazy to have the Russian athletes participate. I have time upon time sent invitations to Mr. Romanoff, but he does not answer. Perhaps he does not care, but probably he does not know that one should answer a letter.[20]

The Soviet Union, in its attempt to join various international sport federations, had made certain demands as the condition for its own entry. The most common were that Russian be an official language of the federation, that Russian officials be placed on the executive board, and that the federations revoke affiliation with "representatives of profascistic organizations of the Franco-Spain."[21] Brundage's assessment of Soviet intentions was expressed to Edström by quoting a letter he had received from a friend.

My own guess is that the real object of the Russians is to humiliate the West. . . . Every time they force a Federation to break its own rules in order to let them compete, Russian prestige is increased and Western prestige is decreased.

The trouble at the moment . . . is that about half the countries don't want to annoy Russia, and any country which is anxious to obtain a World Championship or a World Congress is reluctant to annoy the Eastern bloc. Finally, there are the individuals with personal ambitions who . . . dare not oppose the Eastern bloc.[22]

Brundage thought the overtures to the Russians were unprecedented and that the Olympic committee had gotten along fine for the thirty-five years since 1912 without the Russians and could continue to do so. He thought the Russians should conform to the rules of the Olympics and the federations, not vice versa.

The question of Soviet participation in the Olympics was involved with the question of Eastern European participation. Beyond that, and more basic still, the real issue was the presence in the Olympics of Communists and Communist countries and the fear of mixing politics with sport (a constant issue in Olympic history). In a telling letter from Edström to Brundage, this point is clear:

There are three Olympic Committees at present asking for recognition, Poland, Hungary and Yugoslavia. . . . The political influence in said countries is now communistic as a communistic minority has the political power in each country supported by Russia, but politics must not mix in with sports, therefore we cannot turn them down because the political influence in their country is communistic. We have even shown friendly tendencies towards Russia which is the most communistic country of all.

I am against turning people down for political reasons. The greatest trouble will be to find men that we can have present in the IOC. I do not feel inclined to go so far as to admit communists there.[23]

For the 1948 Games, the issue of Soviet participation was easily solved. The Soviets, failing to form a national Olympic committee and not asking for recognition, simply did not participate. Instead, they sent observers to the Games. Similarly, the issue of recognizing Germany and Japan did not pose a problem since no national Olympic committees had been formed in those two countries.

The recognition of Palestine, however, did pose a problem.

Before the war Palestine had participated as a separate committee but still, since it was a mandate territory, flew the British flag. Invitations from the 1948 organizing committees had been sent to the Palestine National Olympic Committee. In the meantime the United Nations had recommended the partition of Palestine, and the State of Israel was quickly declared. The Palestine committee then changed its name to the Olympic Committee of Israel and announced its intention to compete under the Israeli flag. The Arab countries threatened to withdraw, however, if the Zionist flag were flown. "In Egypt's opinion, admission of the Israeli team would imply partial recognition of the Jewish state."²⁴ The IOC, faced with a possible boycott, not to mention a potentially volatile situation, solved the immediate problem by declaring Israel ineligible because the Israel Olympic Committee had been given recognition under the national designation of Palestine. Since the Palestine committee no longer existed and since Israel had not applied for recognition, it was declared ineligible.

The general issue of recognition was to play a strategic role in the future. The IOC, by recognizing a country's committee or by recognizing a certain name, in effect was conferring political recognition although the IOC had no formal diplomatic status. An Olympic participant was competing in the name of his country by virtue of his affiliation with the national committee, which in turn was affiliated with the IOC. The Olympic Games, grand and world-renowned, were providing a superb forum for the countries of the world. Each country that participated thereby received de facto recognition, even though formal affiliation was not with the state apparatus. The national name, and participation under that name, became all-important.

Incidents at the Olympic Games have often manifested larger political issues. The 1948 Games, for instance, were characteristic. Tension between the Soviet Union, the United States, and their respective satellites (marking the beginning of the cold war) became demonstrative at the 1948 Games. In 1947 several members of the United States Olympic Committee suggested that it would be a nice gesture for the United States to offer to feed all the Olympic athletes at the London Games. The Soviet magazine *Ogonyak,* interpreting the gesture as provocative, denounced the offer as a "Pork Trick," made to bring profits to American capitalists on their "canned pork" and to provide an excuse in case the United States team were defeated. The magazine predicted that the United States track and field and swimming teams would lose and argued that by offering food to European athletes the United States could later claim, if it lost, that the food had enhanced the physical power of European athletes.[25]

At the Winter Games a controversy arose over recognition of the ice hockey federation from the United States. Two groups were vying for official recognition as the sole, legal United States representative in Olympic competition. The magazine *Soviet Sports* responded to the issue by accusing the United States and Avery Brundage of trying to dictate to the Swiss organizing committee and the IOC which organization they should recognize.[26]

Other incidents included a protest by the Greek Olympic Committee of attempted interference by Communist Greek guerillas with the Greek ceremonies preceding the London Games.[27] In another, an Italian reporter accused the British government of barring him because he was a Communist. The British reply was that, after careful interrogation, they had determined he was a possible saboteur.[28] Finally, because of the failure of the Olympic organizing committee to accede to Russian and East European requests for seats on the committee, Rumania pulled out of the Games.[29]

All these incidents, however trivial, were indicative and symptomatic of larger problems. The XIII Olympiad marked the beginning of the postwar Olympics. In the future the Olympics, as a global media event, would have greater worldwide impact as the ideal forum for the expression of political issues. The formative period for the postwar Olympics—1944 to 1948—was also the formative period for the postwar world. Their beginnings corresponded in terms of the sets of relationships, actions, and attitudes that prevailed. An increasing division into two armed camps was forming with the beginning of the cold war, reflected in the apprehensiveness of the IOC concerning possible Soviet participation. The process of decolonization, producing new patterns of relationships and new enmities, was beginning. Here again this process was illustrated in the Olympics in the context of the Palestine issue.

Nationalism predominated in all of these issues, not the chauvinistic nationalism ordinarily seen in the Games themselves, but a nationalism concerned with sovereignty and political loyalty and manifested through the medium of recognition. The question of recognition thus reflected the political trends and relationships in the world—the beginnings of the Soviet and American/Western European estrangement and of the Middle Eastern conflict over Palestine. Later Olympiads would demonstrate other trends in the progress of nationalism.

XIV OLYMPIAD (1948-1952) AND THE 1952 OLYMPIC GAMES

The 1952 Summer and Winter Games were set, respectively, for Helsinki, Finland and Oslo, Norway. The Summer Games that year would mark the first Russian participation since 1912. More importantly, the XIV Olympiad would be a period of precedents that would haunt the IOC for the next twenty-four years.

The period 1948 to 1952 was the height of the cold war. The Berlin Blockade failed, a separate West German state was formed, the city of Berlin was split, de facto, into two sectors—East and West—and the NATO alliance was consolidated. In the Far East the communists achieved power on the Chinese mainland, forcing what was left of the Nationalist forces to flee to the coastal island of Taiwan (Formosa) and surrounding islands. There the Nationalists set up a government in exile, claiming sovereignty over all of China, to which the United States and the United Nations concurred. The communist Chinese held de facto control, however, and were given de jure recognition by the Soviet Union and its satellites. The Korean situation continued to deteriorate to the point that, in June 1950, armed hostilities broke out between North Korea and South Korea. The United States, seizing the opportunity presented them by the Soviet boycott of the United Nations Security Council, pushed through a resolution committing United Nations forces on behalf of the South to repel the North. The forces, nominally under the auspices of the United Nations, were composed mainly of United States troops and were commanded by the American, General Douglas MacArthur. The Korean conflict lasted until 1953, pitting primarily the United States against Chinese forces and Soviet arms and advisers.

On other fronts the year 1949 brought the successful explosion of a Soviet atomic bomb, sending reverberations of fear through the West; now the United States no longer held a nuclear monopoly. At the same time the Soviets were having problems of their own. The recent defection of Yugoslavia from the Russian fold induced the

Soviet Union to look more circumspectly on its satellites, potential satellites, and border areas.

The IOC was faced with the task of finding solutions to the political problems created by the cold war, primarily to the problem of recognition of new national Olympic committees. The key issue was raised over the recognition of a committee from Germany. Before the war Germany had been a longtime member in good standing. Because of the postwar split, however, two committees had requested recognition from a nationalistic/cultural area that traditionally had been considered one country. Under IOC regulations, only one committee from any country could be recognized as the Olympic representative of that country.

In 1950 at the general session of the IOC in Copenhagen, a committee from West Germany requested recognition. Because much residual bitterness from World War II remained, the membership thought it inadvisable to grant full recognition at that time for fear of a boycott of the 1952 Games.[30] The present composition of the West German committee was the same as that of the former, prewar German committee; thus the new committee was not new in the ordinary sense of the term.[31] During the session an early discussion regarding Japanese recognition reiterated that the primary purpose of the Games was to bring the youth of the world together, and that, as had been the case following World War I, animosities and political machinations should be set aside in favor of this higher principle. Considering all these factors, the IOC granted provisional recognition on the condition the West German committee meet with the executive commission before the next general session to determine if full recognition were in order. In the interim the members of the IOC, in particular Avery Brundage, received considerable pressure from political sources in Europe (i.e., the Allied High Command and the US Embassy in Switzerland) to grant full recognition to the West German committee so that the newly created Federal Republic of Germany (West Germany) could participate in 1952.[32]

At Lausanne (the headquarters of the IOC) in October 1950, the executive commission met and received the delegates from the West German committee. There the West German delegates publicly apologized for World War II and the German atrocities. The executive commission was satisfied the Germans were sufficiently repentant, so they decided to propose the recommendation of full recognition, to be acted upon at a full session of the IOC in 1951. The executive commission further recommended German participation at Helsinki, but not at Oslo, because of the bitterness that still existed there against the Germans.[33]

The political situation in Germany, however, would complicate matters, for while a West German committee was being formed, one was also being formed in East Germany. The IOC learned of this alternate committee when separate East German sport federations sought affiliation with various international federations. In an attempt to cope with the situation in a judicious fashion, and in order not to produce conflicting arrangements, the IOC urged the international sport federations to withhold recognition of the East German federations until the IOC could confer and reach a decision on the matter at its full session in Vienna in May 1951.[34]

The IOC was faced with a dilemma. According to their rules only one committee could be recognized from a single country. In Germany two states had been set up in what had once been one state. Each state had achieved recognition from only a handful of nation-states, and neither could abide the existence of the other. Furthermore, United Nations membership had not been conferred on either. Therefore the IOC, in an effort to get Germany back into the Games and as a favor to old friends from Germany, by means of an executive commission recommendation for full recognition gave provisional recognition to the West German committee. The recognition, however, was not meant simply for the West Germans but for all of Germany. The IOC could have granted full recognition to the East, but that would have acknowledged the existence of two separate states, which the Germans themselves would not accept; further, the IOC would have had to overlook its own rules and to enter the realm of politics.

At the Vienna session the IOC gave full recognition to the West German committee and then took up the question of recognizing the East German committee, whose request had included a proviso for creating only one committee from the German territory. Committee opinion varied along political lines. The Soviet delegate at the same session (the Russians had been recognized and had placed a member on the IOC) stressed that because two states existed, there should be two committees. The Western delegates on the whole disagreed, noting that recognition of two committees from Germany would be contrary to their statutes. Instead, they argued for negotiations whereby the two groups could find a common solution and form a single team for Helsinki. Finally, the IOC president proposed letting the executive commission handle the whole problem, even to the point of annulling, if necessary, the grant of full recognition to the West Germans. This proposal was accepted.[35]

A meeting was arranged in Hanover, but no agreement could be reached. The East Germans, although they had a much smaller population, demanded equal representation; their demand was summarily refused. A second meeting was arranged for Lausanne, by which time the East German position had mellowed. They noted that the West Germans had the requisite number of affiliations with international federations (at least five) whereas the East did not, but that there were a million athletes in East Germany. Furthermore, there were three governments in Germany—West, East, and the Saar—and since the IOC had recognized the West and the Saar, and since reconciliation between the sides was at the moment impossible and premature, the East Germans thought they should receive at least provisional recognition.

The point was well taken. In 1950 the IOC had recognized the Saar region, although it had traditionally been part of Germany. The IOC had done this only to please the French, and now the decision was coming back to haunt them.[36] The IOC position was on infirm ground, but the only response the East German representative received (from Avery Brundage, who was conducting the negotiations) was that the IOC had not recognized a separate West German committee but rather a committee for all of Germany. Under IOC rules another German committee could not be recognized. An agreement was drawn up wherein the two sides would attempt to form one team, while the formation of one committee would remain for the present an internal matter.[37] The East German representatives were reluctant to affix their signatures to the document; as soon as they returned home they were demoted by their government and the Lausanne Agreement was subsequently denounced by the East Germans. Further negotiations would be necessary.

The Soviet entrance into the Olympic fold was less troubled but was nevertheless viewed with apprehension. The IOC was concerned that Soviet athletes might not be amateurs in the Western sense and that the satellite countries might follow the same pattern. A letter from Edström to Brundage evidenced this apprehension.

From the Western point of view we must question ourselves if the Russian athletes can be considered as amateurs. We must face the fact that many of them are professionals. We have thus a different idea of Sport in Eastern Europe and in the West. The question is how shall we proceed in the future.[38]

The Olympic officials (those from the West) would have much preferred Soviet abstinence from the committee, indeed from the Games altogether, thereby eliminating certain problems. At the same time they thought that if they could reach an agreement with the Russians to adhere to Olympic rules, the satellite states would follow suit to the advantage of the Olympic movement itself. The Soviet Union submitted its bid for recognition, and the question was taken up at the Vienna general session of 1951. Much debate centered on whether the Soviets in fact lived up to the Olympic statutes, but most of the members agreed it was necessary to include so important a country in the Olympic movement. The result was a vote of thirty-one in favor with three abstentions. At the same time, a Soviet member was appointed to the IOC to be the IOC ambassador in the Soviet Union.

The East German denunciation of the Lausanne accords was met in Olympic circles with great consternation. The hoped-for single German team had been seen as a great triumph for the Olympics. Now all that effort had been wasted. President Edström called for a February session of negotiations in Copenhagen in a last effort toward conciliation. The West Germans and the IOC members (Brundage and Edström) and Chancellor Mayer (a paid employee of the IOC) arrived at the hotel in Copenhagen early in the morning ready to negotiate. The East Germans, however, because of the circuitous route they had to take from Berlin through Prague, were exhausted from the long trip. While the IOC mediators and the West Germans waited, the East Germans rested. Several times, Edström telephoned the East German delegation in its room, demanding its attendance. After waiting seven hours, the IOC members and the West German contingent gave up and left.[39]

Edström, as a result of this breakdown in communications, resolved that henceforth only one German team would be allowed at Helsinki. Since an athlete could participate in Olympic competition only if he were a member of a national federation affiliated with an international federation and a national Olympic committee —both in turn having to be recognized by the IOC—East German athletes would be able to participate only through the recognized organizations. One German team was thus essential and would be selected by a special tryout, regardless of whether the athletes came from East or West Germany.

The East Germans, however, adamantly pursued separate recognition. The IOC, confused and a little irritated, decided simply to put off the matter until after the Games. All West German overtures to East Germany for joint tryouts were refused and, as a result, no East German athlete participated in the Helsinki Games.

While the situation of the two Germanies preoccupied the IOC during the XIV Olympiad, a similar problem arose in early 1952 regarding China, reflecting political conditions in the Far East. Ever since the communist victory in China in 1949 and the nationalist exile to Taiwan, both factions had claimed to be the sole legal governing body of China. The outbreak of the Korean conflict served to intensify this controversy.

Before World War II the IOC had recognized a Chinese Olympic committee. After the communist takeover this committee, with the nationalist government, moved its headquarters to Taiwan, still claiming jurisdiction over all Olympic sport in China. This committee, despite its change in address, was still recognized by the IOC. Meanwhile the communist regime on the mainland created an All China Athletic Federation, claiming jurisdiction over all Chinese Olympic activities. Complicating matters, both groups became affiliated with certain national sport federations that were affiliated with the corresponding international federations, which in turn were recognized by the IOC.

In early 1952 the All China Athletic Federation began making overtures to the IOC and the Helsinki organizing committee for recognition and for an invitation to participate at the Helsinki Games. An attaché from the mainland Chinese embassy (People's Republic of China—PRC) in Oslo, Norway, was sent to the February session of the IOC to present the PRC case. Knowing nothing about IOC procedures or principles, he spoke "politics rather than sport" and drew the ire of all the delegates. As a result, nothing came of his visit.[40]

That was not to be the end of the matter. Throughout the year, until the Summer Games, the PRC kept up the pressure. In the meantime the IOC heard nothing from the nationalist Chinese or the IOC members for China. One Chinese IOC member lived in exile in New York City, another in Hong Kong, and a third was reputedly in Shanghai. Finland, the site of the Summer Games, recognized the regime of the PRC but not the nationalist regime. Finally, after repeated requests from the All China Athletic Federation, the Helsinki organizing committee sent an invitation. Both Chinese committees sent word they intended to send athletes to the Games which, since China had traditionally sent few if any athletes, Edström and Brundage viewed as pure politics.[41]

Only one committee was formally recognized, as per IOC rules, and there was considerable difference of opinion among IOC members as to which committee this should be. Neither committee was willing to negotiate and form a single team, as had been tried with Germany. The issue was so complicated the president proposed that neither committee be allowed to take part in the Games, thereby alleviating the immediate problem and allowing the IOC to tackle the situation at a later date. This proposal, however, did not satisfy the other IOC delegates. An alternate proposal was passed, permitting both committees to participate in the Helsinki Games in those events in which they had been recognized by the international federations. This latter proposal was presented partly in response to the news the PRC athletes were already on their way to Helsinki.

The Nationalist Chinese, upon hearing of the resolution, immediately withdrew from the Games in opposition. Their presence at the Games, since they only had one competitor, was not sorely missed. The PRC, although reportedly enroute at the time of the decision (July 17, 1952), did not arrive until July 29, too late to compete in their events. So no Chinese participated in the 1952 Games, although they did put on demonstrations.

The IOC decision was immediately controversial. Several observers interpreted the IOC decision as a means of placating the PRC for its failure to obtain United Nations recognition.[42] In Western circles, particularly in the United States, the decision was denounced. Avery Brundage, the IOC vice-president and member from the United States, was castigated for the action. A rather biased observer, the Disabled American Veterans, wrote to Brundage saying:

This organization condemns your action in approving the participation of the Communistic Chinese in the Olympic Games now taking place in Finland. This action is strictly not in accordance with the American way;

particularly so while our American boys are in Korea fighting these same fellow Chinese.[43]

The IOC decision was an expedient designed to solve the immediate situation as amicably as possible until a permanent solution could be found. The IOC was faced with a political situation which it had not created but, by failing to recognize the political situation in time, had nevertheless helped to foster. The IOC had simply not been in step with the times, refusing to acknowledge that the world had changed since 1896 and that sport was no longer divorced from politics. The military conflict in the Far East was bound to have worldwide repercussions because it had been going on for two years and had involved the major powers and many other nations. For the IOC it was not just a matter of taking sides on the issue; it was a failure to recognize a potentially explosive situation.

The 1952 Games were noteworthy in that the Soviets participated for the first time. They only sent observers to the Winter Games in Oslo, but competed in Helsinki. The Soviet contingent remained apart from the Olympic Village where, during the Games, all team contingents normally resided. Instead they set up their own encampment, shut off from the others and unavailable for visitation by anyone, ushering the cold war into the Olympics. In previous Olympics public accusations had been made between the two sides, but now there was open competition on the playing field for the whole world to witness. Nationalism had always been endemic to the Games—their structure reflected and even induced its pervasive influence—but now the nationalistic fervor had reached a high pitch. To the chagrin of the IOC, point totals were kept in the press by both sides and ingenious scoring systems were devised to manipulate the totals. Even the athletes could not escape the nationalism. Bob Mathias, the Olympic decathlon champion, described the mood of the United States team at Helsinki:

There were many more pressures on American athletes because of the Russians than in 1948. They were in a sense the real enemy. You just loved to beat 'em. You just had to beat 'em. It wasn't like beating some friendly country like Australia. This feeling was strong down through the entire team, even [among] members in sports where the Russians didn't excel.[44]

The nationalism that was now becoming prevalent on the playing field was also becoming more evident within the IOC itself. As early as 1947 Avery Brundage noticed in the meetings an increasing split on issues along bloc lines.[45] Member nations which lost a representative through death or attrition automatically expected another member to be appointed from that country, prompting a rebuke from Brundage that members were ambassadors to a country or area, not vice versa, and that a member from a country did not have to be replaced. Member states requested more representatives, and the Russians and Latin Americans requested that their languages be made official languages of the IOC, although French and English were and always had been so designated. The IOC member from Switzerland retorted that he understood the request of the Latin American countries but that, since the Russian language was spoken only in one country, however extensively there, he did not think it was necessary. "We are here to practice sports," he asserted, "and not nationalism."[46]

Finally, the XIV Olympiad and the 1952 Games were noteworthy because a new president was appointed—Avery Brundage, an American, who would preside for the next twenty years. Before his appointment, the Olympic presidency had been strictly a European province. The change was symbolic in the sense that it reflected the changed power structure in the world, just as did the inclusion of the Soviet Union on the committee and in the Games.

The 1952 Games were dominated by the rivalry of the United States and the Soviet Union. Henceforward these two states and their rivalry would remain a factor in the Olympic Games system, but through the process of decolonization, numerous other members would join the Olympics and would increasingly make their presence felt.

XVI OLYMPIAD (1952-1956) AND THE 1956 OLYMPIC GAMES

On the eve of the Melbourne Summer Games of 1956 the Soviet Union moved militarily into Hungary to put down a rebellion. Soon thereafter the British, French, and Israelis crossed into Egypt in order to seize the Suez Canal. Both actions precipitated worldwide outcries and flooded the Melbourne Games with political agitation and tension. In an attempt to curb the political excesses, Avery Brundage, presiding over his first Olympic Games, made the following statement:

Every civilized person recoils in horror at the savage slaughter in Hungary but that is no reason for destroying the nucleus of international cooperation.... The Olympic Games are contests between individuals and not between nations.

In an imperfect world, if participation in sports is to be stopped every time the politicians violate the laws of humanity, there will never be any international contests. Is it not better to try to expand the sportsmanship of the athletic field into other areas.[47]

On the face of it Brundage's statement was a plea for a measure of sanity in the world, but it was also an assessment of the role of the Olympics in the changing political conditions of the time. The Hungarian and Suez incidents were primarily reactions to altered circumstances. The presence of the Olympics in their midst demonstrated—actually and symbolically, because of the particular structure of the Olympic system—the emergence of internationalism and transnationalism on the political scene.

It could be said the Hungarian incident was a product of the Korean conflict—not so much of the action itself, but of the effect it had on perceptions and policies. For the West, in particular for the United States, Korea represented a coordinated Communist offensive dominated by the Soviet Union that had to be more effectively challenged. For the Soviet Union the duration of the conflict, with its small success, induced a reassessment of policy. The death of Stalin in 1953 would hasten this process.

The United States, through a series of military alliances that formed a cordon around the Soviet Union, sought to consolidate its position worldwide. NATO was strengthened, although a European Defense Community (EDC) was defeated because of French intransigence. German rearmament and participation in NATO was assured. The German Federal Republic became sovereign, and the Allied occupation was terminated. In addition to the various security treaties the United States had entered (e.g., SEATO, ANZUS), dual policies were implemented: the policy of "liberation," to "develop a resistant spirit within the captive peoples...as the only effective check on aggressive despotism short of general war";[48] and the policy of "massive retaliation," to contain Soviet probes, as in Korea, to reduce reliance on military manpower, and to increase emphasis on nuclear air power.[49] In effect the United States, through its various maneuvers, announced to the world that the policy of containment of Communism was going to be more actively pursued.

The Soviets, especially after the death of Stalin, began taking a different approach in the pursuit of their objectives. Like the United States, they increased their nuclear arsenal with the addition of thermo-nuclear weapons. For the first time, however, the Soviet Union began to give both moral and economic support to nationalist leaders and movements around the world. Previously the Soviet position had been to denounce the nationalist leaders in the emerging states as bourgeois lackeys of imperialism. At the same time the Soviets began loosening controls on their own satellites and in their own country, while making diplomatic overtures of friendship to such countries as Yugoslavia and Greece and concluding a peace treaty with Austria. The Soviet Union was presenting a more amenable visage to the world while, on the other hand, the United States position was becoming more intractible.

In Europe from 1952 to 1956 the trends of detente and containment were both active. The threat of Soviet aggrandizement was still felt in Western Europe but changed conditions facilitated an altered assessment. Economic conditions were improving; the Korean conflict had ended; there was a thermonuclear stalemate, a balance of terror, and the Soviet Union seemed less averse to negotiation. All these factors pointed toward less reliance on security arrangements. At the same time, fears of Soviet expansion were still prevalent, arguing for more security. Both trends and their implementation depended upon the issues of the EDC and the future military and political status of Germany. The French were concerned about the question of German rearmament and the creation of an EDC, which had the potential for a supranational political control threatening French sovereignty. The French felt NATO would be sufficient to ensure European security, with certain controls over the German role, although it was agreed West Germany would be an equal partner. The result was the defeat of the EDC with an alternative proposal for the reactivation of the Western European Union (the predecessor of NATO) with the power to set maximum force levels for all members.[50] West Germany was restored to full autonomy and, in an agreement between France and West Germany, the Saar region was to be internationalized for production purposes, dependent upon the approval of the Saarlanders.

In the meantime the Soviets had been clamoring to no avail for an all-European security arrangement and for free elections in Germany. They threatened to retaliate by creating an organization of their own in Eastern Europe comparable to NATO. In May 1954 in Poland the Warsaw Treaty was signed by the eight states of Eastern Europe, as a direct consequence of the German rearmament. The German situation was solidified with two definite states. The question of unification, for all intents and purposes, was void. In 1955 West Germany and the Soviet Union exchanged ambassadors, and East Germany in September of the same year became the German Democratic Republic (GDR). All formal controls were ended. The GDR became a full fledged member of the Warsaw Pact, and future questions concerning relations vis-à-vis the two Germanies would be considered between them.

As in prior years in the Olympics, East-West relations in the years 1952 to 1956 were manifested primarily in the German and Chinese issues. The German question was particularly interesting for it closely paralleled local political developments. Soon after the Helsinki Games the East Germans requested that the IOC, at its session in Mexico City in 1953, again consider East German recognition. Their request was at first refused by the chancellor of the IOC for the stated reason that there was not enough time to put the issue on the agenda. The chancellor had been at the aborted Copenhagen meeting where the East Germans failed to show. He, like other IOC members present at Copenhagen, was quite irritated with the East Germans and wanted nothing more to do with them.[51]

On the other hand, the East Germans thought the IOC was playing politics with the issue and persisted in their demand. While politics might have influenced the IOC behavior, the real reason appears simply to have been that the IOC—in particular Brundage—was insulted, both by the East German repudiation of the Lausanne accord and by their failure to appear at the meeting in Copenhagen. Nevertheless, the matter was taken up at the Mexico City session in 1953 only to have any decision put off until 1954. At Mexico City the IOC asked its Russian members to look into the situation and to apply pressure to eliminate the continual attacks levied in the East German press against the IOC and Avery Brundage.

At the Athens session in 1954 the question of East German recognition was again considered. The press attacks had not ceased, and, despite a favorable Russian report regarding the Olympic committee of East Germany, the committee was not recognized. At the Paris session in 1955, Brundage, in reviewing the situation, pointed out that he had told the East Germans that in the future the IOC would not deal with the "Lausanne repudiators." A new committee would have to be organized and, in order to receive recognition, it would have to submit to the Lausanne accords.[52] By the time of the Paris session in July 1955 the East Germans had fulfilled all of these provisions. The representatives from the Eastern bloc strove for full recognition of the East German committee, but they conceded to Brundage's proposal that if the East Germans agreed to one German team for the 1956 Games, provisional recognition would be granted if the agreement were carried through. The agreement was put into effect and a united German team participated in the 1956 Games. Brundage would always view this agreement as a great victory for sport, stating, "We have obtained in the field of sport what politicians have failed to achieve so far."[53]

Despite Brundage's jubilation, the IOC's accomplishment was hardly at variance with political events. By 1955 two German states were assured and, though unification might have been desired by both sides, it was no longer considered feasible. Though the IOC achieved unification for the Olympics, in reality this accorded with the mutual toleration practiced by the two German states. In fact, when in September 1955 the East German state achieved de jure control as the GDR from the Soviet Union, the West Germans did not actually object. They merely threatened to revoke diplomatic relations with any state that formally recognized the GDR, although this provision was not applied to the Soviet Union. In essence there existed two German states with corresponding national Olympic committees.

During the debate regarding East German recognition, the Bulgarian delegate said that he could not understand how the German situation differed from the Chinese, where two committees had been recognized at the Athens session of 1954. He stated:

I cannot see why we should apply two different scales of judgement depending upon whether we are concerned with one country or another. We have in our midst the representatives of People's Democratic China based on Pekin [sic], and those of Nationalist China based on Formosa, although the division of China is of a political nature.[54]

At Helsinki it had been decided to let both Chinese committees participate to expedite a confused situation. It was thought the situation could be sorted out after the Games. Brundage thought it would be unjust to the Formosan (Nationalist) committee to recognize the Mainland (PRC) committee,[55] basing his belief on the notion there was only one China, as in the case of Germany. The political situation was in essential agreement as far as one China was concerned; each of the two countries recognized itself as the sole, legitimate China.

The IOC was put in the middle. Among its membership were those who considered Mainland China legitimate and those who chose Formosan China. The international sport federations were split the same way. Because both Chinese committees had the requisite number of federations for IOC recognition, it was a question of barring either 600 million people or 10 million. Complications delayed PRC recognition. One problem was that the delegates sent to plead the PRC case were, in IOC eyes, political agents and not sportsmen. Each time the PRC delegates appeared before the IOC they expounded political issues rather than sport, frustrating and incensing the IOC membership.[56] Brundage would later state that his main reason for opposing PRC recognition was that he "had not yet met a sportsman from Red China with whom I could discuss athletic matters, but only diplomatic representatives."[57]

Another complication was that the IOC totally lacked knowledge of the athletic situation in China. Of China's three IOC representatives, two were in exile. The third, each time he appeared before the IOC, was accompanied by an interpreter who refused to let the delegate speak in English, which the IOC knew he could do from past experience with him, and the interpreter refused to leave the room when the IOC requested to speak to the delegate alone. At Helsinki in 1952 the president of the IOC, Sigfrid Edström, became so incensed that he banged his cane on the table and demanded they both leave the premises at once![58]

Finally, at the 1953 Mexico City session, the IOC in frustration asked its Soviet members to check on the athletic situation in the PRC and to report back at the Athens session in 1954. This was done and a favorable report was rendered, stating that the PRC Olympic Committee conformed to all IOC rules. There were no Nationalist Chinese IOC members at the session to rebut the report, although before the session, Brundage had privately urged that the exiled members attend. Only the president of the Formosan Olympic Committee was present, and his report was regarded as politically biased because he was not an IOC member. In his rebuttal to the Soviet report he charged that the PRC Olympic Committee was under army control, and that a soccer goalie had been persuaded by a fee of $3,000 to leave Hong Kong for Canton to play "behind the Bamboo Curtain." At this point, Andrianov, the Soviet IOC member, leaped to his feet calling the Formosan committee president "a political leftover," to which the man shouted back, "This is not a political congress!"[59]

In a close vote, 23 to 21, the IOC chose to recognize both committees. In this way they followed the political developments of the day. Their ruling, for all intents and purposes, recognized two separate states: Peking-China and Formosa-China. To that extent they did not sacrifice their rules, for the rules stated that there could be only one committee per country. By recognizing two committees they recognized two countries. Entry into the realm of politics was contrary to Olympic principles and to the Olympic charter, so if one took a neutral stand, as the IOC did, the ruling was in conformity to its regulations and principles.

The recognition was immediately denounced by the Formosan Olympic Committee. The president of the committee complained to Brundage that it was an unfair decision because no Nationalist Chinese IOC member had been present to rebut the Soviet report; he added that the PRC committee was dominated by the government. In reply Brundage said:

. . . don't forget that, according to the Olympic charter the Olympic Games assemble amateurs of *all nations,* no discrimination being allowed on ground of color, religion or politics. When the Red Chinese made application and agreed to respect the Olympic rules, it was difficult to exclude them. Don't forget, also, that if Dr. Wang and Dr. Kung [IOC members from China in exile] had been in attendance as I urged, the score would have been different.[60]

The recognition of China was an expedient. Despite the obvious similarity to the German issue, and hence the contradiction, the IOC was in no position to deny a nation of 600 million people, nor could it run counter to its oath of noninvolvement in politics. The best solution was to recognize both, as the world did in a fashion, and hope that the situation would settle. The situation would not, however, and did not—to the continual frustration of the IOC.

The apparent Soviet relaxation was clarified at the Twentieth

Party Congress when Khrushchev publicly denounced Stalin and announced the policy of "peaceful coexistence." The door seemed open for increased contacts between East and West and for a more independent posture for Eastern Europe. United States policy, however, remained adamantly anti-Communist and, in combination with the Soviet relaxation of control, was bound to precipitate displays of independence in the Soviet satellites that would necessitate some sort of Soviet action.

During Stalin's reign intensive heavy industrialization had been the policy in the Soviet bloc, producing great strains in countries such as Hungary and Poland where the previous economies had been predominantly agricultural. Malenkov, Stalin's immediate successor, concentrated on light industry and consumer goods. In Hungary this change brought in Nagy as the head of the government, producing anti-Stalinist reforms. Malenkov fell from power in 1955 and, in Hungary, Nagy was summarily replaced by the Stalinist, Rakosi; but the reforms had unleashed latent nationalistic sentiments. The Soviet rapprochement with Tito in Yugoslavia and the sweeping anti-Stalin campaign in the Soviet bloc forced Rakosi to resign, to be replaced by the less Stalinist-tainted Erno Gero. The call for reforms in Hungary and the demands for the replacement of Gero by Nagy continued. Combined with Western pressure and other reform movements in Eastern Europe, notably in Poland, a rebellion broke out in Hungary in October 1956, placing Nagy back in power. For the Soviet Union the situation had gotten completely out of hand. If Hungary were to remain in the Soviet orbit, which was in doubt, the Soviet Union would have to step in and put down the rebellion. This they did.

As already noted, during this time (1952 to 1956) the Soviet Union had begun to support nationalist movements throughout the world. The Hungarian incident and the subsequent Soviet intervention delivered a blow to this policy, but the blow was softened by the Suez crisis, which came right on the heels of the Hungarian affair.

During this time decolonization had been progressing in earnest. As new countries and new leaders were emerging, an alternate, nonaligned force or bloc was forming, which was changing relations between the Western and non-Western worlds and was opening up possibilities for other sets of relationships and spheres of influence.

The thrust and significance of this new force is illustrated by two events—the Iranian oil nationalization and the Bandung Conference—both leading ultimately to the Suez crisis. The Iranian nationalization of the Anglo-Iranian Oil Company, although it eventually failed, taught the emerging countries that nationalization was an effective weapon with which to achieve economic independence and express their growing nationalism. The Bandung conference of April 1955, sponsored by the Colombo Powers (Burma, Ceylon, India, Indonesia, and Pakistan) assembled representatives from twenty-four countries of Asia and Africa. No startling agreements were achieved at the conference, but declarations of future cooperation for the achievement of economic objectives, the end of colonialism, and other goals were enunciated. The significant result was the establishment of a sense of common cause as a force to be reckoned with in the world.

The nationalism exhibited by these two events manifested itself throughout the non-Western world. French North Africa was in turmoil, leading to Moroccan and Tunisian independence. In Kenya, the Gold Coast, Nigeria, and French Africa, nationalism was on the rise. Events in the Middle East, particularly in Egypt, most vividly illustrated the emerging nationalism and its accompanying forces.

As a result of the 1952 revolt in Egypt, Gamal Abdel Nasser was able to achieve power, institute needed reforms, and become the beacon for emerging nations. In 1955 he concluded an arms deal for Egyptian cotton with the Soviet Union and simultaneously negotiated with a Western consortium for the financing of the Aswan Dam, effectively dramatizing the non-Western world's desire for nonalignment. The Soviet deal underscored the new policy of Soviet overtures of aid to new nations. The Soviets also made an offer to Nasser on the Aswan Dam. The United States reacted in typical fashion to the arms deal. They did not like it, but above all they did not like Nasser's policy of "riding the fence." For various reasons, though the arms deal was the primary reason, Secretary of State Dulles announced that the United States was withdrawing from the tentative agreement already reached with the consortium for the financing of the dam.

Nasser received the news while he was in Yugoslavia conferring with Tito, another leader of the nonaligned nationalist forces. A week later Nasser announced the nationalization of the Suez Canal.

The immediate reactions were as expected. The French and British denounced the action and called for the internationalization of the canal. Economic pressures such as the freezing of Egyptian assets in Britain, in which the United States joined, did not work. In order to show that the Egyptians could not run the canal, Western pilots walked off the job. They were replaced by Egyptian, Russian, and Yugoslav pilots who managed quite capably.

In the meantime the role of Israel, always a sore point in Western-Arab relations, became important. Recent armed border exchanges had heightened tensions in the area. The Soviet supply of arms caused the Israelis to feel increasingly threatened. Jordanian pronouncements for an attack on Israel propelled the Israelis on October 29, 1956, to mobilize and attack Egypt while it was embroiled in the controversy over the canal.

The French and British, the Western states most actively interested in free passage through the canal, gave an ultimatum to the Egyptians and Israelis to withdraw ten miles on either side of the canal. Failing this, on October 31 France and Britain bombarded Egyptian targets and invaded, moving toward the canal. Egypt blocked the canal with scuttled ships. The United States, despite the Tripartite Declaration of 1950,[61] sided with the Soviet Union in calling for a cease-fire. Through the combination of the possibility of direct Soviet intervention, the military and economic pressure on both Britain and France, the wreckage of pipelines by Egyptian sympathizers in Iraq and Syria, which effectively cut off Britain's and France's oil supply, and the creation of UNEF as a peace-keeping force between Israel and Egypt, the hostilities finally ceased.

The Suez affair was important for several reasons. It signalled the decline of European influence in the Middle East and the rise of American and Soviet influence. Nasser's prestige was heightened, not only in the Middle East but in the non-Western world, as a symbol of the nonaligned nationalist forces in the world. The unlikely Soviet-United States collaboration illustrated the processes of lessening cold war tensions and of instituting peaceful coexistence. Soviet influence, increasing in the Middle East, represented a process that had been occurring throughout the non-Western world. The Suez incident was a face-saving device for the Soviet Union, because it drew attention away from the Hungarian intervention. With the United States pledge not to interfere in Hungary and with the United States-Soviet alignment on Suez, peaceful coexistence had become in part a reality. United States policies of liberation and massive retaliation had been shown to be mere rhetoric.

In conjunction with the processes of decolonization and of increasing nationalism on the world scene, there was an increase in nationalism in the Olympics. While nationalism in the Olympics was the product of an increasing number of national Olympic committees, the issue of nationalism, as in the political sphere, was imbued with elements of the East-West conflict. Of course there were always political accusations, but in the Olympics the issue of nationalism and its attendant elements was exhibited in such issues as government interference and amateurism.

Nationalism was never a stranger to the Olympics. As noted before, the issue had been discussed numerous times, and by the very structure of the committee and the Games, some nationalism was bound to interfere. The 1936 Games in Germany were a prime historical example. What was becoming more prevalent in the postwar period, particularly as the size of the committee and the number of national affiliations increased,[62] was nationalism within the committee and government interference both in the IOC and in the national committees. In a communiqué sent by Brundage to members of the IOC, the president detailed these trends and the reasons behind the creation of the committee structure.

The original committee members were chosen by the founder, Baron de Coubertin; later members were elected by the committee at large upon nomination by one of the existing members. They were selected for their devotion to sport and to the Olympic movement (which to the committee were one and the same thing), and they were considered ambassadors *to* their countries. They were financially independent and had no political connections. Members were to be free from economic and political pressures and their viewpoints were to be international.

They could be counted on to support whatever was for the interest of the Olympic Movement even against their own country or the particular sport or sports in which they had a personal interest. The committee was made self-perpetuating.[63]

At the beginning the members, in many cases, established national committees in their countries, assuring fidelity to the Olympic principles. There were to be only three members from a country on the

IOC, and the character of the individual, not his country, was the criteria for selection. The homogeneous character of these individuals produced a type of "Olympic family."

Following World War II, these considerations for selection and the viewpoints of the individuals changed. Many new countries insisted on having representatives on the committee, and, among the members on the committee, blocs were forming such as the European bloc, the Latin bloc, and the iron curtain bloc. In addition numerous countries insisted on choosing their own representatives.

The impact of the blocs was evident on particular issues, such as voting for the recognition of various national Olympic committees, as with East Germany and the PRC. It also was apparent in issues such as the voting on new members, or the voting on and nominating of members for positions on the executive board. For example, at the general session in Mexico in 1953 a replacement board member was needed. The Cuban delegate had been nominated. The Bulgarian member nominated one of the Soviet delegates, "in order that the countries belonging to the popular Democracies' group should be represented on the E.C. (Executive Commission or board), no political reason being implied by this."[64] The Cuban delegate was elected, twenty-seven to five. After announcement of the result, another delegate expressed the wish that in the future no member would be put forward as the representative of a particular group. "We are here," he said, entreating all the members, as "above all, an Olympic family, representing one group only: that of the Olympic ideal."[65] Brundage's concern was well taken, but would not necessarily be heeded in the future.

In the affiliated national organizations, nationalism was becoming an even more prominent factor than in the IOC. Part of the reason, as Brundage noted, was a general lack of understanding of Olympic principles; and many national committees had been created by individuals not associated with the IOC. But the overriding reason was the propaganda effect of the Olympics. As an Olympic participant, a country received recognition. If it were successful in the Games its prestige was enhanced. As an IOC member expressed to Brundage:

L'esprit de nationalisme entre les concurrents a toujours existé et ne pourra jamais être évité. Le nationalisme stimule l'athlète qui fournit tout son effort pour vaincre. Les anciens se battaient pour l'honneur de leur ville et aujourd'hui ils se battent pour l'honneur de leur Nation.[66]

In many countries each national Olympic committee was almost entirely, if not completely, financed by the state. In such instances, for the price of financing the committee, the state demanded some choice in how the committee was going to be run. As of 1952, sixty-nine committees were recognized. Of the forty who answered a financial questionnaire, thirteen received total government support; six received support from public contributions only; the rest arranged financing through a combination of government support, lotteries, and public donations.[67] By 1954 the number of committees had grown to eighty, and most of the new committees were from non-Western, former colonial areas. The majority of these were state financed.

Nationalism and the question of political interference went beyond the mere control of a national committee into the whole conduct of sport. This was most evident in the issue of amateurism. Under Olympic principles and rules an athlete was to receive no compensation for competing other than for the everyday expenses incurred while participating; the theory was that an athlete's participation was purely an avocation and not a vocation.

Soon after the 1952 Games and the participation of the Soviet Union, state amateurism became a burning issue. Stimulated by the East-West controversy, there was much concern that the Soviet bloc countries had an unfair advantage because their athletes were financed by the state; further, they trained so extensively that sport in those countries was really a vocation. In a letter on the issue to all national committees, international federations, and IOC members, Brundage cited as an example the Polish training camps, of four months' duration, for boxers preparing for the European championships. He noted that "only very few professionals can afford a preparation like that of the Polish boxers."[68] Brundage received so much vitriol for this letter that in order to mollify certain groups he was forced to retract and modify his statements. Newspapers such as *Soviet Sport* attacked his statements as products of the "ideology of American imperialism and intelligence organs of the United States to help...undermine the bases of European national sovereignty."[69] In response, Brundage argued that his statements were not solely directed at iron curtain countries, and that reports had been received telling of less than amateur activities on either side of the curtain.

The question of state amateurism also involved what was deemed "payment for broken time," wherein an athlete would receive compensation for time lost from his vocation and expenses for his family. Such compensation was strictly prohibited by the IOC. The most common argument in support of broken time was highly nationalistic, "that an athlete [was] like a soldier defending his country's athletic reputation. . . ."[70] But even Brundage could not resist some nationalistic sentiment. After the strong Soviet showing at the 1956 Winter Games, he warned the United States that if it hoped to meet the Russian challenge it must alter its concept of amateur sports. "It is against the Olympic idea to throw one nation against another," he argued, "but we cannot ignore the fact that Russia is putting tremendous emphasis on the development of its athletes."[71]

The IOC, faced with the growing problems of state amateurism and excessive nationalism leading to government interference in the IOC and control of national Olympic committees, saw that the problems concerned not only the IOC but the sport world in general. Because the IOC considered the Olympic movement and sport to be one and the same thing, it sought to coordinate policies among itself, the national committees, and the international federations through various rule changes and increased conferences between the organizations. All of this was to facilitate closer cooperation. In several instances, this cooperation had already been rendered automatic through the process of waiting for an IOC decision on an issue, such as East German recognition, before the major federations proceeded accordingly. A prime example was the action taken on the East German question by the International Amateur Athletic Federation (IAAF), the largest and most influential federation. The IAAF president was Lord David Lloyd Burghley (later the Marquess of Exeter), also an IOC member, who in 1956 persuaded the East German Athletic Federation to agree to one body, called "Germany," to be affiliated with the IAAF with two addresses—one for the West Germans and one for the East. Of the five delegates, three would be West German and two would be East German.[72]

Because not all federations followed the IOC lead, situations arose, as in the case of the recognition of the two Chinas, where some international federations recognized and affiliated with one committee and others with another. In an effort to remedy such discrepancies, particularly with regard to governmental control of national committees, the IOC inserted the provision in its rules that national committees must be composed of delegates elected by national federations and that the national federations must have voting control of the national committees. At the same time, no member of a committee could also be a member of his government.[73] These changes necessitated closer scrutiny of the national situation by the various international federations concerned.

While the IOC was making rule changes and calling for closer cooperation between the amateur sport organizations, an increasing obstacle was the deep desire of the international federations for sovereignty over their respective sports. The IOC call for closer cooperation was viewed by many delegations as a threat to their authority. This was cogently conveyed by the president of the rowing federation, in response to Lord Burghley's call for a closer relationship between the international federations and the IOC. He could not share Lord Burghley's idea and was of the opinion the delegates of the federations must be able to discuss issues in an openhearted manner among themselves. He disagreed with Burghley's statement that the IOC was the directive power in the world of sports, stating that it governed only Olympic sport.[74]

Cooperation was becoming essential. Governments were directly sponsoring athletic events through diplomatic channels, ignoring national federations and committees. As Brundage pointed out, "This is something the International Federations must stop since the IOC has no jurisdiction. It is easy to see that if competition under political auspices, without control of the Federations, is permitted, the whole structure of amateur sport is in danger."[75] The problem of spheres of authority was to increase, despite efforts for closer cooperation, with the introduction of television and the fight for revenues adding a further dimension to the already increasing variance in philosophy between the roles of national committees, sport federations, and the IOC.

The Olympic Games of 1956 occurred during the Hungarian and Suez crises, and they reflected the prevailing atmosphere of gloom and outrage in the West. Before the Games started, the Nationalist Chinese sent a protest to the IOC claiming that the Peking committee was inviting all Chinese athletes to compete in its tryouts and to participate for the PRC. The PRC in turn threatened to pull out of the Games if Nationalist China were allowed to participate. The IOC ignored such protests as purely political.[76] The PRC sent a protest to the IOC stating that since Nationalist China was to participate in the Games, the PRC would refuse to do so. As the Nationalist Chinese delegation arrived in Melbourne, the PRC flag was accidentally raised. The Nationalist Chinese dragged the flag down, to the cheers of the crowd that had gathered.[77]

Prior to the Games, in early August, the Argentine committee had been barred by the IOC because of government interference resulting from the recent ouster of President Peron; then later that month the situation was corrected.[78]

These types of issues soon became commonplace and were even more or less expected. The extraordinary incidents were the result of the Hungarian and Suez crises. When the Soviets intervened in Hungary, they provoked cries of outrage from the Western world. Immediately, the Netherlands and Spain withdrew from the Games. In the case of the Spanish, their real reason was felt to be financial. The Hungarian affair had simply afforded them a good excuse. In the case of the Netherlands, the president of its national Olympic committee criticized the IOC for saying that the Olympic ideal should prevail over political matters. "How can sports prevail over what has happened in Hungary?" he asked caustically. "How would we like it if our people had been atrociously murdered, and someone said that sports should prevail?" In a similar vein, Spain stated that it was "not fitting for Spanish athletes to engage in sports of Olympic character while the liberty of peoples [sic] is being trampled on."[79]

A few Hungarian athletes had set sail with Soviet athletes to Melbourne before the Soviet intervention. News of this sparked much speculation as to the relations between the two groups during the voyage. Upon arrival the Hungarian athletes said, perhaps unaware of the recent events in their country, that relations had been cordial and devoid of incident.

It was reported that some Hungarian athletes had been fighting in the streets during the crisis, and that most could not get out of the country for the Games. The chancellor of the IOC, Otto Mayer, persuaded the Swiss government to intercede with Hungarian authorities in the name of the IOC to provide safe passage to Prague, where the Czechoslovakian government would provide transportation to Melbourne. This was arranged, and for Mayer it was a great personal triumph. Mayer called it an Olympic Truce, though other members of the IOC were more circumspect in their view.[80]

The Swiss Olympic committee joined the Netherlands and Spain, voicing outrage and withdrawing from the Games. This was a severe blow to the IOC, for their headquarters were in Switzerland. Finally the Swiss were prevailed upon to reconsider, but they were unable to arrange transportation in time and did not attend the Games.

The Suez incident, coming close on the heels of the Hungarian crisis, produced similar withdrawals and protests, this time in the Arab world. Egypt had already pulled out of the Games for financial reasons, but lodged protests demanding that the nations "guilty of cowardly aggression against Egypt" be expelled.[81] In solidarity with Egypt, Lebanon and Iraq withdrew from the Games.

At the Games themselves, numerous demonstrations by Hungarian refugees and others were staged, protesting the Soviet action; and in the athletic contests, certain incidents occurred which reflected that atmosphere. The water polo match between Hungary and Russia was a brutal one. A rough sport to begin with, the game was marred by excessive violence and fighting. The Hungarians, who had long ruled the sport, soundly trounced the Soviets, 4 to 0.[82]

In this atmosphere, an announcement was made that reflected the warming of relations between the United States and the Soviet Union. It was announced that United States and Russian track officials had tentatively agreed to home-and-home track meets beginning in Moscow in 1957. Congressional approval was still needed for the Soviet return visit, and a relaxation of the alien fingerprint provision of the immigration laws would be necessary. As it turned out, this was assured. Previous attempts had been made to arrange meetings between the two countries. The United States had turned down an invitation in 1955 and the Soviet Union had turned down a United States invitation in 1953 because of the fingerprint requirement.[83]

After the Soviet success in the 1956 Winter Games, Soviet sport officials predicted their overwhelming domination of the Summer Games, although the concept of countries winning the Games was frowned upon by the IOC. The Soviets did well at the Summer

Games, but they did not dominate the winning. In the final tabulation of medal acquisitions, the Soviets gained thirty-seven gold medals to thirty-two for the United States; for silver medals the score was twenty-nine to twenty-five, and for bronze medals the score was thirty-three to seventeen. The total was ninety-nine to seventy-four.[84] Because the Soviets had not reached their own predicted expectations, they felt compelled to account for the failure. The Soviet magazine *Literaturnaya Gazeta* blamed it on United States "Mata Haris." The magazine reported that United States intelligence services tempted Soviet athletes with beautiful sirens, but that the Soviet men valiantly strove to keep their minds on athletics. "American intelligence tried hard," the magazine averred, "to acquaint Soviet sportsmen with the young women—their agents—who more than insistently proposed having a good time."[85]

The period 1952 to 1956 was marked by a lessening of tension and a general consolidation of positions between East and West. Stalin had died, and his successors began to proceed more vigorously in other directions, leading to the denunciation of Stalin himself and the announcement of the policy of peaceful coexistence. Their counterparts in the United States were less magnanimous, proceeding to encircle the Soviet Union with a nuclear strike force. Nonetheless, the Korean conflict had made the United States less willing to step boldly into direct confrontation with the Soviets, despite pronouncements and policies to the contrary. Both the Soviets and the United States continued to replace European influence in the former European colonial areas. The Middle East was a prime example and was to become a hotbed of contention between the two sides in the future.

Questions about Europe became for all intents and purposes moot points. On the one hand, the United States indicated by its unwillingness to assist Hungary that it regarded Eastern Europe as, if not de jure at least de facto, a Soviet sphere. The Soviets, on the other hand, had to face the fact of a West German state and its membership in NATO. They countered with an East German state and the Warsaw Pact.

The process of decolonization continued with an increased nationalistic zeal which spurred an increasingly independent attitude, most manifest in the Middle East during the Suez crisis. Along with decolonization and the growth of an alternate force in the world, closer regional cooperation developed in many areas.

Latin America already had the OAS (Organization of American States) and Europe had the European Coal and Steel Community, not to mention the Benelux area and other economic and financial arrangements. Although an EDC was defeated, deferring into the future a European supranational political organ, NATO represented a form of political/military union. The Warsaw Pact also represented this trend. Outside of Europe the process was continuing mainly in security treaties—SEATO, ANZUS—and in the Middle East the Arab League was still prevalent.

Olympic affairs during this period exhibited these trends. The provisional recognition of the GDR was an example of the consolidation in Europe of East-West relations and, at the same time, of peaceful coexistence. The continued influence of nationalism and governmental interference in Olympic affairs illustrated the East-West conflict and the differences in philosophy, as well as the growing independence of primarily non-Western areas and their more nationalistic outlook on the uses of sport than that of the IOC. The call for closer cooperation between sport organizations, the rule changes to facilitate this, and the jealous guarding of authority by the sport organizations symbolized the conflicting trends of nationalism and internationalism.

The IOC, in that it is private and extends beyond national boundaries, is technically a transnational organization; but by virtue of its nation-state structure, its outlook combines nationalism and internationalism. The affiliated sport organizations are, to a great extent, the same. While the Olympic movement, which includes all the amateur sport organizations, maintains its independence as a transnational movement, it strives simultaneously, in its capacity as an international organization, to integrate the world's countries and people despite increasing nationalism. In essence, it reflects the pull of the forces of nationalism as opposed to those of inter- and transnationalism. All are consolidating, organizational tendencies, differing only in areas, realms, and degrees of emphasis.

Despite the Hungarian and Suez incidents, the period of 1952 to 1956 was one of general relaxation of tension. The Hungarian and Suez incidents were essentially unsuccessful efforts to reassert lost influence. Both were lapses in a general trend of changing patterns. The United States and Soviet Union agreed to joint track competitions, but perhaps the real indicator of the general reduction in tension was to be found in the closing ceremonies of the Melbourne

Games. The IOC changed its traditional closing ceremony, in which each national contingent had marched behind its own standard, to one in which a token 500 athletes out of the 4,000 that participated in the Games marched as a single cavalcade, with no regard to order or country, mingling in the spirit of international friendship.[86]

4

1956-1968

THE PERIOD 1956 to 1968 WITNESSED THE end of the colonial system and the emergence of a power bloc composed of the states newly created from the former colonial areas of Asia and Africa. In the Olympics this process manifested itself in the issue of South African participation in the Games and in the Olympic movement.

The unsolved cold war questions of German unification, the two Chinas, and the two Koreas solidified in the 1956 to 1968 period as both Eastern and Western blocs sought to consolidate their positions with little hope of negotiated settlements. Under such conditions both sides began not only to tolerate the division but to accept it. The German people, in particular, moved toward acceptance and by 1968 both Germanies competed separately in the Olympics.

Political and military circumstance as well as economic prosperity were factors behind the consolidation and acceptance of positions, which in turn promoted evolution of the concept of nationalism. Since neither side was willing to risk nuclear destruction but was content to keep pace in the arms race, a stalemate ensued that was conducive to the establishment of alternative forms of confrontation and to the opening of new avenues of communication. Since the interests of each side, however, were basically non-negotiable the only real alternative was acceptance of the status quo. This situation was reinforced by the factor of economic development. As the economic position of Western Europe steadily improved, a more self-reliant attitude was possible. In the case of West Germany the view that unification was essential to the welfare of the German people was considerably lessened.

The essential development in the concept of nationalism was from a cultural linkage to a more objectively defined economic and institutional linkage. Establishment of the European Common Market, based on economic rather than cultural criteria, created machinery seen necessary for gradual European political unification. Looking beyond the system of autonomous units loyal to a culturally or territorially defined political affiliation (the nation-state), the aim was to develop loyalty to a regional organizational construct defined objectively rather than emotively. This was a strategic step in the organizational evolution of nationalism.

Important in this process were the linkages or networks that bound and reinforced the system. The individual unit became more closely tied into the regional system. Since the conceptual evolution had gone beyond such cultural foundations as language and race to an objective foundation, the political and cultural ties between, for example, East and West Germany became increasingly remote. The regional institutional networks served to solidify both Eastern and Western Europe as distinct units.

The nationalism that spurred decolonization outside of Europe also provoked the nonaligned orientation of the emerging areas in Africa and Asia and stimulated regionalism in reaction to the East-West conflict and the increased postwar prosperity in the world's developed areas. As both an offensive and defensive measure, the East and the West sought to extend their respective influence in Third World nations. Meanwhile, conditions fostering economic prosperity in the industrialized areas spurred the development and refinement of the multinational corporation,[1] which in turn enhanced economic prosperity in these regions—a cyclical process. The spread of the East-West conflict and of the multinational corporation into the former colonial areas was viewed with apprehension in the Third World. The emerging nations did not want to become embroiled in the East-West estrangement, becoming mere satellites of the Great Powers, nor did they want to be dominated economically through the mechanism of the multinational corporation. Both conditions were seen as nothing more than neo-colonialism, but the underdeveloped status of the Third World precluded independent action in response to such perceived threats. As a result, the very nationalism that spawned the Third World nationalistic movements also created a type of internationalism in the form of regional arrangements based essentially on common alliiance for defensive purposes. Organizations such as the OAU or LAFTA were created.

In the Olympics these trends were manifested through the issue of South African participation and the role of the OAU, and through the Games of the New Emerging Forces (GANEFO) in opposition to the established Olympic Games. Both cases presented an admixture of North-South and East-West political issues, the issue of amateurism, and the controversy over television revenues, manifesting the economic prosperity of the multinational corporation and its worldwide infiltration into numerous spheres of everyday life. The issues themselves were not as important as was their effect on the Olympics. Questions of economics in the Olympics and in sport began to dominate the decision making processes of the sport organizations, and other considerations became secondary.

XVI OLYMPIAD (1956-1960) AND THE 1960 OLYMPIC GAMES

While tensions between the Soviet Union and the United States lessened in these years, competition between the two countries and their respective blocs, East and West, remained intense. There were still opposing ideologies as well as opposing interests on various issues, such as Germany, China, and Korea. In the Olympics several of these issues were exhibited. Perhaps the most controversial issue along this line was the question of Chinese participation.

Developments regarding the PRC in the Olympics over the period 1956 to 1960 closely followed developments in the political arena. The Winter Games of 1960 were scheduled to take place at Squaw Valley, California, and there was some concern in the IOC over whether the United States would curb its restrictions and admit the PRC, a country the United States did not recognize. This problem was not limited to the PRC but extended to Communist countries in general. In 1957 Brundage warned the United States that if it refused any properly IOC-recognized country the right of participation at Squaw Valley, the IOC would be forced to revoke the Games from the United States and award them elsewhere. Also, Brundage had trouble obtaining a visa for the annual general session of 1957 in Sofia, Bulgaria—another country with which the United States did not have diplomatic relations. He warned that such limitations on his activities might force him to retire from the IOC.[2]

The pressure apparently worked, for the State Department in early September relaxed its curbs on Americans, in positions such as Brundage's, entering certain Communist countries. Visits of limited duration, such as Brundage's, would be considered on a case by case basis, as would visits by newsmen to the United States from Communist countries.[3]

The problem of Communist participation at Squaw Valley hinged on the alien fingerprint requirement. Three days before Brundage was to leave for Bulgaria to discuss, among other things, the possible revocation of the Winter Games from the United States, it was announced that bona fide athletes from all Communist countries would be admitted. The fingerprint requirement would be waived but all other requirements, such as health and security, would be enforced. All names of athletes would be screened for past or present espionage activities.[4] Participation in the 1960 Olympic Games now seemed possible for all Communist countries recognized by the IOC but with which the United States did not have diplomatic relations.

Developments in the IOC regarding the Chinese issue proved otherwise. In 1957 there was every reason to believe that the PRC intended to participate in 1960 unless the Taiwan issue intensified. Despite absence from the Melbourne Games, the PRC had participated in numerous international sport events.[5] The climate in the People's Republic was favorable with Mao's decree to "Let a Hundred Flowers Bloom." Apparently too many blossomed, for by 1957 and 1958 the PRC authorities had retrenched and were beginning the "Great Leap Forward." The retrenchment became immediately obvious in Olympic circles. After a relatively quiescent period following the Melbourne Games the PRC began a barrage of demands for the expulsion of the Taiwan committee from the Olympic movement. Throughout that year IOC President Avery Brundage and Tun Shou-yi, the PRC member on the IOC, corresponded on the issue. Brundage emphasized that two committees existed, that political issues were not the province of the IOC, and that Tung was violating his obligations as an IOC member by constantly raising political issues in the meetings and correspondence. Tung replied with demands for Taiwan's ouster and stated that it was not he, but Brundage, who was introducing politics by the continued insistence on two committees. Finally, in a letter dated August 19, 1958, Tung accused Brundage of being a "faithful menial of US imperialists" and concluded by saying, "A man like you . . . has no qualifications whatsoever to be IOC President. . . . I will no longer cooperate with you or have any connection with the IOC while it is under your domination."[6] With that, the PRC withdrew from the IOC and, at the same time, from all the international federations with which they were affiliated.

Their withdrawal corresponded to the hardening of the political line in China and to the incidents of that summer involving China's bombardment of the islands of Quemoy and Matsu. The United States responded by dispatching air, marine, and naval reinforcements to Taiwan. A 1957 agreement between the United States and Taiwan had provided for the placement of surface-to-air missiles on Taiwan.[7]

Despite the PRC withdrawal, the issue of Chinese participation in the Olympic movement and Games was not to be dismissed. The withdrawal from both the IOC and the federations assured that the PRC would not participate in the 1960 Games, even if they had reapplied. The process of gaining recognition from both the international federations and the IOC would have required too much time, and the animosity engendered by their flagrant violations of IOC procedures through constantly injecting politics into the sessions would have been too much to overcome in such a short period.

The change in the political climate regarding broad East-West issues prolonged the Chinese controversy and sent the IOC into a political paroxysm that would not abate even during the Summer Games. The IOC members from the Communist bloc did not like the idea of the Chinese withdrawal and were adamant in demanding Taiwanese expulsion and reinstatement of the PRC. Their position would have had little impact had they not been supported by the Marquess of Exeter, president of the International Amateur Athletic Federation (IAAF), the most important and influential international federation. Lord Burghley (the Marquess of Exeter) felt that the PRC had not really resigned from the IAAF unless Taiwan was still recognized by the IAAF. As far as he was concerned only one China (the PRC) existed. He proposed recognizing the Taiwan committee, but without the name of "China."[8]

Exeter's proposal obtained general agreement at the Munich

session. By a vote of forty-eight to seven it was decided to notify the Taiwan committee that it could no longer be recognized under the name of the Chinese National Olympic Committee, because it did not control sport in China. Its name would be stricken from the official list. Once it changed its name in conformity to the area it controlled, it could reapply for recognition.[9]

The reaction was immediate. Because the press misinterpreted the substance of the decision, it was generally reported that the IOC had expelled Nationalist China from the Olympic movement as a result of Communist pressure in order to make room for the readmission of the PRC. The outcry from the United States buried Brundage in vitriolic correspondence. It did not help that a fellow IOC member from the United States, Douglas Roby, stated that the IOC vote was far from unanimous, as Brundage had claimed to the press. Roby said that twenty-two members had abstained and that there had been much Communist pressure.[10]

Brundage was livid. In a circular to members of the IOC, Brundage responded to Roby's accusations:

If he had listened to the debate he would have known that regardless of any action by the IOC the Chinese of Formosa could not compete in the Olympic Games under the name "China," because some International Federations recognize them only as "Formosa" or "Taiwan" and they already competed in the Asian Games last year as "Formosa."[11]

He went on to point out that the IOC did not "kick out" anyone, it welcomed the youth of the world, but it must face facts. The IOC could not deny that the Peking committee controlled sport in Taiwan and then say that the Taiwan committee controlled sport in China.

Controversy over the decision continued. When the Taiwan Committee reapplied for recognition as the Republic of China, it was turned down. The problem was the word "China." The uproar in the United States was extreme, and with the Winter Games so close a solution had to be found. The State Department, President Eisenhower, the Congress, the United States Olympic Committee, the AAU, UN Ambassador Lodge, and the American Legion, all deplored the IOC decision and, in turn, Brundage's association with it. Some even threatened retaliatory action. The House voted to prohibit use of army personnel at the Winter Games if athletes from any "free nation" were banned, and to restrict army support to only $100,000.[12] The American Legion also threatened to withhold financial support.

With the Games at stake, Brundage said that even though the Taiwan committee might not be recognized if it refused to change its name, it could enter the Winter Games because it had been invited under its old name before the decision. As it turned out, there were no winter sport athletes on Taiwan. Taiwan did not compete, though it did send officials. A disaster was averted by allowing the Taiwanese to compete, even though they had no athletes, but the Summer Games were at hand and the problem of Taiwan's name remained.

During the controversy it was pointed out by opponents of the IOC decision that to restrict the geographic area of the Taiwan committee to Taiwan begged the question, because sportsmen who competed under Taiwan's banner came from all over Asia—Hong Kong, Singapore, Macao. One Australian observer wrote the IOC that because of the numbers and economic strength of the overseas Chinese in Asia, the IOC decision might spawn retaliatory measures by the overseas Chinese, harmful to such countries as Australia with which they had many ties.[13] The overriding issue for the IOC was stated by Exeter in a letter to Brundage, pointing out that one-fourth of the world's population—China—was already out of the Olympic movement. If the process were carried further it might alienate all the iron curtain countries, thereby eliminating one-half of the world's population from the Olympic movement. A firm stand on the Taiwan issue was essential.[14]

In October 1959 the executive board met and considered the Taiwan question. The Taiwan committee had reapplied as the Olympic Committee of the Republic of China, but had been turned down because of the word "China." Because of the furor over the issue the executive board stated that the IOC did not care what a committee called itself internally, but internationally its name had to be consistent with the territory it ruled. It was decided the Taiwan committee could be recognized as the Olympic Committee of the Republic of China, since it was so recognized by the United Nations. But in international competition the athletes from that country had to compete solely under the name of Taiwan (Formosa).[15]

At both the San Francisco and Rome general sessions in February and August 1960, respectively, the executive board decision was approved. The Olympic Committee of the Republic of China at the Rome Games marched and competed as Formosa, but as the placard bearer passed by the reviewing stand in the opening ceremony, he whipped out a sign saying "Under Protest," and then quickly tucked it away.[16]

The decision of the IOC kept the Olympic movement together. The PRC would have nothing to do with the IOC, but by this time the PRC was having problems with the Soviet Union, easing the pressure on the IOC. The decision was significant because it set a precedent for the future. The decision altered the IOC rules so that Olympic committees would only be recognized by the IOC "under the name of the territory in which they operate."[17] The territorial distinction was to become the linchpin on which future decisions regarding the recognition of previously unrecognized political areas such as East Germany and North Korea could be recognized.

Problems similar to the Chinese question arose regarding North Korea and East Germany. Both issues, like that of China, had plagued the IOC in the past. While the Korean issue had never been as serious a problem as the German and Chinese, it was ever-present. Before the Korean conflict an Olympic committee for all of Korea had been recognized, having its seat in Seoul. Subsequent requests for recognition on behalf of a North Korean committee were turned down, the reason being that only one committee could exist for one country. At the 1957 session in Sophia, the Soviet delegate proposed the same conditions of provisional recognition for North Korea as those for East Germany. That is, if a unified team were formed, provisional recognition would be granted; if not, North Korea would not be able to compete in the Games. The provisional recognition, however, would be valid only for internal affairs and not on an international basis.[18] This was accepted. At both the 1958 and 1959 general sessions, Andrianov, the Soviet delegate, and General Stoichev of Bulgaria demanded full recognition for North Korea because of the South Korean refusal to consider a unified team. The IOC was not prepared to go this far. Instead, at the 1959 session the IOC decided to seek a unified team, not through joint competition, as in the case of Germany, but through having the sport federations select the athletes who held the best times in their respective events, thereby eliminating the necessity of having to arrange joint competition. A joint flag, emblem, and uniform would also be required for the joint Korean team. Although South Korea indicated a willingness to form a joint team, negotiations broke down and North Korea did not participate in the 1960 Games; but South Korea did participate by virtue of its full recognition.

Since a joint German team had been formed for the 1956 Games, not much trouble was foreseen in forming another unified team for the 1960 Games. Although pressure for full East German recognition was constant, both from the East Germans and the Communist bloc, the IOC maintained East Germany's provisional status. On the political front the continued separation of the two countries served to institutionalize the situation, making the possibility for unification more remote as time went on. This was evident in the negotiations over a joint team for the 1960 Games.

With IOC mediation the two German committees agreed in November 1959 on a neutral flag and emblem for the 1960 Games. In the 1956 Games the athletes had marched under the West German flag. There was considerable support for the decision in West German sport circles and in the parties opposing Chancellor Adenauer's majority party. The Bonn government was adamantly opposed to the decision, stating that it was "irreconcilable with national dignity," and threatened West German withdrawal. The West German Olympic Committee president intimated the reason for the decision when he said the compromise was "a necessary one which should not be put in question by political considerations." Earlier the East German government had adopted its own flag, precipitating the necessity for the compromise and, as a result, invoking Adenauer's fury. A spokesman for Adenauer's party put the question before the press in the following fashion: "Should 53,000,000 Germans let themselves be blackmailed by a regime that is not even a legitimate democracy?"[19] Nevertheless, the common banner was adopted and both sides competed in the Games as one team.

Further problems were in store for the IOC regarding Germany. Despite United States pronouncements and assurances regarding free entry of officials and athletes of all recognized Olympic committees, fifteen East Germans, ten officials, and five journalists were refused visas for the Winter Games. Protests were raised by the East German Association of Journalists and the East German Olympic Committee. Official contingents for Olympic committees are arranged in proportion to their number of athletes. A total of eighty-five German athletes were going to participate, fifty from West Germany and thirty-five from East Germany. There were twenty in the official contingents, twelve from West Germany and eight from East Germany. These had previously been agreed upon and duly sent to the organizing committee for the Games, but at the last moment the East Germans demanded more representatives and the West Germans reluctantly agreed to raise the East German total to twelve. For the East Germans this was still not enough, precipitating the controversy.

The IOC protested the State Department's refusal of visas for the journalists, stating its belief in freedom of the press without any type of discrimination. It agreed with the ban on the officials, however, noting that the original allotment had been secured and even an additional four. The demand for more was contrary to all prior agreements and was considered excessive.[20] The State Department refused the journalists in order to prevent any propaganda benefits. It stated that East German journalists were paid employees of the propaganda ministry and that all their reporting was politicized. It cited the case of an East German journalist, Gunter Poetschle, who was an accredited correspondent to the United Nations in 1957 and who used that accreditation to imply recognition of the GDR.[21]

In the IOC during the XVI Olympiad, cold war issues and politics were the most prominent features in the discussions and correspondence. This was true despite the trend away from cold war issues on the world political scene and toward problems such as colonialism, which were considered more important by the non-Western states. Even on the world political scene the distinctions as to the nature of issues became blurred with the numerous protagonists involved. The growing nationalistic/neutralist stance taken by the former colonial areas was still evident, particularly in the United Nations, where cold war topics had definitely become secondary for the non-Western states to problems of colonialism.[22] But the policies of the superpowers, particularly of the Soviet Union, had changed to compensate for the growing body of nations. In effect, the extension of an East-West conflict into the former colonial areas was complicating the issues involved. Two forces were at work: the East-West conflict struggling for adherents, and the nonaligned states struggling to retain their autonomy in the face of stronger powers that were seeking to establish satellites.

Nasser's foreign policy in the Middle East was a good case in point. In the 1952 to 1956 period he carried out a policy of playing off the two blocs, East and West. In the 1956 to 1960 period he still sought aid from the Soviets, as in the case of the Aswan Dam, but at the same time he sought to extend Arab nationalism and his own influence by aligning with Syria in the United Arab Republic, where he quickly expelled the pro-Russian elements in the Syrian government.[23]

In Southeast Asia, Sukarno continued his struggle for the control of West Irian, while in India, Nehru opposed the Indian Communist Party in order to limit Soviet influence.[24] The United States was getting more deeply imbedded in the Vietnamese conflict, which was essentially a nationalistic struggle. With the United States presence bolstering the South Vietnamese regime, the North Vietnamese received aid from China and the Soviet Union.

Africa, in the process of gaining more and more independent states, was a hotbed of nationalism. With the development of these new states, the United States, the Soviet Union, and others such as China tried to gain influence.

In the Olympics this convergence of forces was evident, especially regarding the issue of racial discrimination in South Africa. The problem was first brought to the attention of the IOC in 1955 by the International Boxing Federation. The issue was tabled, however, until 1959 when the Soviet IOC member reintroduced the problem at an executive board meeting with the delegates from the national Olympic committees. In the meantime the IOC had been corresponding with its South African member and the South African National Olympic Committee (SANOC) to obtain information regarding apartheid in sport, which would have been contrary to the Olympic principle and to rule twenty-five, proscribing discrimination of any kind.

The Soviet delegate accused the South African committee of discrimination against black athletes. The South African delegate replied that the charge was unfounded and that the South African government guaranteed that any athlete could receive a passport to participate. The South African delegate went on to state that SANOC was prepared to assure that all athletes of Olympic standing could participate in the Games.[25]

At the general session in Munich the South African member elaborated further, stating that only within the last two or three years had "coloured" athletes taken an interest in Olympic sport, so none had achieved Olympic caliber. The real issue the South African delegate failed to consider was not whether an athlete had achieved Olympic standing, but whether discrimination was practiced in the country by the committee. In point of fact, in 1957 SANOC ruled that no mixed competition would be allowed in any of the affiliated bodies within South Africa's borders.[26]

This point was brought out by the Brazilian and the Soviet delegates in reference to recent soccer and table tennis matches. In the case of the soccer matches, a Brazilian team having three black members was not allowed to play in South Africa. In the table tennis case, an Australian team was refused the right to compete against colored teams. The New Zealand delegate, whose country had extensive sporting ties with South Africa, supported the South African member's statements regarding the condition of sport in South Africa. Brundage finally intervened, stating that the IOC was conscious of the importance of the problem, but that the South African delegate's assurances were to be accepted.[27]

The IOC was content to leave the question at that for the 1960 Games. They were applying their nondiscrimination rule only in terms of whether athletes of Olympic caliber were allowed to participate in the Games, and not whether internal discrimination had led to the absence of black Olympic caliber athletes. The problem would remain and would become the most volatile issue the IOC would ever confront.

The fact that the Soviets introduced the whole question and were most vehement in pressing the issue is indicative of the overlapping and intermixing of forces on the world political scene. The nationalistic movement in Africa was just beginning, and the Africans were preoccupied with the colonialism issue. Although the practice of racial discrimination was linked to colonialism, it was not until later that the African states began to exert themselves more forcefully on the issue in the IOC. The reason for Soviet rather than black African pressure on the issue of South African apartheid in sport was that there were no black African delegates on the IOC. This European-centered composition of the IOC, harkening back to previous times, was being changed by the inclusion of numerous new Afro-Asian committees in the Olympic system. In the Olympic Games themselves the African athletes had not yet become competitive on a world class scale. More competitive states, such as the

Soviet Union, were better able to use their athletic strength as a political tool. By the time of the Rome Games that would begin to change. In the meantime, as evidenced by the Munich session of 1959, the issue of discrimination would be propounded mainly in cold war terms, with the Soviet delegate charging discrimination and the rest of the IOC, composed mainly of members from the Western states, preferring to table the issue.

Amateurism has been a perennial problem for the IOC and for amateur sport in general. The problem of the commercialization of sport, forever a thorn in the side of the IOC, was a favorite subject of Avery Brundage. In the period of the XV Olympiad the controversy had been over "broken time." During the XVI Olympiad the controversy involved the distribution of revenues among the various amateur organizations. For Brundage this was merely another reflection of the growing "materialism of our times."[28]

Several factors set this revenue sharing problem apart in importance: (1) it reflected the growing monetary benefits and costs of the Games, (2) it reflected the growing participation in international sport, increasing the operating costs of the organizations, (3) the economic aspects of the Games and sport in general were beginning to become overriding factors of concern, producing something of a "profit and loss" outlook on the part of the organizations involved, (4) the economic impact and viewpoint reflected the profitability of the Games and sport for business interests, and (5) the economic aspect served further to divide the amateur sport organizations, leaving the Olympic movement even more susceptible to the forces of nationalism and political conflict.

The revenue sharing controversy began soon after the 1956 Games. The growing operating costs for the international federations, because of the increase in the number of members, necessitated alternate forms of raising capital; the proscription method was no longer adequate. The federations felt that since they lent their world championships to the Olympic Games they had a right to share in the revenues. The Marquess of Exeter, in his capacity as president of the IAAF, proposed a five percent surcharge on tickets at the Olympics, with three percent going to the international federations and two percent to the IOC. Brundage was adamantly opposed. He argued that all the federations would have to be accorded the same treatment and not all received the same gate. Furthermore, if it were not for the Games, half the federations would not even hold a world championship and very few would ever have been able to if it had not been for the revival of the Olympic Games. They were not really giving up anything in his opinion.[29]

For Brundage and the IOC this was the crux of the matter. The tax was seen as blatant profiteering, not just as compensation to cover operating expenses, which would have been justifiable. Brundage believed the world, in particular the press, would not look favorably on the tax. In opposition to the proposed tax Brundage said: "...it is going to be misunderstood and we are going to be torn to pieces by the journalists of the world. They are [already] looking for some pretext to attack us." In the same statement Brundate noted that he had received a letter from a journalist inquiring about the rumor and stating, "I hope you succeed in preventing your co-committee members from voting themselves into taking funds, which will certainly be the end of amateur sport."[30]

Against the proposed tax, Brundage further argued that if the federations demanded shares, so would the national Olympic committees, the officials and judges at the Games, and, finally, the athletes.[31] The IOC could not very well defend amateurism and then turn right around and do the opposite.

In defense of the proposal Exeter said that the federations, because their operating costs were becoming so high, could not "founder into insolvency" just for the sake of the IOC.[32] The IOC would also benefit because their costs were increasing and the supposed self-sufficiency of the membership was becoming an anachronism. Only the extremely wealthy members of the committee could afford to pay the costs of transportation and other aspects of membership in the IOC. The IOC share could go into a fund to help defray the expenses of those members who could not afford to pay, and those members were becoming more and more numerous. Exeter's argument was essentially that the sport organizations, because of increasing costs, would be susceptible to feeble membership or government control in the future if they could not find a way to cover expenses and maintain their independence.[33]

Brundage was not averse to this idea, for he was well aware of the increasing costs all around. For years he had lobbied to no avail to decrease the size of the Games because they were becoming unmanageable. Invariably the Soviets attacked his efforts as attempts to harm their Olympic program in favor of the United

States.[34] In addition both the federations and the Soviets were constantly urging that more sports be included in the Olympic program. In 1958 Brundage summed up what the Games had become when he said, "In 1912 the Games at Stockholm operated on a budget of 80,000 pounds. For the 1960 Games it is reported that the Rome Organizing Committee will spend in the neighborhood of $30,000,000. The Games have become 'Big Business' with [sic] obvious danger to Olympic ideals."[35]

The Games had indeed become big business, not only with regard to the costs but to the interests concerned. In 1956 television refused to broadcast the Games, arguing that the rights should be granted gratis since the Games, as a news event, were a matter of public interest. For the 1960 Rome Games total television revenues were approximately $1.2 million.[36] Television revenues would escalate in the future, becoming an increasing part not only of IOC revenue but of the revenue of other sport organizations; this produced more conflict between the organizations. Not only television but business interests in general were involved. For the Summer Games in Rome, forty-six firms donated goods or made services available to the Games.[37] Future contributions to the Games would become greater and more involved—an important source of revenue, but with serious risks of excessive commercialism. As the Games were big business, a business-like attitude began to pervade the sport organizations' approach to the Games and the Olympic movement, leaving it open to attack from various external forces.

Capitalizing on the rift between the federations and the IOC, the Soviet committee proposed a complete reorganization of the IOC. Their proposal was facilitated by the national committees' growing disenchantment with the IOC, not only because of the monetary factor but as a result of the growing ideological rift between them and the IOC. Basing their program on the premise of closer cooperation between all concerned, the Soviet committee proposed enlarging the IOC to include not only the present members but also presidents of national Olympic committees and international federations. These two organizations would be given the right to replace their own members on the IOC, thus taking the choice of membership out of the hands of the IOC and putting it into the hands of the government of the country of the respective sport organization. IOC finances would come from annual fees of national Olympic

committees and international federations, and IOC member sub-
scriptions would be paid by their respective national committees; a
percentage of the gate receipts, as in the Exeter plan, would go to
the IOC and to the international federations; members' travel
expenses would be paid by the national committees and the federations.[38]

The plan, in effect, called for a United Nations of sport. Since
the trend was for increasing government support of national committees, the Soviet plan meant making the IOC a government operation. By appointing the delegates and paying all the expenses, the
chances for government influence and political control would be
greatly enhanced. This was completely opposite to Olympic principles. Needless to say, the membership from the Western states
looked on the plan with some trepidation.

In summing up the basic features of the plan, Brundage gave a
brief history of the International Olympic Committee, giving the
reasons why the IOC chose not to structure itself along the lines of
the Soviet plan. He stated the Western objections to the plan. He
said that at first the IOC had been structured along the lines of the
Soviet plan, but for purposes of efficiency, autonomy, and confor-
mation to Olympic principles, the IOC had split the organization
into three parts. The international federations were to direct all
technical aspects of sport, the national committees would administer Olympic sport, and the IOC would ensure the coordination of
activities.[39] The Soviet proposal would eliminate the autonomy of
the organizations and would put everything under one roof subject
to government scrutiny. Implicit in Western objections was the fear
of Soviet domination. Exeter noted that they ought to settle the
financial question before the Rome meeting, where the plan would
be laid before the federations and national committees for, he cautioned, "goodwill as opposed to badwill [sic] will obviously be a
great help in handling this very thorny Russian proposal."[40] Two
years later Exeter was more emphatic when the Soviet members
again proposed a reorganization. "This is purely and simply a
rehash of what they proposed before," he exclaimed. "The whole
aim seems to be to try and take over the Games from the IOC to
whom, after all, they belong."[41] The delegate from Finland
implored Brundage not to turn the committee into a "Russian
street meeting."[42]

The Soviet plan achieved considerable support from the international federations, the national committees, and the Eastern European delegates on the IOC. Also, to Brundage's dismay, the Exeter plan was widely accepted by the federations. In both cases, however, the decision was to be made by the IOC, and both plans were defeated. In the case of the Exeter plan, a compromise settlement was reached in which the finances of the various federations would be examined in order to determine their respective needs. For the 1964 Games each federation would negotiate separately with the organizing committee, but nothing could be done for the Rome Games.[43]

Because neither issue was solved adequately, increased problems and bitterness seemed likely. The strong support each proposal received was indicative of the growing rift in the Olympic movement as a result of the forces of commercialism, nationalism, and political conflict.

During the XVI Olympiad the People's Republic of China withdrew from the Olympic movement, compelling the IOC to take a second look at the question of Taiwan. That reappraisal set the stage for subsequent recognition of previously nonrecognized territories, indicating a reappraisal of East-West relations.

Cold war tension had lessened, although competition between the sides remained. The issues of colonialism and its corollary, racial discrimination, were raised over the question of South African apartheid policy. The absence of black African delegates on the IOC reflected the fledgling character of black nationalist movements in Africa. The issue of South African apartheid was couched primarily in East-West terms, with the Soviet Union leading the fight against South Africa. The Soviet stance derived from its anticolonial policy and its interest in black Africa.[44] With increased African representation on the IOC in the future, the anticolonial fight would be carried on primarily by black Africa.

Dramatically symbolic of the changing IOC membership and of the increasing voice of Africa in world affairs was the marathon victory of Abebe Bikila, a palace guard from Ethiopia. As the final event on the Olympic agenda, the marathon is a run of 26 miles and 385 yards. Bikila ran the course barefoot, becoming the first black African ever to win a gold medal. The course ended at the Arch of Constantine in Rome, a dramatic victory by an Ethiopian in a country that two decades before had sought to dominate his native land. Bikila's victory signaled that Africa and the other non-Western countries would continue to make their presence felt.

XVII OLYMPIAD (1960-1964) AND THE 1964 OLYMPIC GAMES

The Summer and Winter Games of 1964 were scheduled to take place in Tokyo and Innsbruck, respectively. The Tokyo site was significant in that it would mark the first hosting of the Olympic Games in Asia and would herald the successful emergence of Japan from its defeat of World War II. The Japanese organizers and the government were sparing no expense for the Games, spending over $2.7 billion.[45] For the Olympics, the period 1960 to 1964 would be marked by three major events reflecting the world political scene: the refusal of visas for East German athletes to world championships in France and the United States in 1962, the barring of South Africa from the Tokyo Games, and the establishment of GANEFO (Games of the New Emerging Forces).

In August 1961 the Soviet Union and the East Germans erected a wall in the city of Berlin, dividing the Eastern sector of the city from the Western sectors. Such action had been threatened since 1958 and the United States, under the Eisenhower administration, had been attempting to negotiate the issue at the foreign ministers' conference in Geneva to forestall a unilateral move by the Russians. With the U-2 incident of 1960, however, Chairman Khrushchev of the Soviet Union denounced Eisenhower and the United States for engaging in espionage activities. Khrushchev broke off any further dealing with the Eisenhower administration, stating that negotiations would have to await the next administration.[46] At the start of the Kennedy administration, without waiting for the renewal of negotiations, Khrushchev simply reasserted the 1958 threat to resolve unilaterally the issue of Berlin within six months, before the end of 1961. Unless the West signed a treaty with East Germany establishing West Berlin as a "free city," Khrushchev guaranteed that the Soviet Union would in effect abrogate the West's right to be in Berlin. Russia would unilaterally sign a treaty, turning the whole matter over to East Germany.[47] The United States took no action toward a treaty with East Germany, and the wall was erected.

The United States, France, and Britain did not respond militarily with another Berlin airlift. Instead they issued assurances of support for the West Berliners and retaliated diplomatically, using such methods as the denying of visas for East German athletes to take part in the 1962 world championships of hockey and skiing in the United States and France, respectively.[48] The denial of visas, while motivated directly by a specific political act, was at the same time a barometer of political relations between the East and the West.

The International Olympic Committee was again placed in the middle as an unwilling participant and referee. In a statement to the world press regarding the visa incidents and the subsequent IOC stance, the IOC stated that it regretted incidents which threatened the existence of organized amateur sport and it considered such political incursions intolerable. French, United States, and Canadian cities had submitted bids to host the 1968 Games. The sites were still to be determined and the IOC threatened "not [to] award the Olympic Games to any city unless free access for all recognized teams" was guaranteed. The IOC was also going to suggest similar regulations for the international federations.[49]

In a subsequent statement to the Allied Travel Bureau, the IOC was more pointed in its threat.

Next year, we are to announce our decision as to the choice of city desirous of organizing the Games of the 19th Olympiad in 1968. Of the prospective towns either for the Summer Games 1968, or for the Winter ones, we have named, amongst others, towns in France, Canada and the United States. We need to know immediately, therefore, if these candidatures may be retained, for according to our statutes, entry into these countries by *all sportsmen* wishing to participate in these Games, must be assured.

...we would respectfully request you as Ultimate Authority to exercise your prerogative and guarantee that all athletes, whoever they may be, and from whatever country or territory they may come will receive the visas necessary to participate in the Olympic Games of 1968.[50]

In reply the Allied Travel Bureau gave the necessary assurances "provided that the present conditions remain unchanged, as they are, when the time comes," that is, that a Pan-German contingent participated as in 1960.[51] A Pan-German contingent was the real issue. By insisting on a joint German team since 1956 the IOC had only helped to perpetuate the cold war conflict over Germany. The NATO countries had come to expect a joint team as a means of reaffirming their position in Berlin and their stance against East Germany. In effect, whether the IOC liked it or not, the NATO countries were using the IOC to fulfill their own political ends. This became quite clear when the IOC tried to receive similar assurances of "free entry" into NATO countries for the various international federation world championships.

In early 1964 the IOC sent requests of "free entry" to the ministers of foreign affairs of France, Great Britain, and the United States. The requests were denied, the responses from all three being nearly identical. An assistant secretary of state responding for the United States said that recent adjustments in the rules for issuing temporary traveling documents to East Germans would facilitate greater East German participation in sporting events in NATO countries, provided the athletes did not purport to represent the GDR or engage in political activities. Unfortunately, he went on, the East German regime brought politics into sport by insisting on separate East German teams whenever possible, "despite the fact that there is only one German people. The all-German formula," he stated, "has indeed been successfully applied by your own committee for many years, and if it could be adopted also by the various international sport federations, the hindrances to the issue of temporary travel documents to East German athletes would largely disappear." Regarding the denial of visas in 1962, he admitted that it was a result of the erection of the Berlin wall, and that because of it and subsequent East German strictures on West Berlin—the denial of exit permits—there had been much human suffering and hardship. He hastened to add that in light of such suffering the "inconvenience to sportsmen resulting from the NATO regulations is very small."[52]

The IOC replied by deploring the policies of the NATO countries, and issued a directive depriving the same countries of holding any federation championships.[53] It was obvious that it made no difference to the NATO countries if they received the federation championships, but the Olympic Games were another matter. As a showcase for the nations of the world, the specific nature of German participation mattered a great deal. Many considered that the Olympic Games ranked in stature very close to the United Nations, and the nonaligned non-Western states were intensely interested in participation both in the United Nations and in the Olympic forum.

A united German team for the 1964 Games was assured. In fact

Brundage was so adamant on this policy that when the subject was mentioned at the Tokyo general session right before the Games, he said he would hear no talk of separation at Tokyo. The subject would be deferred until the following year—and that was how it would stand![54]

The question of separate teams, however, was becoming not only an East German but also a West German desire, at least in Olympic circles. Willi Daume, the president of the West German National Olympic Committee, said in a 1962 newspaper interview for the *Frankfurter Allegemeine Zeitung* that in view of inter-German difficulties the formation of separate teams was the only possibility. "In this way we render a better service to the Olympic spirit," he admitted. "This solution is practically nothing else than the legalization of an existing state of affairs, because as early as 1960 in Squaw Valley and in Rome the combined German team was only a fiction for the outside world. In reality we had two separated teams behind one flag." In a television interview in April 1964 Daume made similar statements noting that it would be much more pleasant if both could go separately to Tokyo, but that they should put up with the inconveniences for the time being so as not to afford "the other side" opportunity for the acknowledgment of two German states "before the public of the world, before the gigantic spectacle of the Olympic Games."[55]

Nevertheless, a united German team did go to the 1964 Games, but by 1963 the possibility for a joint team in 1968 was seriously in doubt. Both sides were coming to the conclusion, as a result of political events, that realities should be faced. This presented a problem for the IOC, because if they could not arrange a joint team, the East German athletes might not be allowed to participate in the 1968 Winter Games in France (the Olympic sites for 1968 were chosen in 1963). The Marquess of Exeter voiced the concern of the IOC in a letter to the IOC chancellor, Otto Mayer. He said the IOC should get NATO to modify its travel rules, that since a "thaw" seemed to have set in between the two Germanies since 1961, perhaps a joint team might still be possible. They would have to wait and see, but covering all contingencies was a good idea.[56]

The possibility for a joint team in future years would become more remote. The Berlin issue had set the stage for the final act of a joint German contingent in the Olympic Games. The Berlin controversy and the denial of visas was not an isolated phenomenon during the period 1960 to 1964. It had its counterpart on the other side of the world in Indonesia.

In the summer of 1962 the IV Asian Games[57] were to be held in Indonesia. The Indonesian government refused to issue visas for the athletes of Taiwan and Israel. The practice of discrimination against Israel had become commonplace. In 1952, as a result of a technicality, Israel had been successfully barred from the Mediterranean Games, their rightful regional Games. The Indonesian action was nothing new. Coming as it did, on the heels of the Berlin visa affair, the IOC could not tolerate such insubordination where its name was at stake. In February 1963 the IOC suspended the Indonesian Olympic Committee for not having protested its government's discriminatory action against Taiwan and Israel.[58] Within the same month the Indonesian Olympic Committee withdrew from the Olympic movement.[59]

A double standard was apparent in the IOC suspension. It suspended Indonesia for virtually the same crime committed by France and the United States. Perhaps the severity of the punishment was because the Games in question were sanctioned to use the Olympic name, involving the national committee, whereas in the French and United States cases the events were merely world championships not sanctioned by the IOC. Probably the reasons were threefold: (1) the Indonesian action came on the heels of a similar action, (2) government interference in the newer states was a constant problem, and (3) Indonesia did not hold the same Olympic standing as France or the United States, which were charter members of the movement. France was the birthplace of the modern Olympic Games' founder, Baron de Coubertin. As for the United States, it was the strongest country in the world, it had always held the most Olympic prestige, and it was a lucrative source of revenue, particularly with the potential American television market as coverage of the Games burgeoned. Indonesia was but a newcomer, and as such, not very significant.

Perhaps it was this double standard, combined with the IOC's and the world's (industrialized countries) condescension towards Indonesia and other non-Western areas, that prompted Indonesian President Sukarno's next move. Sukarno proposed the establishment of GANEFO (Games of the New Emerging Forces). At a preparatory conference in April 1963, participated in by Cambodia, the PRC, Guinea, Indonesia, Iraq, Mali, Pakistan, North Vietnam, the United Arab Republic, and the Soviet Union (Ceylon and Yugoslavia sent observers) the purpose of GANEFO was spelled out. GANEFO was to be "based on the spirit of the 1955 Bandung Conference and the Olympic ideals, and was to promote the development of sports in new emerging nations so as to cement friendly relations among them."[60]

Even before Sukarno's announcement of the establishment of GANEFO, the IOC suspension, and Indonesia's withdrawal from the Olympic movement, the PRC was urging the establishment of alternative Games. On October 4, 1962, in an editorial in the biweekly sports newspaper *T'i Yu Pao,* the Chinese proposed an organization and Games that would help develop sports in Asia and Africa and would combat the "forces of imperialism and sports organizations manipulated by imperialist countries."[61] There is some evidence supporting the idea that the Indonesian proposal was actually Chinese. The Chinese were reported to have paid the transportation costs of all the delegations at GANEFO, and to have given the Indonesians an $18 million gift for the Games.[62]

Whether the PRC was behind GANEFO made no difference to the IOC and to the international federations, for the purpose of the Games was made clear in Sukarno's opening speech denouncing the IOC for working contrary to its rules and mixing politics in sport. He said, "Let us declare frankly that sport has something to do with politics. And Indonesia now proposes to mix sport with politics."[63] To Sukarno the Olympic Games were but a tool of the old established forces who engaged in discriminatory actions against Asian, African, and Latin American nations. Sukarno stated that in Indonesia sport was used to further the country's political aims, namely, world friendship and peace. GANEFO would be a tool to oppose the old established forces.[64] The IOC and the international federations could not tolerate a sport movement whose aim was strictly political, nor one in direct competition with the Olympic movement.

It was a complicated situation owing to the structure of the Olympic movement. The only power the IOC had in controlling the practices of regional contests, such as the Asian Games, was over the practices of the national Olympic committees. This depended in large measure upon whether a regional Games sought IOC patronage. If this were not the case, the IOC had nothing to do with the Games unless a national committee went contrary to its rules. If the

Games did not have IOC patronage they could not be linked to the IOC. The international federations controlled the athletes in their respective sports and could withhold permission for the athletes to take part in certain contests if the contests did not meet their qualifications.

GANEFO was not under IOC patronage but was avowedly political. The presence of the PRC in the Games, which at least two federations (the IAAF and FINA, the international swimming federation) did not recognize, presented problems. If the federation athletes participated against PRC athletes, this would be contrary to federation rules, and federation athletes would not be able to compete in federation sanctioned contests, such as the Olympic Games.

Fifty states participated in GANEFO, including the Soviet Union, but the fear of being barred from the Olympic Games prevented most of the participating states from sending official teams. In general only athletes of less than Olympic caliber were sent. The Games were hailed as a great success, foiling the forces of imperialism, and were scheduled to take place, like the Olympic Games, every four years. The next GANEFO would be held in Cairo in 1967.

GANEFO was a clear attempt to compete with the Olympic Games. More important, according to its stated purpose, GANEFO was to unite the new emerging forces and to emphasize their presence on the world scene. The absence of the United States and the Western European states, save France, was a clear indication of this purpose as well as of East-West estrangement. GANEFO took place in November 1963, but its impact would still be felt and would cause problems at the Tokyo Games in 1964.

Before the GANEFO Games in November 1963, the IOC held its annual general session in October. With the Tokyo Summer Games in mind, roughly a year away, the IOC decided that it was prepared to reinstate the Indonesian Olympic Committee as soon as it had apologized and "had undertaken to respect the Olympic rules."[65] Since the Games were going to be held in Asia for the first time, the IOC wanted all the national committees from the area to participate. The GANEFO Games being held a month later complicated matters. Not only was there a possibility that Indonesia might not participate, but also that North Korea might abstain.

The Tokyo Games would mark the first time that North Korea would participate in the Olympic Games. In 1962 it received provisional international recognition like the GDR. Under the conditions laid down by the IOC, North Korea was to form a united team with South Korea, as in the German case. The North Koreans agreed, but South Korea said such a team was impossible. Impatient with the South Koreans' intransigence, the IOC issued an ultimatum to the South Koreans stating that if they refused to form a joint team, North Korea would be allowed to compete independently. They refused and the IOC carried out its threat.

GANEFO had operated without IOC patronage, so the IOC had no jurisdiction except insofar as any national committees were involved. On the other hand, the Games were carried out through diplomatic channels, bypassing the federations. In addition two countries, the PRC and North Vietnam, which were not members of any federations, had participated. As a result the federations issued warnings to their national members not to take part in GANEFO. Several Olympic caliber athletes from North Korea and Indonesia, affiliated members of the two federations IAAF and FINA, took part anyway. They were subsequently barred from the Tokyo Games.

In April 1964 Indonesia was still suspended from the IOC and refused to apologize for its action in the Asian Games. By June, with the Summer Games approaching, the Indonesian committee hastily agreed to abide by the Olympic rules and was reinstated. The athletes from Indonesia, however, who were affiliated with the IAAF and FINA and had taken part in GANEFO, as well as those from North Korea, were still barred by these two international federations from participating in the Tokyo Games. At the IOC session in Tokyo, right before the Games, several national committees (the USSR, North Korea, UAR, and Morocco) tried to prevail upon the IOC to lift the ban on the Indonesian and North Korean athletes. The reply they received was that it was not the intention of the IOC to keep athletes out, but that the rules existed to maintain necessary order. The international federations also had rules which must be followed by anyone who intended to participate in the Olympic Games. The IOC respected the autonomy of the international federations, but its position was that the national committees should work to protect the Olympic movement, and therefore should prevail upon their governments not to interfere in sport.[66]

The two committees, Indonesia and North Korea, threatened to pull out their whole contingents if the barred athletes were not allowed to compete. They were not and the two committees withdrew, but only after they had caused much consternation to all concerned. GANEFO's impact, however, was still to be felt. The possibility of an alternative athletic movement gaining wide adherents in the non-Western world was very real, particularly in Africa, and very much a threat to the Olympic movement.

Regional Games for Africa had been planned and were organized in Brazzaville. Some African states were excluded, notably South Africa, and consequently the IOC would not issue its patronage as the "African Games." The name would have to be changed. In view of the GANEFO episode, possible alienation of the African countries through the IOC stance on the African Games might have steered the African countries into the GANEFO camp. This fear was voiced by Brundage in a letter to the Marquess of Exeter.

If we want to hold the Olympic world together we must not let these 37 African countries be led into the GANEFO camp, which may easily happen. Peking, China is very active now in Africa, and Congo Brazzaville has recently received from it a $20,000,000.00 loan. The Egyptians are organizing the second GANEFO Games in Cairo in 1967. . . . The Indonesian Embassy in Switzerland is inviting the National Federations and the Swiss NOC to a reception on the anniversary of the First GANEFO Games. This is probably also taking place in other places. The Arab countries and a few others are sympathetic.

. . .Africa is today a battleground for conflicting political creeds, they know little about Olympic principles and they are supersensitive anyway. The fact that we are inconsistent in insisting that they invite a Federation (South Africa) that we refused to invite to Tokyo has already put us in a very bad light and will probably drive them all into the receptive arms of the GANEFO crowd if we are not most careful.[67]

Brundage's fear was well founded, but the alienation of the African countries did not result in a stronger GANEFO. Instead, the result was trouble in the future for the IOC and the Olympic Games over the issue of South Africa.

The GANEFO movement intended to divide and fragment the Olympic movement, to emphasize the political realities of the world structure, and to dramatize the political ambitions of the new and nonaligned states. At the same time GANEFO was a product of East-West estrangement as it existed in the early 1960's. By the time of GANEFO the Sino-Soviet split had taken place, halving the Communist camp and creating three power blocs, each vying for the attentions of the nonaligned emerging states. This was evident in GANEFO. The PRC was its main supporter. The Soviet Union participated, but not enough to jeopardize its stature in the Olympic movement. The United States and Western Europe, save France, did not participate. French participation was illustrative of France's growing independence with de Gaulle at the helm, reflecting the United States-French estrangement during this time.

The issue of South African participation in the Olympic Games exemplified the emergence of the new states on the world scene and indicated the competitive interest accorded to this area by the industrialized world and by the power blocs. South Africa's participation in the 1960 Olympic Games had been guaranteed by the IOC through Brundage's insistent acceptance of the assurances of nondiscrimination given by the South African representative. These assurances were contradicted in February 1962, when the new South African minister of the interior, Jan de Klerk, announced that "the government policy is that no mixed teams should take part in sports inside or outside this country."[68] The meaning was clear, but the IOC, or at least Brundage, was not convinced. At the March executive board meeting Brundage noted that the assurances given in Rome in 1960 had not been carried out, and that the IOC would communicate with SANOC to get an explanation as well as confirmation of the earlier assurances.[69]

The South African government, however, kept up its strict apartheid stance, prompting the IOC representative from South Africa, Reginald Honey, to absent himself from the June general session in Moscow, for he thought South Africa would surely be suspended.[70] That was not to be, at least for the present. Instead, at the Moscow session the IOC decided to issue a stern warning to SANOC, stating that because the assurances given in Rome had not been carried out, the IOC was informing SANOC that if the government's policy of racial discrimination did not change before the IOC's Nairobi session in 1963, the IOC would be obliged to suspend the South African committee.[71]

Subsequent events regarding the holding of the Nairobi session would set the stage for South African suspension. Nairobi had been selected as the city for the 1963 IOC general session, the first time such a meeting was to be held in Africa. The IOC member from Kenya, Reginald Alexander, had lobbied hard for the IOC to pick his city in order to show Africa that it was really wanted and recognized by the Olympic movement. It was one way to avoid fragmentation.[72] The city of Nairobi and the Kenyan government were looking forward to holding the IOC session and were diligently preparing the facilities. By 1963, however, the African countries were taking a strict stand to discontinue any relations with South Africa. They declared in an OAU decision that they would boycott any conference anywhere in the world if South Africa or Portugal were present (Portugal still had colonies in Africa—Mozambique and Angola) as they had already boycotted a United Nations conference in Geneva on labor and education over the same issue.[73] The Kenyan government let it be known it was conforming with the decision of the OAU made in early July 1963, and it would not allow the South African delegates of the IOC into Kenya for the October session.[74]

Upon receipt of this information, the IOC decided the African action was discriminatory and could not be tolerated. As a result, the session was moved to Baden-Baden, West Germany. After the Kenyan government's decree there was some agitation for expelling the Kenyan committee. Brundage stated, however, there was no justification for such action. The Kenyan committee, he reasoned, could not be held responsible for the decision of its government.[75] Yet the IOC had seen fit to suspend the Indonesian committee and was threatening the South African committee. Both instances involved crimes neither committee supposedly had any control over, whether they agreed with their governments or not. It would appear the IOC action was not motivated by its charter and by noble principles but by political expediency, using the charter when it supported IOC action and conveniently neglecting it when it was contrary to the IOC's purpose.

The events in Nairobi clearly expounded the African position and forced the IOC, if it did not want to alienate all of Africa and numerous sympathizers, to take a stand against apartheid. At the Baden-Baden session the representatives of SANOC made the IOC decision considerably easier. They declared that apartheid was purely an internal matter and no business of the IOC. They would hold trials outside of South Africa if necessary, though they would have to be segregated, and the South African government would grant passports to all worthy nonwhites.[76] It was apparent from government statements and the conditions laid down by SANOC that the whites of South Africa would not be allowed to compete against nonwhites of South Africa in any forum, even the Olympic Games. Refusing to suspend South Africa outright, the IOC gave SANOC until December 31, 1963, to change the apartheid policy in sport, or face suspension from the Olympic Games.

The IOC extended the deadline into January, to the time of the next executive board meeting. In the meantime, the South African government had restated its position by threatening to introduce legislation to enforce apartheid in sport.[77] At the executive board meeting the Marquess of Exeter pointed out to the SANOC president that his committee had not publicly and officially disassociated itself from the government's policy, to which the man replied that the government refused to see the IOC point of view, reluctantly admitting that "his committee had not alarmed the public opinion on the matter."[78] The rest of the executive board agreed with Exeter's point, declaring that SANOC had not carried out its obligations. Brundage tempered the decision of the executive board, stating that some progress had been made and a resolution to that effect would be proposed to the full session.[79] At the full session following the executive board meeting, the IOC voted to revoke its invitation, agreeing to reconsider if SANOC would declare its opposition to the government's sport policy. SANOC failed to do this and consequently did not participate in the 1964 Games.

The IOC action precipitated some international federation and government action against South Africa. Alex Metrevelli of the Soviet Union and Istvan Gulyas of Hungary refused to compete against South Africa at Wimbledon. In consequence, the International Lawn Tennis Federation (ILTF) passed a resolution barring any racial discrimination in international tournaments. In addition, in retaliation against the Russian and Hungarian actions, it ruled that any entry to a tournament could withdraw only for reasons of health or bereavement, or with special permission from the organizing committee.[80] In September the International Table Tennis Federation met in Prague and censured South Africa. In October the Russians proposed that South Africa be barred from three federations: boxing, swimming, and the IAAF. The Russian proposals were not passed. The International Soccer Federation did, however, resume suspension of its national affiliate in South Africa, a suspension that had been earlier executed in 1962 and then lifted by the executive board of the federation in 1963.[81]

The IOC decision pointed up the growing world concern over events in Africa and other emerging areas. This concern was voiced in extra-political modes, as well, although political motives may have inhered. One such mode was the granting of aid. Of course this could take many forms—military, economic, or technical. In the case of the Congo in the early 1960's, the motive was completely political due to the involvement of the superpowers. The IOC, for reasons that will become clear, joined the parade to aid the African countries by establishing in 1961 an International Olympic Aid Commission, proposed by Comte de Beaumont of France and Constantin Andrianov of the Soviet Union. The purpose of the commission was to promote the Olympic ideal in such areas as Africa where it seemed lacking. This was designed to bolster the Olympic movement and to keep amateur sport free from politics. Unfortunately the Olympic aid program had to compete with the programs of organizations that did not necessarily share the Olympic ideals. The Comte de Beaumont, head of the Aid Commission, related this problem in an open letter to the IOC.

There is no doubt that the whole world is now turned toward Africa and that the interests of all kinds—in spirit as in quality—mingle there.... Information coming from different sources have [sic] confirmed our belief that one expects the International Olympic Committee to fulfill its international task in matter [sic] of sport. However the IOC must be aware that other organizations feel concerned with the development of sport in Africa, for such reasons that we shall not define here, but the tendency of which is not necessarily that of the IOC and of its rules. Therefore it is most important that we do not relax our action, but that, on the contrary, we make it alive by the pooling of our common efforts in a constant and constructive prospect.[82]

It was Comte de Beaumont's and Andrianov's idea that the IOC should do more than merely give encouragement, but any offers of coaching or of technical aid were derided by the international federations as being only in their province.[83] At the same time the African countries were not content with only moral support. They requested financial aid, which the IOC could not and would not give. Andrianov was quite enthusiastic about the aid commission, but his enthusiasm was viewed with suspicion by other members of the IOC. In a letter to Brundage, Comte de Beaumont voiced his fears of the Soviet interest.

...it is my private opinion that the USSR are only keen about this effort in so far as it is part of their political objective of extending their influence in Africa, and they see in the IOC a means to that end. We must not forget that the overwhelming influence of the USSR in the United Nations affairs has been accentuated by their support of the African States, and we have to beware that too much influence on the IOC of increased African membership could have the same effect.[84]

The combination of political exploitation, the risk of embarrassment of the IOC by any financial considerations, and a lack of funds spelled the end of the aid commission. At the Baden-Baden session the residue of the funds for the commission was paid over to the IOC and put into a special account. The commission was finished without really having started.

The politics involving the aid commission were symptomatic of the excessive politicization of the period, which pervaded the Olympics. The problems of GANEFO, NATO, and South Africa brought to the forefront the necessity of a common policy between the federations, the national committees, and the IOC if the Olympic movement were to retain its standing in amateur sport, but all that ensued was a series of joint declarations for mutual cooperation. The Soviet committee persisted in its proposals for changing the structure of the IOC. These, in turn, were interpreted as efforts by the Soviet Union to take over the IOC; they were therefore turned down.[85] On a similar matter there was considerable concern in the IOC that a bloc existed to rally countries of Eastern Europe. This feeling had been conveyed before, but in 1961 Brundage assembled the Soviet members for the first time to discuss the issue. They categorically denied that such a bloc existed. When the executive board meeting was convened the issue was brought up by the French delegate, who mentioned that at each session when the USSR members made a proposal they were backed by the members of the Eastern European countries who, "one after the other, raise from their seat to punctuate their assent." The French delegate found this type of proceeding somewhat unusual. Andrianov, the Soviet delegate, replied that no such bloc existed or was necessary. One after another, the Eastern European delegates rose to confirm his assertion.[86]

An Olympiad would not be complete without some controversy over China. The IV Asian Games with the denial of Taiwan's participation, plus the GANEFO episode with the PRC's involvement would have been enough in and of themselves, but one more incident with a comical side was a factor in closing out the Chinese problem for the XVII Olympiad. At the Baden-Baden session of 1963 it was decided to allow the athletes from Taiwan to wear emblems designated "ROC" (Republic of China), but in all other matters the committee was to be called Taiwan. The Taiwan committee, when designing the emblem, also placed above the letters "ROC" some Chinese script. The committee sent the emblem to the chancellor of the IOC to get it approved. The chancellor, noticing the Chinese script in addition to the lettering "ROC," wondered about its real meaning. The only authoritative Chinese source in Switzerland was the Chinese embassy in Berne, but this embassy was the PRC's and not Taiwan's. The chancellor, suspecting that the script said "Republic of China," which was forbidden, sent the emblem to the PRC embassy. Sure enough, it said "Republic of China!" The Taiwan committee was duly notified to leave the Chinese script off the emblem.[87]

The Olympic Games, in addition to being a showcase for nationalism that produced much political activity, were becoming a showcase for business interests as well. The Winter Games of 1964 were expected to be a great boon to the Austrian economy, provided of course the Austrian skiers did well. An Austrian trade delegate to the United States estimated that a good performance by the Austrian skiers would result in a substantial increase in exports of ski equipment, a large part of the Austrian economy. They had experienced a boom in exports after the 1956 Games, when Toni Sailer of Austria took the triple crown in skiing, winning all three skiing events: downhill, slalom, and giant slalom. Even beyond exports, the Austrians figured to increase their major tourist industry by making Innsbruck, site of the 1964 Winter Games, a sport center as well as a tourist attraction.[88]

Another example of the increasing business interest in the Games was the aspect of donations of equipment and sundry items. In this case the textile and apparel firms were involved, donating outfits to the United States Olympic Committee. There had been no real coordination in the apparel of the United States squad, which had caused negative comment. In an effort to smarten the appearance and to bring greater glory to the American "ready to wear" industry, the apparel was revamped. A subcommittee was formed in the

United States Olympic Committee to meet with clothing representatives and design a common costume. For the donation, the industry would receive a favorable public service image, a tax deduction, an international fashion showcase, and the opportunity to merchandise the article as "contributed to" the Olympic team. It was estimated the dress parade uniforms for the opening and closing ceremonies would exert a strong influence on high school and college-age Americans in the fall.[89] All this came at a time when the American textile and apparel industries were beginning to meet heavy competition from imports.

The aspect of having "contributed to" the Olympic effort was a very important selling point. With the increasing costs of the Games, national committees as well as the organizing committees came to rely much more on industry contributions. In turn, such contributions were seen by industry as beneficial due to the principle of positive identification on the part of the would-be buyers. Here, the element of nationalism became a factor. If the team should do well, as in the cases of Austria and the skiing industry, or the American team and its apparel, industry would benefit because it could market those items as having contributed to the Olympic team with the connotation of having contributed to the team victory. This factor is very important in sporting equipment, and large sums of money are spent by manufacturers to get their products tried out and identified with the top athletes in international and Olympic sport. This was a problem for the IOC because of the question of amateurism. It would develop into a major issue, particularly in Alpine sport, after 1964.

Meanwhile, problems attendant upon television coverage of the Games had continued to escalate. By 1964, with the proposed use of satellite coverage for the Tokyo Games, television had become a major issue in Olympic discussions not only for the IOC but also for the federations. The possibility of reaping tremendous revenue from the sale of television rights to the Games was seen as the panacea for Olympic financial problems, but with such a panacea came problems of allocating the revenue. The international federations were demanding that after the 1964 Games they should receive one-third of the revenue. Their reasoning was the same as in 1960, that they were donating their championships to the Games and thus deserved a share.[90] The national committees, the organizing committees, and the IOC were also demanding shares of the revenue.

For the 1964 Games the revenue was to be distributed by the executive board of the IOC to "each according to his need." This scheme would soon become inadequate and would produce much controversy in the future, particularly as television revenue skyrocketed.

The major issue at the 1964 Games regarding television was over satellite coverage, mainly because it involved a conflict of interest between corporate and public/state interests. NBC television had the American broadcasting rights to the Tokyo Games. Tests were carried out by NASA and NBC, at United States and Japanese government prodding, as to the feasibility of live satellite coverage. The Communication Satellite Corporation was asked by the State Department, in the national interest, to look into live television coverage. Syncom III, developed by the Hughes Corporation, was chosen by the Communication Satellite Corporation as the most advanced satellite for the purpose, but it still had to be orbited before the Games and had to be put into place.[91] The arrangements were made, after months of negotiating between foreign and domestic agencies and companies, to show the satellite coverage on the American continent and then to fly the broadcasts across the Atlantic on the same day for European audiences. The White House said the transmissions, if successful, "would be an outstanding demonstration of technological partnership by the United States and Japan. It would be the forerunner of the coming establishment of the global communication satellite system bridging the Pacific as well as the Atlantic."[92]

NBC had other plans. They had shown little interest in the project from the beginning and took part only at the urging of Averell Harriman, Under-Secretary of State for Political Affairs. NBC's plan was to show the opening ceremonies live and to limit the satellite's use after that. Instead, the satellite pictures were to be recorded for later use on sponsored shows along with pictures flown from Japan. The fourteen-hour time differential was seen as a major obstacle because it would interfere with the lucrative evening program schedules.

As it turned out, the opening ceremonies were seen live on the East coast of the United States, but were delayed on the West coast for three hours until 1:00 A.M., instead of the originally proposed 10:00 P.M. showing, because they did not want to interrupt Johnny Carson's "Tonight Show." The State Department voiced concern over the matter because coverage of the Olympics was a source of

Japanese and American national pride and had been hailed as a great achievement and source of international peace. NBC announced there would be no more live telecasts, despite all the efforts that had been made. This angered not only the State Department and Japan, but also the Hughes Aircraft Company. There had been an intense rivalry between Hughes, the manufacturers of Syncom, RCA, the manufacturers of Relay satellites, and AT&T, the manufacturers of Telstar. All three had vied to be chosen by the Communication Satellite Corporation. The corporation picked the Hughes satellite, but RCA owned NBC. NBC also expressed concern over the time differential, noting that the event would come at odd times in the United States. The State Department disagreed. They were concerned that Europe and the Soviet Union might televise the Olympic pictures before the United States because of the time differential. This was viewed as a matter of United States prestige.[93] Nevertheless, NBC's programming schedule prevailed.

The XVII Olympiad was characterized by increasing incidents of nationalism representing the changing face of the nation-state system. No longer did only an Eastern and a Western bloc exist, although their conflict permeated many of the issues and leaders on both sides still tended to view world affairs in cold war terms. Now there was a split in the communist camp, and a split was developing in the Western camp with the increasing independence of France and the EEC. In addition the new emerging states were vying to be heard. The Olympic movement was forced to contend with each of these power centers while struggling with dissension in its own ranks. The financial interests were continuing to intrude upon the Games, and the attendant problems would only increase.

XVIII OLYMPIAD (1964-1968) AND THE 1968 OLYMPIC GAMES

The most controversial issue confronting the IOC and the Olympic movement during the XVIII Olympiad was the question of South African participation, not only because of the immediate political conflict but because of extrinsic issues that developed around it. The whole complex of problems reflected the main political events and trends of the period.

The South African controversy represented the reaction of world opinion against the exploitation of the underdeveloped areas. Apartheid as practiced by the white ruling regime in South Africa was widely considered to be an extension of colonialism. The growing opposition to apartheid by the black African states and by the world at large reflected not only the emergence of black Africa onto the world scene at that time, but also the responsive attention paid to the African states by the rest of the world. The particular forums of opposition further illustrated the changing organizational relationships. Regional and global alignments against apartheid, such as the OAU and the United Nations, evidenced growing cooperation in the face of adversity by means of the integration of states, that is, the formation of larger units for a more efficient solution to common problems for the benefit of each individual unit. The focusing of global attention on the problems of Africa took some of the pressure off other troubled spots in the world, facilitating a lessening of tension in those areas, such as Europe, and creating a more conducive atmosphere for the solution of prolonged conflicts.

The Question of South Africa

Following most Olympic Games there is a lull in Olympic activity, which rebuilds gradually to a crescendo in the next Games four years hence. The aftermath of the 1964 Games was no different. Certain movements were in the works, however, that would alter Olympic relationships and would inhibit the IOC's ability to cope with various issues. The major issue was South Africa. The decision that had been taken to exclude South Africa from participating in the Tokyo Games had no bearing on its continued membership in the Olympic movement. The pressure to refuse South African participation had come mainly from within the IOC as a result of South Africa's intractible attitude toward IOC rules. The indirect threat of an African boycott had not been the foremost concern of the IOC. Following the Tokyo Games the situation had changed. The South African attitude was as stubborn as ever, but direct pressure was being applied by the African states.

Early in 1965 a conference was held in Rome by eighty national Olympic committees to discuss common problems, presenting resolutions to the IOC as a body rather than as individual units, hoping by this means to get more effective national committee input into the IOC. Similar movements were developing among the international federations and among regional groupings of national committees, such as those from Africa. At the conference the African delegates threatened to walk out of the meeting if the South African representative, Reginald Honey (also an IOC member), were admitted. Not wanting to risk aborting the conference, the delegates voted unanimously to bar the South African delegate from the meeting. In addition, the African national committees proposed a resolution to be presented at the IOC general session in Madrid later in the year, which called for the complete exclusion of the South African committee from all Olympic institutions.[94]

At the executive board meeting before the general session the African position was noted; it was also noted that the South African national committee had not taken a stand against discrimination. For this reason, a recommendation to suspend SANOC until its rules accorded with the IOC's was presented to the general session.[95] The general session ruled that since the laws of South Africa prevented the observance of Olympic principles, at the next meeting in 1966 the South African committee would be suspended and its officials would no longer participate in the meetings. Until the 1966 meeting, as an attempt to keep the national committees in line, the decision stipulated that at any meetings under the aegis of the IOC, representatives of all recognized national committees had to be permitted to participate.

The IOC decision was clearly aimed at the South African government and did eventually bring certain concessions. At the Rome general session in April 1966 Brundage tempered the tone of the meeting and the IOC demands by pointing out that the South African committee risked sanctions if it violated its government's laws of apartheid. He stated, "...we must reexamine the question realistically. If we expel them, we shall never see them again. If we suspend them immediately, this could cause the arrangement that they are desperately trying to make with their government to miscarry." He wanted no decision made at that session but preferred that the issue be considered when invitations were sent out for the Games.[96]

In their attempt to conform to the IOC rules, the South African delegates proposed to form a committee composed of an equal number of white and colored officials that would concern itself with the selection of their Olympic team. This committee would be presided over by SANOC. It was estimated such a move would

constitute a basis for SANOC's continuation in the Olympic movement and was a real step forward. Because of this concession the
IOC decided to put SANOC to the test to see how the committee
would function, deferring its decision until the following year at the
Teheran session. An IOC commission was to be formed to go to
South Africa, investigate the situation on the spot, and report later
at Teheran.[97]

Brundage's view of apartheid as being a political issue totally
removed from sport[98] was not shared by all his colleagues. Andrianov, the Soviet member of the IOC, disagreed openly. In a letter
to Brundage he pointed out that, "trying sometimes not to take any
notice of the surrounding present-day life, the IOC unfortunately
doesn't pay attention to the existing reality. We can't keep ourselves away from and shut our eyes to flagrant discrimination on
racial grounds," he went on, "under the pretext that apartheid is a
governmental policy inside the [sic] South Africa."[99]

Brundage's reply is interesting for the contradiction that he failed
to recognize. He agreed with Andrianov that racial discrimination
was denounced by practically everyone, but apartheid was a government policy, and the IOC was not concerned with governments
or politics. "There is no government yet that is perfect," Brundage
emphasized. "Our concern is whether the South African OC
[Olympic Committee] can function according to Olympic rules."[100]
It had already been noted that the government of South Africa prevented this, and that SANOC would not declare its allegiance to the
Olympic principle of nondiscrimination. It was clearly unwilling
and unable to conform to Olympic principles. A mixed team and
trials were still not forthcoming.

If Brundage and the IOC had their heads in the sand, then so did
the international federations. In July 1966 the Soviet Union proposed the exclusion of South Africa from the International Lawn
Tennis Federation (ILTF), but the ILTF established a "weighted
voting" system, whereby the major tennis playing nations (predominantly white) would control the majority of votes. As a result,
the Soviet proposal was defeated eighty percent to twenty percent.
The USSR proposed a similar motion in the IAAF, the largest and
most prestigious federation, but the IAAF had also adopted a
weighted voting system. In their organization thirty-seven predominantly white states had 244 votes and ninety-nine predominantly
nonwhite states had only 195 votes. The motion was defeated.[101]

It is interesting to note the origins of the weighted voting system. The increase of participating members in international sport had altered the "complexion" of the sporting world. International sport had been predominantly white-ruled and centered, but the new members came chiefly from the emerging areas (predominantly nonwhite) and the white membership in international sport was being outnumbered. Future voting decisions would probably favor the nonwhite membership. It would simply be a matter of a majority of votes in the sense of "one member, one vote." Much the same process was taking place in the United Nations General Assembly and subsidiary bodies. The IOC, because of its unique structure, could delay this trend by appointing its members from only certain areas of the world. The international federations could not. In a June 1963 executive board meeting with the international federations, Brundage commented on this situation. "If we accept 25 new African countries, the countries with a strong Olympic tradition will risk being outvoted," he cautioned. "It would be prudent perhaps to give certain countries with a large sporting population more votes than a country only recently affiliated."[102]

The IOC, despite its unique structure, was not completely immune to the trend. The Soviets had proposed the alteration of the IOC to include representatives from each member committee. This had been defeated. For the April 1966 session the Soviets were proposing a modification of this plan by reorganizing the executive board to include a representative membership from around the world, with two members from Asia, two from Africa, two from America, two from Europe, and one from Oceania.[103] In addition the national committees were lobbying for more input into the IOC, and movements were afloat to form organizations of national committees for this purpose. The Rome conference, which was mentioned earlier, is an example. The IOC was concerned about such movements because of the threat to its authority and the possibility of political interference. Brundage was particularly concerned, warning that the new African committees simply did not understand that one could not use sport as a stick for achieving political objectives, and that the IOC would have to be very careful.[104] The problem was compounded by the fact that because of general inexperience and lack of money many African governments had to initiate and administer sport. The instrument chosen for administering sport was normally a national sport council, government dominated. For purposes of affiliation to the IOC, the sport councils or their subsidiaries would simply be termed national olympic committees.[105]

The fears of Brundage and the IOC were confirmed in December 1966 in Bamako, Mali, when the Supreme Council for Sport in Africa (SCSA) was formed with thirty-two African states. Its general purpose was coordination and promotion of sport throughout Africa, but its specific objective was the attack against South African apartheid in sport. At the founding conference the SCSA resolved:

...to use every means to obtain the expulsion of South African sports organizations from the Olympic Movement and from International Federations should South Africa fail to comply fully with the IOC rules.

Finally, the Supreme Council invites all its members to subject their decision to participate in the 1968 Olympic Games to the reservation that no racialist team from South Africa takes part, and to ask all national Olympic committees to support the attitude of the Supreme Council for Sport in Africa.[106]

The SCSA was a semi-autonomous subsidiary organ of the OAU (Organization of African Unity) whose members were not only governments but also national Olympic committees, owing to the special relationships involved. The motives of the SCSA were obviously political and were contrary to the IOC. Brundage's opinions were clearly anathema to the Africans. What Brundage failed to recognize was that sport was in fact a terrific stick for achieving political objectives, particularly when leveled against South Africa, a country highly sensitive to sport issues. The Africans were certainly not the first to seek political objectives through the use of sport. Brundage knew this very well. The Africans were simply the most recent and, as it would turn out, among the most adept.

Considering the forthcoming Teheran session, the IOC commission to Africa, and the continuing problems of South Africa in its sporting relations abroad, Frank Braun, the SANOC president, made the following concessions for the Olympics: (1) South Africa would send a mixed team to the Games, (2) all members would march under the same flag and wear the same colors, (3) South Africans of different racial groups would compete against each other at the Games, and (4) a nonwhite Olympic committee would be formed and each racial group would designate its candidates for selection.[107] The IOC viewed these concessions as a definite improvement. The Marquess of Exeter said it was a very great step forward and was pleased to hear it. The same sentiment was voiced even by the nonwhite South African sports circles.[108]

The SCSA, however, did not hold the same view. It vowed that the African states would boycott the 1968 Games if a "racist team" from South Africa was admitted.[109] The Ethiopian sports director underscored this when he threatened that if the IOC "dared to allow" South Africa to participate, his country would definitely boycott. He called South Africa's new policy "a farce."[110] Braun's statement was followed by an official government policy statement made by Prime Minister Vorster, where he substantiated that South Africa would send a mixed team and would allow nonwhites from other countries to compete in South Africa against whites because these contests, he said, involved interstate relations. But Vorster emphasized that the internal policy of separate development (apartheid) would still be enforced.[111]

Before the Teheran general session of the IOC, at the executive board meeting with the national committees, the African national committees made clear their stand against South African participation. They said it made no difference whether the black population in South Africa was inclined to accept the changes; the African committees would not accept any South African team, mixed or not mixed, as long as SANOC could not fully comply with all IOC rules. "Only complete independent Olympic committees could be recognized by the IOC," and it was their opinion SANOC was not independent from government interference.[112]

Their position was a bit incongruous considering their own relationships with their governments. Andrianov pointed out that governments were not to interfere in the affairs of national committees and federations, but governmental assistance must be accepted in countries where only the government had the means to promote sport.[113] For the African committees the distinction was clear. South African internal policy prohibited SANOC from abiding by the IOC charter, and this internal policy had not changed.

At the Teheran session the IOC heard Frank Braun's detailed proposals and decided to make no decision until its Grenoble session in February 1968, where it would hear the report of its three-man commission to South Africa. The IOC was very much encouraged.

Meanwhile, the South African question had definitely become an international incident. In 1966 the Brasilia seminar of the United Nations recommended that "all states should refrain from cultural and sports relationships with South Africa as long as apartheid and white supremacy prevail in that country."[114] In the United States the American Committee on Africa (ACOA) composed a letter signed by thirty prominent Americans, including Jackie Robinson, Arthur Ashe, Roy Campanella, I. W. Abel, Langston Hughes and Reinhold Niebuhr, to Douglas Roby, president of the United States Olympic Committee (USOC), asking the USOC to commit itself to keeping South Africa out of the Olympics.[115] The First National Conference on Black Power was held in Newark, calling for a boycott by blacks of athletics, including the Olympic Games.[116] The conference later would demand Brundage's resignation because of his alleged racism and anti-Semitism, an end to discrimination against blacks and Jews in the United States, reinstatement of Muhammad Ali, appointment of an additional black coach to the United States Olympic team, appointment of a black to the USOC, and the end of competition between United States teams and those of South Africa and Rhodesia.[117] At a British track and field meet, the teams from Kenya, Nigeria, Pakistan, and India withdrew, refusing to compete against the two teams from South Africa— white and nonwhite.[118]

The handwriting was on the wall. Now the decision was completely in the hands of the IOC. In September the IOC commission, composed of Lord Killanin of Ireland, Reginald Alexander (who was white) of Kenya, and Sir Ade Ademola (the only nonwhite IOC member from Africa) of Nigeria, went to South Africa. In December the SCSA stated that "if, in spite of the country's [South Africa] segregationist tendencies in sports, the Committee [IOC] decides to admit it [South Africa] we will withdraw from the world body."[119] Everyone anxiously awaited the Grenoble session.

The IOC Commission report was released on January 30, 1968, just before the Grenoble session, and was favorable to South Africa. It stated that from the evidence compiled from sport administrators and competitors in South Africa, the Teheran proposals were "an acceptable basis for a multi-racial team to the Mexico Olympic Games.... Sportsmen of all communities in South Africa were prepared to accept the selection by the joint body as provided for in the Teheran statement."[120]

All those against South African participation stepped up their efforts in opposition. New appeals were directed to Brundage. In a statement for the American Committee on Africa, Harry Edwards, a professor from California State University at San Jose, a former world class athlete and the leader of the black American boycott movement said:

I am deeply opposed to the presence of South Africans or Southern Rhodesians as team members or as individuals at international sporting events or events in the United States if there is any form of racism and on that there can be no compromise. Black athletes will refuse to participate in the Olympic Games if South Africa or Southern Rhodesia are permitted into the Games while racism still exists at any level.[121]

Because of the absence of so many delegates at the Grenoble session the IOC decided to send out a postal vote on the South African question. The decision of the delegates was to be based on the following motion:

Having studied the report of the Commission on South Africa, the International Olympic Committee notes with grave concern that racially-discriminatory internal policies of the South African Government prevent the National Olympic Committee of that country from achieving fully the aims of the IOC under Fundamental Principle I of the Olympic code. It is, however, encouraged that positive efforts by the S.A.N.O.C. have resulted in a firm undertaking to implement the proposals announced at the IOC session in Tehran in May 1967 whereby a multi-racial team will be selected on merit. It now resolves that the S.A.N.O.C. may enter a team which conforms with Fundamental Principle I in the Olympic Games in 1968 in Mexico and on the understanding that it continues vigorously its efforts to have all forms of racial discrimination in amateur sport removed, the IOC will reconsider the question by the end of 1972.[122]

By February 15 all ballots were in, and by an absolute majority it was decided to readmit a mixed South African team to the Games of the XIX Olympiad in Mexico.[123]

Delighted pandemonium broke out in South Africa, but elsewhere storm clouds appeared on the horizon. In the United States, a New York Athletic Club (accused of being racist and anti-Semitic) track meet was boycotted. The seven member Soviet contingent to the meet withdrew, and Harry Edwards, the leader of the black American boycott, in justification of the boycott, stated: "We deplore the use of black Americans in the NYAC track meet for the same fundamental reason that we deplore the exploitation of black

Americans in the Olympic Games and in Vietnam. These black Americans are being used to further the racist attitudes of the USA...."[124] Two days after the IOC decision Algeria and Ethiopia withdrew from the Games. The Ethiopian sport director said the IOC decision was a victory for apartheid, not for SANOC. "What happens after the Games?" he asked. "Each athlete will return to South Africa and join his segregated club. What has the IOC achieved if the status quo is maintained in South Africa after the Mexico Games?"[125] The USSR called the IOC decision a "flagrant violation of the Charter of the IOC,"[126] but withheld any action until after the Winter Games. One by one the countries began to withdraw. A mass exodus was in progress. On February 25 the OAU recommended that all African countries boycott the Games;[127] two days later the SCSA agreed.[128]

By February 28 almost all of Africa had withdrawn and numerous other states were joining the process. The IOC was ridiculed from all sides. The Belgium Olympic Committee castigated the IOC for relying on a mail vote on such an important question and brought up the perennial issue of inadequate national committee input, noting that the national committees had not been consulted and that over half were not represented on the IOC.[129] In the United States the top black athletes, many of whom were world record holders, were boycotting the Games. On March 6 the Soviet Union threatened to join the boycott unless an emergency session were held to reconsider the issue.[130]

The Mexico Games were now definitely in jeopardy. Before the IOC decision Brundage had shrugged off the boycott threats by telling the American athletes they would not even be missed.[131] Now the problem was serious. The Associated Press had polled various national committees to get a consensus view. Most were against the decision and were hoping the IOC would reconsider.[132] There was a very real possibility only a handful of states would go to the Games. Of those, large segments of their contingents would be missing.

The Mexican organizers of the Games were desperate and called on Brundage to reconvene the IOC. Five members of the executive board called for a full IOC meeting. Instead, on March 12, Brundage summoned a meeting of the executive board. In the interim he went to South Africa, ostensibly to visit a game park but also to confer with South African sport officials and to hint at a voluntary withdrawal. Frank Braun told Brundage he would "rather be shot in Mexico City than lynched in Johannesburg."[133]

At the executive board meeting on April 21, 1968 Brundage laid the situation before the membership—to leave things as they were or to throw South Africa out. The former was obviously inadequate, so only one course was open to the IOC—to withdraw South Africa's invitation. The question was how? To Brundage, the integrity and dignity of the IOC were on the line. They had to carry out the action like gentlemen and sportsmen. The subsequent debate centered around withdrawing the invitation on the rules of the IOC, but the board wanted South Africa to be able to withdraw gracefully. Brundage pointed up the possibility the Mexicans would not be able to protect the South Africans, to which the Mexican delegate objected. It was decided to recommend unanimously that, due to the international climate, the executive board was of the opinion it would be most unwise for South Africa to participate. For this reason, they requested the IOC endorse the recommendation, which the IOC subsequently did.[134]

As a result of the reconsideration, the 1968 Games were saved and the boycotts were called off. The IOC had based its decision on the international climate, which Brundage elaborated on in an interview to mean "the present atmosphere of violence around the world."[135] This was to become apparent in Mexico City as the Games drew near. Lord Killanin, when questioned about the decision, noted that numerous factors had been weighted, the boycott threat, the question of the Olympic's future, and possible "incidents" against the South Africans. Killanin said that although the Mexicans assured the IOC they could guard the South Africans' safety, they could not guard the South Africans against embarrassments. What all this really implied was a fear of embarrassing the Mexicans.[136] The United States boycotters rescinded their boycott but vowed to make some sort of protest at the Games, ultimately fulfilling Killanin's fear.

In June, the Mexican organizing committee of the Games announced that because of the recent resolution passed by the United Nations Security Council, which stated that all member states should deny admittance to any person traveling on a Rhodesian passport, Rhodesia would be unable to participate in the Games.[137] It is interesting to note Brundage's reaction to this development. "Here we have another case," he lamented, "of throwing

the Olympic Movement into the middle of an international controversy when the cause is political and has nothing at all to do with
sports.''[138] This is in sharp contrast to a statement Brundage made
in 1953 regarding the violation of Olympic principles and rules:

> If and when a Government determines to take over its national Olympic
> Committee there is, of course, very little effective opposition that can be
> offered by the national amateur sports organizations. The only correction
> for situations of this kind when the *letter and spirit* of the Olympic rules
> are not followed is for the rest of the world to refuse to play with countries
> which are in violation of Olympic principles.[139]

Apparently because the IOC based its South African decision on
the international climate rather than on a violation of its rules by
SANOC and the South African government, the IOC did not feel
that racial discrimination was in violation of its basic principles. In
any event, the way was clear for nearly full world participation in
the Summer Games.

The South African question and the boycott threat had brought
together numerous events and movements on the world scene. The
opposition of the African states to South Africa's participation
portrayed both substantively and symbolically the Third World
estrangement and anticolonial fight. Alignment with the black
movement in the United States reflected the dissident voices in the
developed world—the United States, Western Europe, Japan—that
were crying out for internal reforms and against postwar foreign
policies. There had been many student protests and riots in recent
months in Paris, Japan, and the United States, as well as black riots
in the inner cities, underscoring Brundage's claim and the IOC's
fear of violence or "incidents" at the Games. As it turned out,
Mexican students, who had been striking for months, rioted just
before the Games in protest against the vast outlay for the Games
at the expense of needed internal reforms and social programs.

In the United States, and to a certain degree in Western Europe,
much of the protest was over the war in Vietnam. The linkage of
the black American and African boycotts was, as such, no accident.
The American action in Vietnam was viewed essentially as an extension of colonialism (imperialism), the very thing the Africans were
fighting in South Africa in the form of white racism. In this connection the Soviet position was significant, as opposed to the
United States position. In the IOC the Soviets had consistently lob-

bied for the expulsion of South Africa, which was in line with the black African position but contrary to the United States stand. At the IOC meeting with the national Olympic committees at Mexico City just prior to the Games, this same alignment on the South African issue remained despite the cancellation of South Africa's invitation.[140] The Soviet delegate supported a joint African national committee proposal for expelling SANOC, while the United States delegates opposed it. At the Grenoble Games the president of the Central Committee of Soviet Sports called a special news conference solely to denounce American "aggression" in Vietnam.[141]

The Soviet Union's position regarding the African boycott of the Games is interesting for the political cross-pressures it faced. The Soviet Union never committed itself until it was assured of action. The Soviet Union could not support the boycott too early for fear of losing its position in the Olympic movement, where it had gained considerable prestige. The Soviet action must be seen in light of the political conditions at the time. The Soviets were in competition with the West throughout the world to gain the favor of the Third World countries by supporting their causes. At the same time their split with the Chinese produced a state of high tension between the two, similar to that of the early cold war period. In turn the PRC viewed itself as the champion for the Third World and was in competition with both the Soviet Union and the West for the favor of the emerging states. The Soviet Union could not totally alienate the West for fear of creating a coalition of opposing forces. This is where the African boycott became important. As an editorial in the *New York Times* pointed out:

The Russian dilemma involves more than just a decision that may kill the Games. It bears directly on their rivalry with the Chinese for the loyalty of the left in the underdeveloped world. If Moscow turns its back on Africa now, in the face of the South African challenge, it would be a major victory for Peking, which does not even participate in the Games.[142]

The Soviet Union was forced to play a waiting game and juggle its foreign policy so as to not upset its position vis-à-vis all the parties concerned.

The African boycott clearly demonstrated the strength of numbers unified into a single force. The African states were able to utilize their collective power through their regional organization, the OAU, and through the United Nations to achieve the desired results. The African's desire to form into a collective whole, in turn, spurred similar movements in the Olympic system itself, that is, in the General Assembly of National Olympic Committees, and the General Assembly of International Federations. The African integrative movement was but a part of the same trend taking place all over the world, mainly in the form of economic arrangements such as LAFTA, EEC, and COMECON. Significant in this trend was the desire, rising out of necessity, to form arrangements that went beyond the nation-state. It represented an ideological acceptance and sophistication that was rooted in nationalism but that went beyond a national perspective. A measure of autonomy was handed over for the collective good and, ultimately, for the good of the individual unit.

The German Question

As has been indicated, the desire for a joint German team in the Games was steadily meeting opposition from both German states. As early as 1962, Willi Daume, the president of the West German committee, had voiced some apprehension on the continuation of the plan. For some time the East Germans had been lobbying for separate representation. The changing climate of opinion in sport circles followed its counterpart in political circles. The erection of the Berlin Wall lessened the interest in reunification and further consolidated the East German state, thereby widening the gap between the two Germanies. Previously there had been a considerable number of defections from the Eastern zone, confounding the ability of the East German authorities to develop a sense of national consciousness. The erection of the wall limited these defections to a small number. The reaction of the Western powers to the Berlin Wall was a significant change in attitude toward a divided Germany. The Western powers' cries of protest, as opposed to direct military confrontation, signaled a tacit acceptance of two states. The East German leaders' change in emphasis, from reunification to a consolidation of a distinct East German state, was accompanied in West Germany after Adenauer's departure by a policy of reconciliation with Eastern Europe—the building of bridges with Eastern Europe. This policy was echoed in the conciliatory pronouncement by President Johnson of the United States calling for healing of the breach between Western and Eastern Europe.[143]

The Soviet recognition of full East German sovereignty with the erection of the Berlin Wall facilitated a reduction of superpower entanglement in the two Germanies, leaving the problems existing between East and West Germany mainly to the Germans. The process was abetted by the continuing expansion of Soviet and United States interests in other areas of the world. The Soviet Union was involved not only in Third World concerns but also in the Sino-Soviet conflict, decreasing its ability to concentrate as intensely as in previous years on the European theater. Also, the establishment of effective military security arrangements (NATO and the Warsaw Pact) had successfully deterred the threat of military aggrandizement by either side, permitting a consolidation of positions since the war.

All these factors had progressively altered the attitudes toward reunification and had a similar effect on the sporting relationships in the Olympic Games. For the 1964 Games there had been a unified team, but almost immediately after the Tokyo Summer Games the East Germans were clamoring for full recognition and separate participation by 1968. They were joined in their demands by the majority of the international federations—twenty out of twenty-four.[144] Several problems persisted. The NATO countries were still averse to allowing separate East German teams within their borders for international sporting events and made it plain to the IOC they expected a joint German team for the 1968 Winter Games in Grenoble, France. In addition the problem remained of fully recognizing the East German committee without conferring on it any political recognition. This problem had been solved in the case of China and Korea—by using a geographic rather than a political representation for the teams—China and Taiwan, North Korea and Korea. In 1965, at the IAAF session in Tokyo the East Germans had asked for the same type of recognition and had received it.[145]

In October 1965 at the IOC general session in Madrid, it became clear the IOC could not compel a unified team. The West Germans still advocated one, but the East Germans were adamantly opposed. The international federations were also against a unified squad. France, however, was balking at admitting a separate East German team. In light of the IOC declaration that all candidate cities for the Games had to assure that all recognized national committees could participate, the IOC was threatening to revoke the Games from Grenoble. In 1963, at the time of the selection of Grenoble, French Prime Minister Pompidou had given the IOC his assurance of freedom of participation for all recognized committees, specifying that it would be "under existing conditions," which the IOC had interpreted as meaning under IOC rules. The French specification, however, meant a united German team.[146] Under the IOC threat the French government relented and gave assurances that a separate East German team would be admitted on the strength of Olympic identity cards.[147] In the IOC a solution was agreed upon whereby East Germany would receive full recognition, two teams would compete in Grenoble and Mexico City (as Germany and East Germany, geographic recognition bypassing the political) but both contingents would have a common flag and anthem.[148] This latter provision was interpreted as a conciliation to the Allied Travel Bureau. After Mexico City the common flag and anthem would be terminated.

The problem of the name of the committee persisted. The East Germans, as well as the North Koreans and the Taiwanese, objected to the geographic description instead of the names they actually called their committees. Brundage insisted the three questions be considered together. It had been argued that since all other committees were allowed to use rightful names, to deprive these three committees of the same right was an act of political discrimination. Finally, at the Mexico City session in October 1968, the IOC decided that after November 1, 1968, each would be referred to by its proper name—East Germany, German Democratic Republic (GDR); North Korea, Democratic People's Republic of Korea (DPRK); Taiwan, Republic of China (ROC).[149] For the 1968 Games they would participate under their geographic names. The North Koreans did not like the arrangement, calling it a decision of the "reactionary ruling circles of the International Olympic Committee in collusion with the U.S. imperialists...."[150] As a result they did not participate in the opening ceremony, refusing to march under the banner of North Korea. This was a violation of the conditions of the agreement and consequently, on October 14, 1968, the IOC declared that the agreement for the name change of North Korea to the DPRK was null and void.[151]

It is interesting to note that during the period 1964 to 1968, throughout the whole drama of the Korean, German, and South African questions, Andrianov, the Soviet member, stopped referring to the Chinese situation as a means of supporting his arguments for Korean and German recognition, or even for South African expulsion. Before 1960 Andrianov had consistently referred to the Chinese question in order to pressure the IOC to expel Taiwan, but during the 1960's he was conspicuously silent over the Chinese issue. Obviously the question of China during the 1960s was not as compelling an issue as it had been during the 1950s, except for the occasion of GANEFO, and there the emphasis was primarily on Indonesia. Even on that issue, Andrianov was silent about PRC participation. He did, however, vote against the Mexico City resolution that would change the name of Taiwan to the Republic of China as of November 1, 1968. He stated that such a resolution was in violation of the 1959 resolution, which he said recognized only one China—the People's Republic of China.[152]

The IOC and GANEFO

As was the case during the XVII Olympiad, the IOC and the Olympic movement had to contend with GANEFO during the XVIII Olympiad. GANEFO II had been scheduled to take place in Cairo in 1967, with Peking as an alternate site. In September 1965 the second session of the council of GANEFO was held in Peking. Thirty-nine delegations were present at the meeting.[153] The scope of GANEFO was expanded to form an Asian committee, which decided to hold an Asian GANEFO from November 25 to December 6, 1966, in Cambodia. Like GANEFO itself, the Asian GANEFO was designed as an alternative Games and was strategically timed to take place at the same time as the Olympic sanctioned Asian Games.

The Asian GANEFO, underwritten in large measure by the PRC, like GANEFO I, was hailed as a great success.[154] As in GANEFO I, the majority of the contingents were not official bodies since certain international federations were equally opposed to Asian GANEFO and to GANEFO I. The international weightlifting federation sent out a circular warning of suspension if any of its affiliates participated, since normal channels for invitations had not been followed (governments were used instead of national sport federations). Also, Cambodia was not a recognized member, and a regular affiliate was not supposed to compete against a non-member.[155] North Korea officially participated, again getting in trouble with the IAAF, this time for the 1968 Olympic Games. The

IAAF suspended the North Koreans, preventing their participation at Mexico City in the events under the auspices of the IAAF.[156] Unlike GANEFO I, Indonesia sent only fifty-seven athletes to the Asian GANEFO,[157] presumably because of the overthrow of Sukarno in 1965 and the attempt to resume an Indonesian Olympic Committee.[158] In fact, the Asian Games, which were held nearly simultaneously with the Asian GANEFO, were refusing Indonesian entry because of difficulties between that country's Olympic committee and the Asian Games Federation. The IOC warned the federation that since Indonesia was back in good standing with the IOC any refusal would prompt an IOC lifting of its patronage.[159] The Asian Games Federation complied.

But GANEFO was definitely approaching the end of its existence. Cairo announced it could not hold GANEFO for financial reasons. The PRC was in the throes of the cultural revolution, effectively shutting off that country from any international contact.[160] GANEFO died a quiet death. During its existence, however, it had posed a real threat to the IOC, especially in the Third World.

Before the first African Games at Brazzaville in 1965, the threatened exclusion of South Africa, Mozambique, Angola, and Rhodesia raised the problem of a possible conflict with the IOC. The IOC was concerned not only about the possible exclusion but also about the fact that if it took action against the Africans it might drive them into the GANEFO camp.[161] As it turned out, the four countries mentioned above were excluded. The IOC got around the issue by taking the stand that since South Africa had not participated in Tokyo and did not respect Olympic rules, it was not authorized to participate in the African Games. As for the others, they were not independent countries.[162]

The nationalism exhibited by GANEFO presented a real threat to the Olympics, which was generally associated with the more established nation-states and more developed parts of the world. In Africa, intense nationalism combined with intense superpower rivalry on the continent made GANEFO a very dangerous force for the IOC, at least as far as the IOC was concerned. If the IOC alienated the African countries, forcing the superpowers and their satellites to take action commensurate with their interests in Africa, the potential for destruction of the Olympic movement was very great indeed. This had almost happened over the issue of South Africa in 1968, even with the absence of GANEFO. In fact, at the announcement of the Grenoble decision on South Africa, plans were under-way for a separate set of Games to take place in Africa that year.[163] Had the IOC not rescinded its Grenoble decision on South African participation, GANEFO or its equivalent would probably have been revived, this time superseding the Olympic Games.

Integrative Organizational Forces and the IOC

Nationalism and the threat of GANEFO had its counterpart dur-ing the XVIII Olympiad in the nationalism of the African coun-tries. In this instance the amount of government interaction in the national Olympic committees was so great the committees were but subsidiary organs of governmental sport bodies. Anticolonialism in Africa had spurred the creation of a regional alignment based on the common purpose of combating colonialism. As such, the Orga-nization for African Unity (OAU) was born in 1963. The OAU, like other regional organizations, such as the EEC, was at first designed to cope with specific problems. The integrative effect developed mechanisms and opportunities for solving other common prob-lems, thereby expanding the scope of the organization. One such sphere was the Supreme Council for Sports in Africa, established in 1966 by thirty-two African states whose membership essentially comprised the national Olympic committees from those states. The ongoing process in Africa was one of organizational development extending beyond the national perspective. Similar movements were occurring throughout the world in numerous spheres of activ-ity. The Olympic movement was no exception. The Olympic move-ment, however, because of its unique character as arena/partici-pant, was susceptible to various international organizational align-ments as well as reactive to this international organizational process.

The organizational forces with which the IOC was forced to deal were the United Nations, NATO, the OAU and its Supreme Coun-cil for Sports in Africa (SCSA), and, in the Olympic system's own ranks, the General Assembly of International Federations (GAIF) and the General Assembly of National Olympic Committees (PGA). In addition the IOC had to contend with television and commercial interests in sport and in the Games themselves. Both the GAIF and its counterpart for the national committees (PGA) were a product of the organizational integrative process as well as a reaction to it.

The activities of the SCSA and the OAU regarding the South African issue have been discussed. So has the role of NATO as it pertained to the question of East German recognition and participation in the Games. The United Nations passed several resolutions regarding South Africa and Rhodesia, the latter being instrumental in Mexico's denial of Rhodesian participation in the Mexico City Games. As the largest international organization, multifaceted and multipurpose, the United Nations was involved in numerous areas. UNESCO, through its interest in sport and physical education as they related to education, science, and culture, created the International Council for Sport and Physical Education (ICSPE). ICSPE's purpose was to promote study and research from a societal perspective, integrating the fields of sport and physical education into modern societal life.[164] In the view of the ICSPE, by virtue of its affiliation with UNESCO, it was supreme over the IOC. The IOC was to remain the organization of competitive sport at the regional and world levels.

The IOC was suspicious of all government-associated sport organizations. The IOC position was that the ICSPE, like other government programs, was designed to supersede it and constituted government interference in the activities of the Olympic movement. The IOC was particularly concerned about Africa. Most African Olympic committees had some government influence. Their association with the OAU through the SCSA prompted the IOC to warn the Africans against further government interference by way of the ICSPE.[165] The IOC wanted nothing to do with ICSPE, considering it like GANEFO to be "a serious threat for the Olympic movement."[166]

Within the Olympic movement itself there had been efforts toward closer cooperation between the various bodies—the IOC, the national committees, and the international federations. For the federations, the main concern had generally been financial. For the national committees, the problems were somewhat more complicated. Not only was there a financial concern, especially from the poorer committees, but there was a general feeling the national committees were not given sufficient consideration in IOC decisions. This was particularly true of the committees from the Third World, notably Africa. Because of the lack of a strong sporting tradition as in the European countries, the financial strains, the nationalistic fervor, and the opposition to old established traditions —perceived as linked to colonialism—the African committees were much more bound to their government apparatus, viewing sport and their role in it from a perspective different from that of the IOC. Because of its established amateur tradition, the IOC merely tolerated the government influence in the African countries, since intense opposition would have served no useful purpose; in fact, it would have been detrimental to the Olympic movement. This toleration, however, did not come to grips with the fundamental problems and issues of the time. The IOC was operating in the twentieth century with nineteenth-century attitudes and through nineteenth-century institutions. The same criticism applied to its relations with the communist bloc committees and to its handling of the problems of commercialism and professionalism with the Western committees. In essence, the IOC was out of step with its time. As a result the federations and national committees were growing restless in their subsidiary role and confining institutional structure.

During the XVII Olympiad the international federations had demanded one-third of the television revenues. This demand was carried over into the XVIII Olympiad. The IOC position remained the same. It had obligations to four revenue recipients—itself, the federations, the organizing committee, and the national committees. In 1966 the IOC came up with a comprehensive table of distribution in which the first million would be divided between the federations, the national committees, and the IOC. Of the second million, one-third would go to the organizing committee, two-ninths apiece would go to the federations, the national committees, and the IOC. Of each successive million, the organizing committee would receive two-thirds, with one-ninth apiece for the other three.[167] While at first this appeared satisfactory, some federations later found it totally inadequate and began lobbying for a separate organization of federations (GAIF) to present the federations' positions. Ostensibly, the main problem was financial, but the issue ran much deeper. Sport and the Olympic Games had become profitable business. The concept and the performance of sport had changed drastically, in large measure through the dynamics and impact of the media. Sport was now worldwide. If the federations were to maintain their status, they had to change and have the ability to adapt. The financial demands were tremendous, and membership fees and solicitations no longer could carry the load. Added sources of revenue were necessary in order to maintain these worldwide organizations.

The face of sport was changing along with the face of the world. The possibilities for profit in sport, especially for those having mass spectator value, such as soccer, basketball, ice hockey, skiing, and ice skating, were altering the concept of amateurism to adapt to the commercial possibilities. The athletes were cashing in and the federations had to change. The soccer federation, for example, allowed both amateurs and professionals, but it was the professionals whom the world followed. The Olympic soccer program was really secondary, yet the IOC was demanding that the soccer federation (FIFA) form a separate amateur body. The federation replied that such a separation would cause serious financial repercussions since the amateur affiliates had no money.[168] The same demand was made of the cycling federation.

The Olympic Games, because of the mass audience and mass exposure, was a forum very much sought after by all the federations, but not all federations were allowed to participate, and of those that did, many did not have all their events included. For the 1968 Games the IOC had limited the program to eighteen sports, but there were twenty-four affiliated federations and many unaffiliated. Each wanted its sport on the Olympic program and more events for each. Judo was not on the program although it had six million participants throughout the world.[169] Skating was on the program of the Winter Games, but one of its most popular events, ice dancing, was not included. The skating federation held its world championships separately, right after the Games, and they were quite lucrative. The IOC stipulated that only those federations who held their world championships at the Games could receive television revenue. For such federations as the skating federation, which was one of the most popular for spectators and received much media attention at the Games, this rule was an affront. The IOC position on limiting the Games had been reiterated many times in the past. The Games were just getting too big, and the recent decline in the number of candidatures for the Games was thought to be a serious indication that the Games were becoming too large and the cities simply could not afford them.[170]

The problems the federations were facing were basically similar. In fact, they were a product of the problems facing the world at large. The increase in the nation-state system, expanding technology, the expansion of economic relationships, increase and change in the transnational economic actors—all these plus numerous other factors made for a world that was smaller, more complex, and tremendously dynamic. In light of this, the older institutional and organizational relationships no longer sufficed. Although the nation-state system had expanded with the consequent growth in nationalism, the very forces that produced this expansion also forced the change in nation-state relationships. A solely nation-state perspective was no longer adequate to cope with the changing forces and relationships. States were forced to look beyond their borders, and give up a measure of autonomy in order to hold on to what little they did possess. It was a process of organizational adaptation.

The international federations, as products of similar processes at work in sport, also felt the need to adapt to the changes. The combination of issues, essentially at variance with the IOC, produced a movement for an organization of federations to present the IOC with a unified position on the issues in order to effect change. Termed the General Assembly of International Federations (GAIF), this organization was viewed by the IOC as anathema to the Olympic rules and idea. The IOC would have nothing to do with it. The IOC stated that it would deal with the international federations only in the traditional fashion—separately.[171] The IOC was not opposed to the federations meeting together before their meeting with the executive board and drawing up joint resolutions. This was seen as an efficient way of handling the matters that confronted them. A separate organization, however, was seen as an attempt to exceed federation authority and supersede the IOC. The federation action was really no different from states joining together, for example, to form free trade areas. It was but a part of a global centralizing process to cope with common problems for the betterment of each individual unit.

There was some dissension among federation ranks regarding a superfederation organization. The IAAF was opposed. Its concern was similar to that of a large nation-state—the fear of a loss of autonomy commensurate with its size, but unequal to that lost by the smaller members. The IAAF and other lesser federations wanted to retain their ability to consult with the IOC separately. The real issue was loss of autonomy, whether actual or not.

By the close of the XVIII Olympiad the matter was still up for debate. The IOC would not recognize the GAIF, and there was dissension within the federation community as to the benefit of such an organization. The IOC still refused a lump sum of one-third of the television revenue. Since many federations preferred a basis of division other than their loss of revenue through giving up their world championships in the Olympic year, the IOC decided to allow world championships to be held separately in the Olympic year without the federations losing revenue from the Games.[172] The IOC also decided to increase the number of sporting events to twenty-one for 1972.[173]

If the federations were a product of the changing world conditions, so were the national committees. As noted earlier regarding the South African question, a special session (General Assembly) of national committees was held in April 1965 to discuss common problems and to present joint resolutions to the IOC in their meeting with the executive board later that year. The national committees' basic complaint was of inadequate representation on the IOC, a complaint issued by the Soviet representatives some years before. In April 1966 the IOC set up a coordinating and study committee to establish the basis for an association of national committees.[174] Later in the year, the IOC decided to set up a special section in the IOC secretariat in Lausanne to deal with increased contact between the IOC and the national committees. The IOC was trying to head off any super-organization of national committees apart from the Olympic structure and traditional mode of conducting Olympic affairs. The IOC felt the formation of such an organization was extremely dangerous to the Olympic movement "as inevitably politics would enter into sports."[175] Naively, the IOC thought it could placate the national committees by announcing that at its next general session in 1967 it would devote one day to the national committees and one day to a meeting among the national committees. Obviously, this would not suffice.

The problem of politics was a crucial one, especially considering that the main protagonists for a permanent organization were the African committees[176] in conjunction with the communist bloc. The leader of the movement, however, was Italian, Giulio Onesti, an IOC member. He and his supporters were adamant in their purpose. Further efforts by the IOC to stem the tide were to no avail. At its 1967 general session the IOC set up a joint commission to advise the IOC, but Onesti was not satisfied, stating that such a commission had neither the competence nor the right to speak for the national committees of each region.[177] He proposed the establishment of a Permanent General Assembly of National Committees (PGA) as a more democratically representative organization, much along the lines of the Soviet proposals for reorganizing the IOC in 1959. The proposed organization was supported by the Soviets, Eastern Europeans, Asians, and Africans. The Scandinavians, some Latin Americans, Western Europeans, and North Americans opposed it.[178] At the Mexico City session of 1968, Brundage proposed a tripartite commission, composed of six representatives from the IOC, six from the national committees, and six from the international federations, as a means of effecting closer contact and cooperation between the various groups. It was an attempt to tie all the dissident claims together and coordinate the activities and problems within the Olympic structure. The federations were in favor of it and, in general, so were the national committees.[179] At a separate meeting, however, the PGA of national committees had been agreed upon by seventy-seven of the national committees present, so the question was still unresolved.[180]

The same factors affecting organizational change in the federations and national committees were pressuring the IOC to make changes in its organizational structure, apart from those dealing with the federations and national committees. Over a period of time, up to the 1964 Games, the operations of the IOC had grown increasingly expensive. The 1964 Games, for the first time in the history of the modern Games, produced a substantial amount of money. Even though the IOC was an organization of international caliber, its staff until 1964 was composed only of the president and two part-time assistants in Chicago (Brundage's residence), and a chancellor and two part-time assistants in Lausanne. The increasing expenses and duties of the IOC necessitated increasing the staff and operations of the IOC. Commissions were created for all facets of the organization including finance, protocol, press and public relations, game site selection, and amateurism. Until 1960 the expenses of the IOC averaged only $10,000 per year for the Lausanne office (the Chicago office of Avery Brundage was operated at no expense to the IOC). By 1964 expenses had risen sixfold, but receipts had also increased substantially due to television. More money could be devoted to expanding the IOC structure to cope with the numerous changes and problems resulting therefrom.[181] In fact, the IOC was moving its headquarters in Lausanne to larger offices in that city to take care of the expansion.[182]

The same processes of expansion in the world at large were hitting the IOC. Television, as a reflection of increased technology, had great impact altering traditional relations in various spheres. The increase in revenue had afforded the IOC the opportunity to conduct and expand such activities as aid to African sport programs, distribution of money to the federations and national committees, structural expansion and diversification, and delegation of authority to an increased staff. With all these new opportunities came some drawbacks. The IOC was forced to become a business with all the problems that follow.[183] The business of the Olympics began to take precedence over the traditional orientation of sport for sport's sake. Instead, a profit and loss mentality began to emerge and dominate numerous facets of the operations of the IOC. This attitude extended outward to the federations and national committees, as was apparent in a letter from Exeter to Brundage. Noting that the IOC needed money, as did the federations, Exeter contemplated that "if the Games were in the USA there would be likely to be a substantial sum available."[184] The United States provided a lucrative market and the Olympic movement could cash in on it. For the 1968 Summer Games, United States television rights were sold for $4.5 million,[185] the largest sum ever and the single largest payment in the world. Future years would see an unbelievable escalation in the price paid for broadcasting the Olympic Games. Financial considerations increasingly occupied IOC sessions, as evidenced by the squabbling over television rights. Not only television rights but also commercial interests and the problems of amateurism would become more and more of a factor in IOC business, forcing the altering of rules and changing the attitudes of amateur sport officials.

The 1968 Olympic Games

As at prior Olympics, the 1968 Games produced some incidents and scandals that reflected conflicts or trends in the world at large. The 1968 incidents, however, like those that would follow in successive Olympic contests, reflected these conflicts with a darkness and intensity that was new. Five major incidents were reflective of three political trends or conflicts. The Winter Games produced a conflict over ski manufacturers' names on skis. The Summer Games had a similar track shoe scandal. Both crises reflected the increasing commercialism of sport, but in addition they manifested the increasing role of business as a semi-independent actor in international affairs and an increasing mentality to view things in economic terms. At the Summer Games, Mexican students had rioted over internal government policies and black American athletes had protested on the victory stand. Both incidents were related in the sense that both were expressions of dissent against internal government policies. Beyond that, however, both represented the voices of opposition to the established order and power structure in the world. Another incident to be mentioned, which occurred before the Games and had a strong effect on them, was the invasion of Czechoslovakia. The cold war intruded once more in the Olympics.

The skiing controversy had been going on for some time before the Games. There had been much concern in Olympic circles over certain skiers being essentially professionals. The IOC charge of professionalism gained credence when the international skiing federation (FIS) altered the entry forms for the Games so that competitors could promise to abide by FIS rules, which were more lenient than the IOC's on the subject of amateurism, rather than to abide solely by IOC rules.[186] An agreement had also been reached between the IOC and the FIS eligibility commission prohibiting trademarks on the skis—a move to eliminate excessive advertising. This was overruled by the FIS council with the claim that covering or eliminating the trademarks would interfere with the running of the skis. Furthermore, the skis had such distinctive coloration they would be recognized anyway. The skiers had been in the habit of posing for victory pictures with their equipment clearly exhibited. It was agreed simply to have no victory photographs taken of the skiers with their equipment. To Brundage the advertising on the skis was a direct violation of IOC rules. The compromise, essentially imposed on the IOC, was viewed as a threat to the power and authority of the IOC.[187] Some members wanted the skiing events deleted, some wanted the blotting out of the manufacturers' names on the tops of the skis. It was generally felt that nothing could be done at that point, the implication being that so much money had already been put into the Games—$224 million[188]—and to eliminate the skiing events, a large part of the Winter Games, would be to court disaster. The problem would have to be taken up later. As far as Brundage was concerned, he was not about to associate with the skiing "amateurs." He refused to attend the events or even to hand out the medals as was customary.[189]

At the Summer Games a similar commercial scandal occurred, though it did not really receive much press until after the Games when its full extent was revealed. It involved two track shoe manufacturers—Adidas and Puma. They were the leading track shoe manufacturers in the world, and their respective owners were brothers. The companies had originally been one, but through sibling rivalry the company had split into two. Apparently in the competition for sales and advertising, the two had paid track athletes to wear their shoes.[190] In the process of investigation it was revealed that many manufacturers were in the habit of paying athletes to use their equipment, and that such payments had become a major source of income for the athletes.[191] All of this was of course contrary to the Olympic rules and principles.

At the Summer Games, in addition to the demonstrations of the Mexican students which had threatened to cancel the Games, there were demonstrations by the black American athletes on the victory stand. After their first and third place finishes in the 200 meter run, Tommie Smith and John Carlos of the United States stood on the victory platform during the playing of the national anthem, black gloved fists raised defiantly in the air and heads bowed. Their salute to black power and their protest of United States policies was seen by the IOC and the USOC as grossly unethical conduct. Within thirty hours of their demonstration, the two athletes were suspended and sent home. They immediately became martyrs. The Cubans extended invitations to them and the Cuban 400-meter relay team sent its silver medals to Harry Edwards, the founder of the "Olympic Project for Human Rights."[192] Of twenty athletes polled on the United States team, white and black, thirteen were in favor of the protest, five were opposed, one undecided, and one had no opinion.[193]

The solidarity for the cause was apparent. Not only did the Cubans support the American athletes' action, but the second place winner on the platform with Smith and Carlos, Peter Norman of Australia, wore the button of the "Olympic Project for Human Rights."[194] Martin Jellinghaus, a member of the bronze-medal-winning West German 1600-meter relay team stated: "I am wearing this medal because I feel solidarity not only for them as persons, but for the movement, the human rights movement."[195]

Similar demonstrations were made by Americans after Smith's and Carlos' protest, but none were as dramatic nor did they require punitive action by the USOC. Harry Edwards had warned before the Games that some sort of protest would be lodged at the Games. The resulting action should not have been a surprise. The significance of the protests could not be ignored. Combined with the boycott held before the Games, the Mexican student demonstrations, the Kenyan strategy in the 1500-meter run (see chapter 1), and the overall Kenyan and African success in the Games, one had to view the black protest not only as an American protest but as a picture of the emergence in world politics of alternate power centers. In conjunction with this, changing attitudes regarding world politics and their orientation were also involved.

The victory stand protest and the African success at the Games may have indicated changing political relationships, but that process was far from complete, and certain prior political relationships remained intact. This also was apparent at the Games. Just prior to the opening of the Summer Games Czechoslovakia was invaded by the Warsaw Pact countries, making for a dramatic reminder of the cold war estrangement between the East and the West. A similar invasion of Hungary had thrown the 1956 Games into turmoil. While the Czechoslovakian invasion did not have the same effect on the Games as the Hungarian invasion in 1956, there was concern that Czechoslovakia might not participate, and there were outcries for the barring of the Warsaw Pact countries—notably by Scandinavia[196] and by Emil Zatopek, the great Czech distance runner of the 1948 and 1952 Games.[197] Zatopek was subsequently stripped of his position in the Czechoslovakian Communist Party, barred from membership, and forced to relinquish his position on the Czechoslovakian Olympic Committee.

Czechoslovakia sent a 100-man contingent, and arrangements had to be changed in Mexico for the housing of the athletes. originally the Czechs were to eat in the same dining room with the GDR, USSR, Austria, Hungary, Poland, Rumania, and Yugoslavia. Instead, it was arranged for the Soviet Union and the GDR to eat separately.[198] The intense bitterness of Czechoslovakia toward the Soviet Union and the GDR was sharpened by remembrances of World War II.[199]

The Czechoslovakian invasion almost coinciding with the

Games, drew an especially poignant contrast between the Olympic ideal of peaceful competition and the harsh certitudes of combative repression. It pointed up, despite the reduction in tensions in Europe and the East-West conflict in general, the persistent East-West, United States-Soviet estrangement. The Games, by virtue of their tremendous visibility, became once again an unwilling forum for the presentation of world political realities.

The Games of the XIX Olympiad climaxed a period marked by the emergence of alternate power centers and changing world political relationships. The period 1956 to 1968 can be viewed as the budding of a new global political structure evolving from the intense cold war era following the war and coming into flower between 1968 and 1976.

5

1968-1976

THE YEAR 1968 MARKED A turning point in international relations, just as the year 1956 had marked a similar change a decade earlier. The United States involvement in Vietnam had become so unpopular and counterproductive that President Johnson was compelled to initiate peace negotiations and to reject for himself a further term in office. The incoming Nixon administration announced the program of Vietnamization accompanied by troop withdrawals and rejected a United States role of world policeman (Guam Doctrine).[1] Under the auspices of Henry Kissinger, Nixon's National Security Advisor and later Secretary of State, the United States embarked upon a program of detente with the Soviet Union and China.

In 1967 China had successfully exploded its first nuclear bomb while still in the throes of the cultural revolution, claiming for itself a de facto position as a third power center to rival both the United States and the Soviet Union. By the time of the Nixon visit (through ping-pong diplomacy) in 1972, China was coming out of the cultural revolution ready to embrace its new power position and to take advantage of the Nixon initiatives. It had been admitted to the United Nations (1971), claiming its rightful place on the world scene.

Under the Johnson administration, the nuclear nonproliferation treaty of 1968 was concluded, setting the stage for further agreements under the new Nixon policy of detente. In the Soviet Union the reception to detente was expressed in the successful conclusion of the SALT agreements (1972), in pressing for MFN status, and in the desire for improved trade relationships with the United States.

The process of detente and a more independent line moved forward at a similar pace in Western Europe. Under De Gaulle, France had retreated from NATO and in 1967 had rejected a second British bid to enter the Common Market. De Gaulle's retirement in 1969 brought to leadership in France men less charismatic but also less nationalistic and somewhat more "European-oriented." Britain successfully entered the Common Market in 1973, further binding the European states. In West Germany, a new policy toward Eastern Europe had been progressing ever since the departure of Adenauer. With Willi Brandt and the Social Democrats at the helm, this policy became one of detente leading to a succession of treaties between the Federal Republic and its counterpart to the East, the GDR, plus other Eastern European states.

In other areas, notably the Middle East, a drastic change in relations with the rest of the world was taking place. In 1967 Israel successfully repulsed its Arab neighbors, seizing considerable amounts of territory in the process. The United States commitment to Israel had greatly increased over the years, with the Soviet Union's commitment to the Arab cause following the same pattern. A growing Western European dependence on Arab oil had chilled the Western European support of Israel, and with the 1973 oil embargo, the United States attitude toward Israel began to be reassessed. The economic strength of Arab oil money was altering the foreign policies of states toward the Middle East and was enhancing the power of the Middle East in general. Arab oil money was invading Europe, Japan, and the United States. The Middle East was a power center to be reckoned with. By 1971 the United States decided to go off the gold standard and no longer to give gold for dollars in consequence not only of the growing economic power of the Middle East but also of changing world economic relationships.[2] The United Sates was no longer as prominent a world power as it had been.

The winding down of the Vietnam conflict, the final reunification of North and South Vietnam, and the increasing voice of the Third World in the United Nations and other forums all evidenced a world power structure diversifying and moving away from the strict bipolar arrangement following World War II. The year 1968 was a turning point, and these trends would manifest themselves in the Olympics.

XIX OLYMPIAD (1968-1972) AND THE 1972 OLYMPIC GAMES

The 1972 Summer Olympic Games held in Munich will probably go down in history with a notoriety comparable to that of the 1936 "Nazi Olympics."[3] Both were scenes of Jewish persecution. During the 1936 Games the persecution was instigated and executed by Germany. During the 1972 Games the persecution was the product of forces beyond German control. Eleven Israeli Olympic team members were murdered by Arab terrorists. The persecution at the 1936 Games, while not sanguinary, underscored the deadly assault carried out on a vast scale outside the Olympic encampment. It is tragically ironic that such persecution should have taken place in the same country, but the irony was not lost on the Germans nor on the Arabs who perpetrated the terrorism. What better place to commit a heinous crime against the Jews, where so many Jews had been butchered a mere forty years before? What better forum than the Olympic Games, the great festival of peace?

While the terrorist attack overshadowed all other events at the Games and pointed up a particular sore spot in international relations, there were other events during the period illustrative of changing developments and processes on the international scene. One such event or issue was the South African/Rhodesian controversy.

SANOC had not been permitted to participate in the 1968 Summer Games, although they were still bona fide members of the Olympic movement. The pressure that had been exerted on the IOC to keep the South Africans out of the 1968 Games increased continuously after the contests.

At the Mexico City general session of the IOC prior to the 1968 Games, the African national committees had presented a joint resolution calling for the expulsion of SANOC from the Olympic movement. This resolution had been supported by the Communist committees as well as those from Asia. The IOC decided to consider the resolution the following year. In December 1968 the United Nations General Assembly proposed a resolution calling for all countries to break off sporting relations with South Africa.[4] The world was clearly aligning to isolate South Africa.

Early in 1969 the IOC learned that South Africa was using the

Olympic rings on insignia and stamps to advertise its white South
African Games. At the executive board meeting in April the IOC
censured SANOC for using the Olympic symbols in games "contrary to Olympic principles and ideals."[5] Commenting on the decision, Lord Killanin warned that such incidents did not bode well
for continued SANOC membership, much less for participation at
Munich in 1972.[6] The prospect of separate South African Games
inviting only white competitors from predominantly white countries, using Olympic symbols to sanction the Games, albeit illegally,
raised the ire of the African states. Kenya threatened to boycott the
Commonwealth Games of 1970 if any states showed up that had
participated in the South African Games. Abraham Ordia from
Nigeria, president of SCSA, said that Nigeria would do the same. A
further threat by SCSA to boycott the Munich Games of 1972 if
West Germany participated in the South African Games prompted
a quick West German reversal. Similar withdrawals by European
countries took place in support of the African position. The Soviet
Olympic Committee protested to the IOC and called for individual
states to boycott. Even the United States got involved. First the
AAU prohibited participation by four athletes under its jurisdiction who had been invited to the Games; the United States embassy
in South Africa also denied two state department employees in
South Africa permission to compete. In March United Nations
Secretary-General U Thant called on all states to break their sporting links with South Africa, and in clear reference to Britain and
New Zealand, which had not withdrawn from the Games, the
SCSA warned that any country that participated would bear the
consequences. Britain sent one participant and New Zealand sent a
full contingent, although New Zealand sport leaders professed they
were not going as representatives of New Zealand but only as
individuals.[7]

The Games took place, but world opinion had swung drastically
against South Africa. The strength of the African countries was evident, for they were the primary lobbyists against South Africa. It
was almost solely the threat of an African boycott that resulted in
withdrawal by virtually all the invited countries. The African
sportsmen, especially in track and field, had become so prominent
that their absence would have been sorely felt, but it was the great
increase in African political strength that had been the persuading
factor. Unified in a bloc and aligned with other Third World states,

they elicited a potent political and economic force, especially in light of the East-West competition. They could play off the two sides to achieve their own political objectives.

At the 1969 IOC general session in Warsaw, the question of South African participation would be discussed. In light of world opinion, Avery Brundage was publicly pessimistic about South Africa's chances for remaining a member of the Olympic movement. He provoked a stinging rebuttal from Reginald Honey, the South African IOC member, who was incensed that Brundage would prophesy the outcome of an IOC meeting before the event. He professed his faith in his committee's innocence, asserting that any decision for expulsion would be for political reasons only and he accused the IOC of having acted illegally for twenty years. "The IOC," he charged, "is a farce today, as they do whatever they want and break their own rules every day."[8]

Honey's referral to illegalities hit a sore point. The IOC executive board, when voting to withdraw South Africa's invitation to the 1968 Games, had argued incessantly over the legalities of the issue, finally settling on a decision that had nothing to do with its charter, much to the chagrin of the membership. If it were going to expel a member, which was more severe than withdrawing an invitation, its reasons had better be legally sound regardless of the climate of opinion. As a result, the IOC requested that the African committees present a list of specific charges with evidence, while at the same time the IOC would await a report from the subcommittee on racial discrimination. South Africa would then be presented with the charges and would have a chance to refute them. The IOC decided to take up this discussion at its next general session in Amsterdam in 1970.[9]

Meanwhile South Africa's position was becoming more untenable internationally. The International Judo Federation refused the South African White Judo Association's bid for membership, and the International Weightlifting Federation suspended the South African affiliate.[10] At an international gymnastics meet in Yugoslavia, the Yugoslav government refused to allow the South Africans to participate. As a consequence the United States, West Germany, the Netherlands, Canada, and Switzerland walked out in protest of the Yugoslav action.[11] In July at a US/USSR/Commonwealth track meet in Los Angeles, because of the presence of athletes who had participated in the South African Games, the Kenyan athletes were barred by their government from competing. A month later Lee Evans, a black American track star, announced that black American athletes, in solidarity with "our African brothers," would not compete against British athletes until they had agreed to boycott events with South Africa.[12]

In October, just prior to the IOC executive board meeting with the national Olympic committees, the fledgling PGA of national committees, composed mainly of African committees, voted to recommend the barring of South Africa from future Olympic competition.[13] This was followed by a vote to prohibit participation by the South African or Rhodesian delegates in a meeting of the executive board with the national committees. As a compromise, they were allowed to sit as observers.[14] This was the first time Rhodesia had been linked to the South African controversy in an IOC meeting, though Rhodesia had been barred from participating at Mexico City by the organizing committee's adherence to the United Nations resolution against Rhodesia. It would certainly not be the last time Rhodesia would be mentioned at an IOC session.

The stage was set for Amsterdam. In the meantime two international events helped the IOC make its decision. The first was the banning of South Africa from the Davis Cup tournament, ostensibly for refusing the black American tennis star, Arthur Ashe, a visa to play in South Africa.[15] The second involved a proposed South African cricket tour of Britain and Northern Ireland. Demonstrations and riots preceded the tour, prompting the British government to suggest a cancellation of the visit. This was acceded to four days after the IOC was to make its final decision.[16]

At Amsterdam the African committees presented their charges. Seven related to discrimination and one pertained to use of the Olympic symbols for an event contrary to Olympic rules and principles. Rebutting the African charges, Frank Braun, president of SANOC, made an inflammatory speech attacking Brundage and the IOC. This sealed the fate of SANOC.[17] By a vote of thirty-five to twenty-eight with three abstentions, the IOC voted to expel South Africa from the Olympic movement, marking the first time any such action had been taken against a member.[18]

The issue of sport was just a vehicle for expressing Africa's general opposition to the South African policy of apartheid and white rule. South Africa's intense preoccupation with sport provided an ideal arena of opposition for Africa's overall campaign, as would be demonstrated in the opposition to Rhodesian participation in the 1972 Games and, conclusively, in the African boycott of the 1976 Games. In essence, sport as such had nothing substantively to do with the African position against political conditions in South Africa, but the Olympic Games and sport as a worldwide forum determined Africa's mode of opposition.

In March 1971, Rhodesia received an invitation to the 1972 Summer Games in Munich. West Germany, not being a United Nations member, had no obligation to abide by the United Nations Security Council decision of 1968 requesting member states not to honor Rhodesian passports. This had been the basis for Mexico's refusal of Rhodesian participation in the 1968 Games. Because Rhodesia was still a colony of Great Britain, in 1963 the IOC had recognized the Olympic Committee of Rhodesia as Southern Rhodesia. The subsequent Rhodesian declaration of independence without British approval ultimately produced the United Nations sanction of 1968. In light of these events the IOC still recognized the Rhodesian committee as Southern Rhodesia, but to facilitate its participation in Munich the IOC decided in September 1971 to have the Rhodesian contingent march behind the same flag that had been used in 1964 at Tokyo before the independence movement—a blue flag with the union jack in one corner.[19] The athletes would participate as British subjects. The settlement seemed agreeable to all concerned, in particular to the British Olympic Association and the SCSA.[20]

Some concern, however, had been voiced by the African countries over Rhodesian participation because of racial discrimination. Upon investigating the charges, the IAAF said they were unfounded and that discrimination in sport like that in South Africa did not exist. The teams and competitions in the country were multiracial and there were more black Rhodesian athletes than there were white.[21] The Rhodesian committee was purportedly not guilty of contravening the IOC rules. In order to mollify any extremists, the IOC decided to have the Rhodesian athletes participate as British subjects. The IOC felt that because the racial situation in sport in Rhodesia was different from that in South Africa, there would be less opposition to Rhodesian participation.

The central issue, however, was not racial discrimination in sport. The opposition to Rhodesian participation was based on the general racial situation in Rhodesia and on minority white rule. No compromise settlement by the IOC would have made any difference. The only decision acceptable to the African countries would have called for the nonparticipation of Rhodesia.

The boycott began in mid-August 1972, just prior to the opening of the Games. First Guyana withdrew, then Ethiopia, Ghana, Zambia, Tanzania, Sierra Leone, Liberia, and Sudan. Kenya was threatening. If neither Kenya nor Ethiopia participated, men's track and field would lose at least ten potential medalists out of twenty-four events.[22]

As in 1968, black American athletes joined in solidarity. The OAU sent an appeal to the African members on the IOC to press for Rhodesian nonparticipation.[23] The situation, within days of the opening ceremonies, had grown desperate. On August 20, the Africans presented the IOC with a petition stating that the Rhodesians had not conformed to the September 1971 agreement, contending that the Rhodesians had entered West Germany on Olympic identity cards issued by the organizing committee rather than on British passports. This referral to a violation of the September accord gave the IOC the opportunity to reverse its decision on a legal basis and thus to circumvent the discrimination issue, which the Rhodesian committee supposedly was not violating. A Rhodesian Olympic official noted sardonically, "We are ready to participate under any flag, be it the flag of the Boy Scouts or a Moscow flag. But everyone knows very well that we are Rhodesians and will always remain Rhodesians."[24]

The United Nations Security Council sanctions committee told West Germany the presence of Rhodesians might violate the 1968 resolution and asked it to inform the IOC that the resolution applied to individuals and private organizations as well as to governments. The West German government, concerned that the issue might damage its relations with black Africa, pressured the IOC to reverse its decision.[25] Using the passport issue as its pretext, the IOC in a close vote (36-31-3) withdrew its invitation to Rhodesia.[26] A crisis had been averted, but much more was in store for the Munich Games. At hand was a controversy centered once again in the Third World (the Middle East) but having worldwide implications.

In previous Olympiads, the cold war had made its presence felt in one fashion or another. Over the course of successive Olympiads since the end of the Second World War the cold war conflict had become less of a factor, reflecting a trend in the world at large.

Nevertheless competition still existed between East and West, the United States and the USSR. During the XIX Olympiad, the competition reflected the atmosphere of detente. Germany was no longer an issue. The two Germanies were participating separately. The Korean committees were to participate separately as in the German case, and the Chinese question had not been an issue for some time. Even over the question of South African participation the two sides had a semblance of agreement, though their motives may have differed. Competition between the two sides centered on narrow issues, having little impact on larger questions.

One such issue was selection of the site for the 1976 Summer Games. Both Moscow and Los Angeles had submitted bids. As an inducement, the Moscow group offered to fly all the gold medal winners home free.[27] Similar inducements had been offered before by cities bidding for the Games. Montreal in its unsuccessful bid for the 1972 Games had offered free room and board for all competitors and officials, stating that (because of Expo '67) Montreal would have to spend little on facilities and could afford to be generous.[28] Little did it anticipate the subsequent outlay for the 1976 Games! The IOC did not look on such "attractions" with much favor, citing the Montreal inducement for 1972 as hardly ethical.[29]

The Moscow officials claimed that no other city could offer such a vast cultural program and the choice of their city would increase the prestige of Moscow in the eyes of the world. Constantin Andrianov said there were no "political, economic, or sporting reasons why Moscow should not be chosen." He said the time had come for the Games to be held in a socialist country and not to be just a privilege for western countries.[30]

Los Angeles officials offered the lucrative American market as an enticement, prompting the Moscow people to charge the Americans with unfair use of "commercial lures." The Los Angeles group offered to reimburse every participating nation for its travel expenses, its per diem expenses, and to turn back to the IOC and the various national committees an estimated $6 million profit.[31] The Los Angeles officials also felt the American bicentennial would be attractive. The American market was a strong selling point, particularly the television revenue. With the facilities Los Angeles had for all aspects of the Games, the organizers might very well have been able to turn a profit and reimburse the IOC and the national committees as they had offered.

Uncertain security was Los Angeles' major drawback. Because it was a large area with a heterogeneous population, there was some concern in the IOC about protecting all the contingents and preventing incidents. The recent Cambodian demonstrations increased the IOC's trepidation regarding Los Angeles. One reason for having chosen Munich for the 1972 Games was its homogeneous character and its smaller size—a better atmosphere for security!

The IOC maintained that its choice would depend on what was best for the Olympic movement. Many felt that what was best for the Olympic movement came down to a matter of money, prestige, and convenience. One analyst, Robert Lipsyte of the *New York Times,* said the "decision may have been made a long time ago by a swing bloc that hates or loves smog, vodka, Disneyland."[32]

As it turned out the swing bloc hated all three, for the third city bidding for the Games, Montreal, was chosen. Montreal won on the second ballot. On the first ballot Moscow received twenty-eight votes to twenty-five for Montreal and seventeen for Los Angeles. On the second ballot Montreal received forty-one to Moscow's twenty-eight, one being blank. The Soviets immediately cried foul. They charged there had been collusion between the two North American cities if either one lost on the first ballot. Sergei Pavlov, Minister of Sport, said the "secret second ballot was not inspired by interests of sport and strengthening Olympic ideals." *Tass* said Moscow had "clearcut and unquestionable arguments in its favor" and during the vote some members "proceeded not from principles of expanding and consolidating the Olympic movement, but from their personal political likes and dislikes." Further, *Tass* said, "it was the first time that a socialist city nominated its candidacy, and the rejection of its request cannot but be regarded as a blow at the Olympic movement and its ideals."[33]

Mayor Sam Yorty of Los Angeles said the vote had strong political overtones and he was obviously disappointed, but was glad the Games remained in the "free world."[34] In an analysis of the decision, Gerry Snyder, vice-chairman of the Montreal delegation, said the reasons the IOC had picked Montreal were the security situation in the United States, the fact that the United States had held the 1932 Games, and the volatility of feeling worldwide toward the United States over Vietnam. Canada held a neutral stature. The Soviet Union was too much of a newcomer to the Olympic movement, as opposed to Canada. Montreal did not propose extravagant offers of financial remuneration, as it had in 1972, whereas the other two did. The IOC, said Snyder, concerned over its amateur status, felt alienated by such offers.[35]

As the IOC would later state, a major reason for choosing Montreal was to show that a smaller city could stage the Games, completely self-financed, which Montreal proposed to do. The IOC hoped thereby to encourage other small cities, particularly in the developing countries, to bid for the Games. This aspect was acknowledged by the Dutch Minister of Cultural Affairs, who stated that the high costs of the Games were keeping smaller cities like Amsterdam out of the Olympic market.[36] In addition, preferential consideration had always been given to cities that had been runners-up in previous selections. Montreal had been runner-up in 1972. Finally, the choice of Montreal eliminated charges of bias by the IOC toward either the United States or the Soviet Union, even though Montreal was a western city.

The East-West conflict also manifested itself in a heightened sense of competition in the Games, pervasive since the end of World War II and intensified with the participation of the Soviet Union beginning in 1952. The 1972 Games had been the most successful for the Soviet Union in twenty years. The three preceding Games had not lived up to Soviet expectations, prompting a Soviet official to chide the Soviet public that it must get used to losing upon occasion.[37] In 1972 this was not the case, as the Soviet Union emphasized. Sergei Pavlov, Minister of Sport, gloated, "In 10 sports the Russians were the best and in 15 others, we were ahead of the Americans." *Pravda* placed special emphasis on East Germany's third place showing in total medals behind the USSR and the United States, and pointed out that Bulgaria, Hungary, and Poland outperformed Britain, France, Sweden, and Canada. *Komsomolskaya Pravda* asserted that the results "show to the entire world the triumph of the personality liberated by socialism."[38] Such exclamations prompted the incoming president of the IOC, Lord Killanin, to disavow such ultranationalistic claims of a better way of life. "I do not think," he chided, "it shows you have a better way of life if you win a lot of medals."[39]

The Soviet Union was not alone in utilizing the Games for propaganda or prestige purposes. The United States and other countries were as guilty. For the United States as for the Soviet Union, considering the intense rivalry between the two powerful countries with opposing ideologies, the prestige to be gained or lost was perceived as of utmost importance.

In the 1972 Games the United States, for the first time in Olympic history, lost a basketball game. To make matters worse, it was lost in the finals to the Soviet Union. A basketball defeat was especially ignominious. The United States lost all the time at ice hockey, soccer, and other team sports, but basketball was an American game, and the United States had the best players in the world. They were all professionals and therefore ineligible, but the United States sent its college players, who, by and large, were more skilled than those from other parts of the world, since the colleges were the farm systems of the professional leagues. In the final game, after being behind most of the contest, the United States squad surged ahead by one point with three seconds remaining. The Soviet team had to go the length of the court in that span of time to score a win. Through a foul-up with the clock and the rules, the Soviet team was given three chances to score. On the third try the Soviets succeeded, ending the United States string of wins and taking away the basketball title. It would not have been so bad had the United States lost to some other team, but a loss to the Soviet Union was intolerable. Because of the argument over the rules, a sense of bitterness over the defeat, and a feeling of having been cheated out of a win, the United States team refused even to attend the award ceremonies or to accept its silver medals. The USOC protested the game to the IOC and FIBA (the international basketball federation). United States sport circles were so upset over the loss they threatened to suspend indefinitely any further United States participation in Olympic basketball.[40] The United States media reverberated with cries of foul play and revenge, which persisted until the 1976 Games and an ultimate American triumph.

Other countries, to varying degrees have exhibited nationalistic fervor during the Olympic competitions. In the 1972 Games, a striking example of this was the controversy among the Alpine skiing countries over the problem of commercialism and professionalism, centering on the Karl Schranz scandal. For some time prior to the 1972 Games there had been much concern in Olympic circles over the problem of commercialism and professionalism in amateur sport, especially in winter sport and notably in Alpine skiing and skating. Most of the controversy had centered on Alpine skiing. The decade of the 1960s had seen a tremendous rise in the popularity of skiing with a consequent boom in the skiing industry. At the forefront were the top international competitors. As spokesmen for the sport, they made great advertising agents. Not only was skiing big business for the manufacturers and sellers of equipment, but tourist revenues were an important part of the economy of the countries where skiing was practiced. All parties concerned had great stakes in the maintenance and growth of the sport.

The IOC did not view the situation in the same light. Because the sport was no longer amateur, as it defined amateur, the IOC wanted to restrict the commercialism or eliminate the sport from the Olympics. Brundage was so soured not only on the skiing situation but on the Winter Games in general that, in one of his characteristically diplomatic moments, he voiced his fervent hope the Games would receive a "decent burial" at Denver, the site for the 1976 Winter Games.[41]

For those countries most involved in winter sport—Austria, France, Italy, Germany, the Scandinavian countries, the United States, and Canada—any proposal to eliminate the Winter Games or skiing from the program was blasphemy. As early as 1960 the Finnish IOC member wrote to Brundage expressing disapproval of his suggested elimination of the Winter Games. He whimsically told Brundage that if he eliminated the Winter Games the membership would put him in a Frigidaire.[42] Not only did the Olympics reap tremendous economic dividends but, for many countries, the Winter Games were the one arena in international sport in which they excelled. To eliminate the sport or the Winter Games was to hurt both business and national prestige.

For the IOC, the problem of commercialism had gotten out of hand and the 1968 Games at Grenoble had been "shameful." Brundage, for one, was not going to let such practices continue. In a circular letter of 1969 he noted the violations at Grenoble, asserting that because no law in France protected Olympic words and emblems,[43] the Games had been completely commercialized with such items as "Olympic butter, Olympic sugar, Olympic petrol. . . . Purveyors names were attached to every item of equipment and supplies and even to the entertainments. It seemed a huge business enterprise instead of another sport event."[44] Brundage also referred to the conflict with the skiing federation (FIS) over advertising. He felt the IOC had been deceived and, worse yet, that individual skiers had been supported by their federations and national committees when they made blatant statements that they were not amateurs. Finally, the expenditures for the Games had become so enormous as to encourage commercialism. "It was reported," Brundage wrote, "that the French spent $240,000,000 in connection with these Grenoble Games and when you consider that this was for ten days of amateur sport, it seems to be somewhat out of proportion. With that kind of money involved there is bound to be commercialization of one kind or another."[45]

The Games had become in fact a huge business because sport had become a huge business. The profits were available for everyone—the state, industry, the competitor, the sport federations, the media, and the IOC. Amateurism, as the IOC defined it, no longer existed, nor was it practical or even desirable. This was bluntly stated in a report on amateurism made in 1969 by the amateurism and eligibility commission of the IOC. Their finding was that the IOC had to change its rules and attitudes or be left out in the cold.

Sport had changed drastically in the past thirty years, not only in the number of people participating but also in its orientation. Commercialism represented only one aspect of the change. More free time was available to wider segments of the population, so sport was no longer restricted to the leisure class. States were creating opportunities for the inculcation of social values and ideologies through the medium of sport. Scientific research was investigating the physiological, psychological, sociological, and biological aspects of sport. Sport was no longer a simple pastime. It was becoming an integral and important segment of societal life. The IOC could not keep its head buried in the sand.[46] As Baron de Coubertin had said, the Olympic movement had to be a part of the times in which it existed, it had to adapt to its environment.[47] It could not hope to survive by espousing attitudes and rules of the past.

The only fundamental change made by the IOC was the loosening of controls over equipment advertising, financial assistance, and training periods for competitors. All such matters would first be subject to the discretion and the rules of the federations and of the national committees, with final approval residing in the IOC. The athletes still could not receive remuneration nor could sport be their basic occupation.[48] The IOC had not confronted the central problem; as a practical matter, championship sport requires nearly full time attention. Skiers, because they are in competition six months out of the year, have no time for an outside occupation. The other half of the year, at least three months of it prior to the opening of the season, is devoted to intensive training. For all intents and purposes, the skiers are professionals.

The FIS tried to adapt its rules to curb the commercialism, but financial support to the athletes from the skiing industry or through state subsidy had become essential to the Alpine and Scandinavian countries' ability to maintain championship levels of performance. The skiing program in these countries differed in character from that in the United States, where skiing, though popular, had not become a major sport. The United States skiing program, privately financed, had not attained the success or prestige levels of its Alpine and Scandinavian counterparts. In France and Austria, for example, the skiing program was state subsidized and the champion skiers were acclaimed as national heroes. The manufacturers of ski equipment sought out the athletes, offering them considerable financial support in return for product promotion. The FIS was faced with having tacitly to accept much of the commercialism in order to retain its position while at the same time seeming to follow IOC regulations.

The problem came to a head at the 1972 Games. In May 1971 Brundage demanded that ten skiers be disqualified for coaching at a ski camp in California. Six Alpine skiing countries—France, Austria, Italy, West Germany, Yugoslavia, and Switzerland—vowed they would boycott the Sapporo Winter Games in 1972 if the IOC barred any competitor for alleged professionalism. The Scandinavian skiing countries were expected to join the boycott,[49] which would have made a shambles of the Winter Games. The FIS sent a letter to the IOC condemning ski camps but noted that the skiers had received permission from their national federations. The skiers had received a fifty dollar daily allowance at the camp run by the Lange Ski Company (IOC rules did not permit remuneration from teaching sport). As a result of the FIS explanation and apology, the crisis was averted,[50] but Brundage remained adamant. He said the IOC had a list of fifty skiers who had allowed themselves to be exploited for commercial advertising, and the IOC would control the entry applications to determine who was eligible. This determination had previously been the prerogative of the national committees.[51]

By the time of the Sapporo Games the IOC was in a dilemma.

Brundage was pressing for expulsion of virtually all the skiers. His committee, seeking to maintain practical objectivity, judged it imprudent to ruin the Games through exclusion of the skiers. They argued that it was unfair to focus on the skiers in a punitive fashion when so many other athletes, such as those from the Communist countries, made their living from athletics. As a compromise, they barred Karl Schranz, the great Austrian skier, from participation. Schranz had been the most blatant in parading his name and picture for commercial purposes.[52]

In response Schranz said, "The Russians are subsidized by their own government and all international athletes get help from one source or another. It's an emphasis on the wrong principle. I think the Olympics should be a contest of all sportsmen, with no regard for color, race, or wealth." His argument was to no avail. Schranz was made a sacrifice to appease an angry president, to save the Games, and to save the IOC. When Schranz applied for an appeal to present his case before the IOC, Brundage denied him this opportunity with a curt dismissal, "We don't deal with individuals!"[53]

When Schranz got back to Austria he received a hero's welcome. One-hundred thousand people thronged the streets to see him. The populace were incensed over the decision. The American embassy in Vienna received bomb threats and dozens of protests. A fire was started at the door of one of the leading members of the Austrian Skiing Association because it was felt he had not sufficiently protected Austria's interests. A well-known Austrian industrialist was singled out for vitriolic attacks because he had cabled a supportive message to Brundage, an old friend, calling him "the last pillar of the Olympic idea." His grandchildren were badly beaten at school, and his products were boycotted. Schranz was given the Order of Merit for Sports by the Austrian Council of Ministers, the first to be awarded.[54] The Austrian team did not withdraw from the Games, however, only because Schranz persuaded them to stay.

The Schranz incident exemplified both the nationalism and the commercialism of the Games and of international sport in general, underscoring the increasing influence and power of commercial interests worldwide. The Schranz incident also dramatized the IOC's repeated failure, in the face of changing conditions and attitudes, to recognize and adapt to the challenges of the times.

For some years the IOC's inflexibility had fostered dissension and division within the Olympic movement. The increased demands on the sport organizations from commercial interests, government interference, growing financial strains with the prospect of alleviation through television revenue, all put pressure on an organizational structure that had been conceived at a time when such problems did not exist or were minor at best.

In order to obtain greater representation in the IOC, two umbrella organizations had been formed, one comprised of the majority of the international federations (General Assembly of International Federations; GAIF) and the other representing the interests of the national committees (Permanent General Assembly; PGA). The PGA was established by the vote of 78 out of 127 national committees in Mexico in 1968.[55] These two organizations addressed themselves to basic dissatisfactions with the IOC. It was felt that the IOC held itself aloof and was inefficient in meeting the demands and needs of the federations and national committees, that there was a lack of dialogue between the IOC and the federations and national committees, that the IOC was intolerant of federation and national committee attitudes and needs, that IOC decisions were arbitrary, and that there was not enough cohesion among the federations and the national committees in working with the IOC.[56]

The IOC had consistently refused to deal with the GAIF and the PGA, but during the course of the XIX Olympiad it became clear that the two organizations could no longer be ignored. The problems they presented merited attention. If a working relationship were not defined, a split away from the IOC by the federations to form their own combined games, or a political takeover of the IOC were real possibilities.

With regard to the GAIF, the IOC was faced with a fait accompli and, although the IOC espoused only direct dealing with single federations, it had to recognize the de facto existence of the GAIF.[57] The problems with the GAIF were not as difficult to handle as were those with the PGA. Since the federations were international and did not directly represent individual countries, they were more immune to national politics than were the national committees of the PGA. The federations each represented a single sport, so their chief concerns were the propagation and funding of that sport. For the IOC, the main problems regarding the GAIF were distributing television revenue, making sure the federation rules not only corresponded to the IOC rules but also acknowledged the particular requirements of each sport, and fighting off the biased demands of each federation for expanding the program of the Games.

The IOC, however, still held an upper hand with the GAIF in the sense that many federations relied for revenue on the Games as well as on the national committees and they held their world championships only at the Games. In addition, by choosing a handful of the federations' most responsible people for inclusion in IOC membership, the IOC could retain federation loyalty.[58] This process of co-optation is a common practice among large organizations for maintaining control. As a result, while the GAIF held de facto existence, the IOC was able to maintain its authority and to keep the GAIF operating within Olympic guidelines.

The situation within the PGA was more complicated. The PGA comprised mainly Third World and communist bloc committees, each striving for a reorganization of the IOC in order to obtain greater committee representation (i.e., the Soviet attempts at reorganization in 1959 and the early 1960s). Under such schemes, a real potential existed for political control in the manner of the United Nations General Assembly.

The IOC considered the PGA to be controlled by unscrupulous individuals out for personal benefit whose motives undercut the ostensible purposes of the PGA. The PGA was ostensibly designed to present the IOC with a coherent program of the needs of the national committees and to advise the IOC on the problems of the Olympics. Through it the national committees hoped they could be better represented in the IOC. The national committees were particularly concerned with sport aid to the developing countries and with television revenue for that purpose to be distributed through an Olympic Solidarity Program. The PGA wanted to control the television revenue itself. The IOC was committed to distributing the money to the national committees, but not to letting the national committees distribute it themselves.[59] Giving the PGA control of the distribution would give it virtual autonomy and would establish it as a separate entity eventually superseding the IOC.

At the 1969 Dubrovnik meeting of the IOC executive board with the national committees, the communist bloc and the Afro-Asian committees requested that the IOC recognize the PGA.[60] The Dubrovnik meeting soured many of the national committees on the concept of a PGA, however, because in that forum it became clear that the controlling purpose was not to facilitate closer cooperation but to achieve an autonomous and superior status. A proposal for PGA control over television revenue was frowned upon by many of the national committees concerned because it placed revenue distribution in the hands of the four organizers of the PGA and set no distribution schedule. In another proposal, Brundage's suspicion about unscrupulous motives behind the PGA was confirmed by a motion to accept a commission report for maintaining the IOC member selection process, which was contrary to many national committee objectives. Since Brundage was not running for another term after 1972, if the PGA maintained the existing selection process, the leaders of the PGA, who were also IOC members, would be able to gain control of the IOC for themselves. By restricting membership in the IOC, any further competition from the many new members that would be admitted under a revised selection system could be averted. Both proposals were voted down, but the credibility of the PGA had been damaged.[61] As a result, by the end of the XIX Olympiad, many national committees looked to the IOC for leadership through the various commissions and programs it had set up in conjunction with the federations and national committees for Olympic solidarity.

The event overshadowing all others at the XIX Olympiad was the terrorist attack at the Munich Summer Games. Arab terrorists, members of the Black September organization, stole into the Israeli team quarters at the Olympic Village in the early morning hours, killing two Israelis and taking nine as hostages. Ambushed at the airport in their attempt to leave with the hostages, the terrorists killed all their hostages. Three of the terrorists were taken prisoner; the rest were killed in the ambush.

The world was stunned and shocked that terrorism could occur at the Olympic Games during a time of supposed peace and friendship. Fear of future attacks spurred immediate preventive action by numerous states. President Nixon instituted extra security measures to protect American citizens as well as visiting Israelis from possible Palestinian attacks. European states closed their borders to incoming Arabs, stranding many for hours while security checks were conducted. The Israeli government warned the Palestinian guerilla organizations and the Arab states that they would be held accountable for the massacre.

President Nixon, Western European leaders, and United Nations Secretary-General Kurt Waldheim began immediate plans for international action against terrorism. Numerous countries sent condolences to Israel. The press in Prague, Warsaw, and Budapest deplored the attack, but the Soviet Union was conspicuously silent. At the memorial service the day after the massacre all team delegations appeared except that of the Soviet Union, and only a few members from Poland and East Germany attended. East German television was the only Eastern European network to carry the entire memorial service.

Demonstrators protested against the Lebanese, Iraqi, Egyptian, and Soviet missions to the United Nations, and they protested outside the Lebanese embassy in Moscow. The Israeli government made its first retaliatory raid into Lebanon two days after the massacre, denying any connection between the raid and the terrorist attack. The following day Israel made sweeping reprisals into Syria and Lebanon, this time acknowledging the connection.

The complex process had begun toward another major war between Israel and the Arabs. Suffice it to say here that a major catalyst, although a year prior to the Yom Kippur War of 1973, was the Munich Games terrorist attack. Following the attack, relations which had become strained between Egypt and the Soviet Union were righted. The military presence of the Soviet Union, which had been cut off by Egypt in June of 1972, was resumed. The Soviets began to supply the Palestinians directly with arms. The newly resumed relations between West Germany and Egypt once again deteriorated. All had augured well prior to the terrorist attack for progress between the two countries, and a strong West German influence in resolving the Arab-Israeli conflict had been a possibility. Now those hopes were dashed.

Israeli raids into Lebanon and Syria increased, as did Palestinian raids into Israel. Espionage activities were rampant in Europe, real cloak and dagger affairs including the killing of attaches, agents, and couriers. Significant throughout this was anti-Arab feeling, particularly in Western Europe and the United States. A Kuwait government official, a graduate of Berkeley, commented on the anti-Arab feeling in the United States resulting from the terrorism at Munich. "It is one thing," he cautioned, "for you in the United States to take the side of Israel. We think you are wrong, but that is your choice. It is another thing, however, when you say, you lousy

Arabs, to hell with you. For that you are going to pay a heavy price one day.''[62]

Perhaps that price came in 1973 with the Arab oil embargo. This is conjecture, but the fact remains that the terrorist attack at Munich elicited a worldwide reaction far more extensive and emotional than any that had preceded. The possibility of settlement in the Middle East had held some prospect before the attack, much more so than at any time since the 1967 war. After the attack, relations deteriorated steadily. Perhaps the intention of the terrorists had been prevention of a settlement that they felt would have been disadvantageous to the Palestinians. It is hard not to view the Munich incident as a catalyst, particularly in light of the conditions existing before it and those that followed. The Olympic Games had once again become the staging ground, this time in a barbarous fashion, for a particular political cause. The Munich massacre vividly underscored the unique simultaneity of the Olympics as actor and stage, participant and arena.

XX OLYMPIAD (1972-1976) AND THE 1976 OLYMPIC GAMES

The XX Olympiad marked the beginning of a new era for the Olympic system. For the first time in twenty years the IOC did not have Avery Brundage at the helm. His age and his growing intractability on various issues had increasingly divided the Olympic world, posing a major threat to the very existence of the Olympic Games. His successor, Lord Killanin of Ireland, was a younger man, aware of the cleavage in the Olympic movement and more amenable to change. During the two previous Olympiads, the IOC and the Olympic Games had successfully weathered two possible boycotts of the Games and two separation movements by the international federations and the national Olympic committees. The IOC and the Olympic system were not left unscathed, though, and it was up to Brundage's successor and his fellow IOC members to heal the wounds and to bolster a flagging movement.

The forces for change in the Olympic movement were the same forces that were at work in the world at large. For the XX Olympiad, these forces continued to gain strength and to press for change in the world and in the Olympic system. The primary issues that illustrated these trends were the entry of the People's Republic of China into the Olympic system and the continued conflict over South Africa and Rhodesia. Within the Olympic system itself an entente was reached between the three groups, the IOC, the GAIF, and the PGA, serving once again to bring the world of amateur sport closer together.

During the XIX Olympiad the groups had demanded formation of an Olympic Congress where all three could come together and air their views. Such an assembly had not been held since 1930. Since that time the IOC had preferred to meet separately with the federations and national committees in order to deal more efficiently with each group's particular problems. Both groups increasingly demanded more input into the conduct of amateur and Olympic sport, and both were faced increasingly with the same problems of financing their operations and protecting their independent existence from political and commercial interests. The IOC reluctantly agreed to schedule a Congress in the hopes of welding the Olympic system together again.

The Congress, originally scheduled for 1971, was put off until after the Munich Games and was rescheduled for October 1973 in Varna, Bulgaria. The theme of the Congress was "sport for a world of peace." A tripartite commission composed of members of the three sport organizations was set up to coordinate the Congress. In 1968 Brundage had proposed a similar commission to deal with the problems afflicting the Olympic movement and to provide a forum for cooperation between the three groups. The 1968 proposal had been voted down since the federations and national committees preferred to work separately in the context of their respective organizations, the GAIF and the PGA.

In addition to the tripartite commission, a program of Olympic solidarity was established in 1972 at the Sapporo and Munich sessions of the IOC in order to provide technical assistance to national committees for building up their sport programs in their respective countries. The Olympic solidarity program focused primarily on the developing areas—Africa, Asia, Latin America—where sport programs were scarce and underdeveloped, and where assistance was needed if these areas were to become effective international competitors. Much of the conflict between the IOC and the national committees had concerned this issue. Recent demands by the national committees for a status independent of the IOC had come from the underdeveloped areas in conjunction with the socialist/

communist bloc. The Olympic solidarity program was to include the president of the IOC, three vice-presidents, and the national committee coordinator (Giulio Onesti of Italy, the PGA president). The commission would contact the international federations to ensure their cooperation with and contribution to the program. Olympic solidarity would have a special section at IOC headquarters in Lausanne, would be funded out of the national committee's share of the television revenue, and would create a foundation with a separate bank account.[63]

Through the establishment of the permanent tripartite commission[64] and the Olympic solidarity program, and through the tacit acceptance of the GAIF and the PGA by the IOC, much of the conflict within the Olympic system was abated. It remained for the Olympic Congress to unite the groups into a working basis for a more cooperative and interactive Olympic system. Under the coordination of the three groups, the key issues discussed at the Congress included eligibility, women's role in sport, the role of the individual athlete, and the participation of the People's Republic of China.

The issue of athlete eligibility for the Games had long been a bone of contention between the federations and the IOC. The federations wanted the IOC to adopt guidelines rather than bylaws, leaving to each individual federation the problem of establishing its own rules of eligibility, conforming to IOC guidelines but acknowledging the particular needs of each sport. The federations felt the problem of determining eligibility for the Games should be left to the federations and not to the IOC or national committees.[65] The issue of eligibility had become essentially a problem of economics and politics and, because the federations felt it was no longer possible to divorce sport from either, each federation had to adapt to the situation according to the peculiarities of its sport. The IOC, more open-minded since the departure of Brundage, was somewhat amenable to this. The Congress moved that the IOC eligibility rule should be revised and updated.[66]

Two other resolutions were adopted at the Congress, requiring that all three groups should consider women members and that each should explore means of maintaining closer contact with the athletes. Regarding the former, as a part of the women's movement, it was noted by a female Bulgarian representative at the Congress that there were no women on the IOC and yet there were seventy-six women for every man in the world.[67] At the session following the Congress, the membership voted to allow women members and then promptly elected four men. Defending the IOC's apparent disregard of the Congressional resolution, Killanin said that a woman would probably be inducted in a year or two, but that he would not support the gimmick of having a woman elected just to make headlines. If a woman were to be elected, it would have to be because she would be good for the IOC and not because she was a woman.[68]

The issue of maintaining closer contact with the athletes was responsive to the increasing dismay voiced by the athletes, particularly in the United States, over Olympic rules and regulations that seemed callously impersonal and totally oblivious to the needs of the athletes. The athletes' needs were considered, if at all, only once every four years. In the cases of the Israeli athletes during the Munich massacre and in the sacrifice of Karl Schranz to the dictates of eligibility, it seemed that the athletes were totally subordinate to the bureaucracy.

At the Congress several athletes were invited to observe the proceedings, marking the first time individual athletes had been given such an opportunity. United States athletes demanded input into United States Olympic Committee (USOC) operations. As a result the USOC established the Athletes Advisory Council in 1973 as an arm of the USOC to be run completely by athletes.[69]

The situation of the athlete in international sport was perhaps best summed up by the statements of three athletes. Tom McMillen, an American basketball player on the 1972 American Olympic basketball team that lost to the Soviet Union in the finals on some controversial rulings, said that unless the current trend were stopped he foresaw the day when determinations of victory and defeat would be made in conference rooms without athletes present. "After the game," he said, "I felt helpless. There was an utter futility as others decided which team had won and which had lost." Donna de Varona, an American Olympic swimmer in the 1964 Games testified, "We have no idea if the Olympic Games can survive after Canada in 1976. The athletes are disillusioned by the excessive nationalism and the politics. No one pays any attention to the athletes."[70] Her thoughts were reiterated by an Israeli athlete, one of the eight to survive the Munich massacre. "Every athlete," he said, "wants to succeed in the Olympics for himself first, and only second for his country. The officials, of course, only care about their countries. They're super-nationalistic. Still, the Olympics is for the athletes, not the officials."[71]

This was the Olympic creed, but it had been increasingly shunted to the side in favor of nationalism and bureaucratic infighting. Brundage's statement regarding the Schranz appeal, that the IOC did not deal with individuals, was stark evidence of this. At the Congress it was emphasized that although the Games ideally had been established for individuals, in recent years everyone knew that this was far from the truth. Something had to be done to make the ideal conform with reality or, if possible, reality with the ideal.[72]

The problem was that, historically, the ideal of the Olympics as being for the athletic youth of the world had never conformed to reality. Time and again qualified athletes had been denied admittance by way of official rulings for reasons that had nothing to do with the Olympic creed. A classic case was that of Jim Thorpe. He participated in the 1912 Games in Stockholm, but because he had played semiprofessional baseball one summer to earn money and to stay in shape, he was stripped of his medals. This dishonor ultimately destroyed his life. He had been unaware of the amateur ruling and his indiscretion was really quite minor. Similar incidents have demonstrated that the Olympics have been far from a humanitarian enterprise and have been clearly an enterprise for the exhibition of special interests.

The question of the participation of the People's Republic of China (PRC) in the Olympic Games was a major topic of discussion at the Congress. The reemergence in the world of the PRC had begun in 1971 with the reappearance of the Chinese table tennis team at the world championships in Japan. At these championships the Chinese invited the American delegation to a series of exhibition matches in China. These matches set the stage for the round of negotiations between the PRC and the United States, culminating in the visit of President Nixon the following year.[73] This "ping-pong diplomacy" initiated a carefully calculated, step-by-step rapprochement by the Chinese with the world of sport and the world at large. In 1971 the United Nations recognized the PRC and expelled Taiwan. This facilitated the reexamination of the PRC by the sporting world.

Early in 1973 the Japanese Olympic Committee, in line with the Japanese government's recent opening of diplomatic relations with the PRC, began writing to various international federations and national committees calling for China's reinstatement in the IOC. The Japanese committee sought the expulsion of Taiwan and wanted the cooperation of the federations and national committees in bringing this about.[74] In March 1973, Willi Daume, the West German vice-president of the IOC, went to Peking to discuss the possibilities of China's rejoining the Olympic movement.[75] He was told the PRC would wait sixty-five years, if necessary, before entering the Olympics as long as Taiwan remained a member of the IOC and the international federations.[76] The renewed interest in China, enhanced by a more favorable political climate toward the PRC, snowballed in the sporting world. At the GAIF meeting in May 1973, the federations sat down to discuss the PRC's entry into international competition.

The PRC was a member of only two federations, table tennis and ice hockey, and only the latter was an Olympic sport. The PRC approached other federations in an attempt to reenter the international sporting arena. In order to become eligible for membership in the IOC and participation in the Olympic Games, the PRC had to acquire membership in at least five recognized federations whose sports were on the Olympic program, and to establish an Olympic committee.

The Chinese strategy for recognition was first to approach those federations that did not have Taiwan as a member. In that way there would be less of a problem of attaining membership. This created difficulties, however, for those federations with Taiwan as a member. In multiple sporting competitions, for example, the presence of the PRC would conflict with some of the federations' nonparticipation rules with nonmembers. This problem became quite clear in 1973 when the State Department proposed sponsoring a trip of ten United States swimmers to the PRC. In the United States, the AAU was the national federation that controlled most of the amateur sport, including swimming. The AAU was also a member of FINA, the international federation for swimming. Since FINA had a nonparticipation rule and did not recognize the PRC, the AAU was compelled to suspend the ten swimmers if they made the trip, or to risk suspension itself if it did not suspend the swimmers or prevent the trip. If suspended, every United States swimmer would be ineligible for all FINA sanctioned events, which included all international swimming competitions.

The United States government was in a quandary. At the time of the AAU announcement the Senate happened to be holding hearings on amateur sport in the United States. Harold Henning, then president of FINA, was called to testify. Senator John Tunney, a prime exponent in Congress for the revision of United States amateur sport, suggested to Henning that in this case FINA might make an exception. Henning replied that it was impossible, that FINA was composed of 103 member states and had reaffirmed the rule on the PRC three times. Responding in a reproving manner, he said, "It's come down to an international political situation. We have invited China to rejoin FINA but they won't unless Taiwan resigns. And Taiwan isn't resigning. We're not the United Nations."[77]

The United States swimmers went on the trip anyway, all having decided before the AAU announcement of possible suspension not to continue their amateur swimming careers. Three of the swimmers had been gold medalists at Munich. PRC participation in international competition was not going to abate. It would only increase as more and more states desired sporting and other types of exchanges, and as the PRC began gaining membership in more federations.

Just prior to the Olympic Congress in October 1973, the executive committee of the Asian Games Federation, the coordinating and supervisory body for the Asian Games, voted to admit the PRC and to exclude Taiwan in the upcoming Asian Games to be held in Teheran. The motion had been proposed by Iran and Japan and was passed just after a protest walkout by Malaysia, Indonesia, Taiwan, and Thailand. It still had to be ratified by the twenty-two member council.[78] The international federations did not look on the motion with esteem and passed a motion of their own in their meeting prior to the Olympic Congress, condemning the Asian Games Federation decision. At the Congress itself they threatened to withdraw from the Asian Games if the PRC were admitted at the expense of Taiwan.[79]

At the Congress pressure was continued for the inclusion of China in the IOC and the international sporting world. The Zambian delegate spoke out in favor of including China in the IOC, and the Japanese delegate reiterated the Zambian's statement when he said, "It is a shame that a country with one-fourth of the world's population is excluded from the world of sports." Not to be denied, the Taiwan delegate responded sharply, calling the speech "purely

political" and "un-Olympian." Disgusted, the president of the
International Judo Federation said he was "sick of listening to
propaganda" and stated that twenty out of twenty-six federations
supported the PRC's entry, but not at the expense of Taiwan.[80]

The matter was far from settled. Killanin, as spokesman for the
IOC, in his closing speech commented guardedly on the issue. He
reproached the Japanese committee, saying that he did not think it
should be the self-appointed task of one committee to write to the
others recommending the suspension of an Olympic committee.[81]
Immediately following the Congress, at the IOC general session,
the IOC position regarding the PRC was further clarified when the
IOC warned the Asian Games Federation that they risked the revocation of IOC patronage of their Games if they proceeded to
exclude Taiwan.[82]

The Asian Games Federation was not to be dissuaded from its
purpose. In February 1974, at the IOC executive board meeting,
the secretary-general of the Iranian organizing committee for the
Asian Games argued that he felt the time had come for China to
match its emergence onto the political scene, by virtue of its United
Nations membership, with a similar "revolution" in the world of
sport. He thought it ridiculous to have the Asian Games without
the largest Asian country. In an attempt to rally support the Iranian
organizing committee courted Andrianov, the Soviet IOC member,
who was reportedly opposed to IOC patronage of the Asian Games
if the PRC were admitted.[83]

The Iranian organizing committee and the Asian Games Federation were not alone in their desire for PRC participation. Recent
developments within the international federations had bolstered
their position. Eleven federations had given licenses or permits of
various types to the Games, thereby sanctioning the PRC's presence at the Games. The IOC decided not to withhold its patronage,
although it deplored the action of the Asian Games Federation in
not inviting a recognized member, basing its decision on the interest
of developing sport in Asia and citing the fact that many of the participating federations sanctioned the exclusion of Taiwan.[84] The
IOC's action was a break with its traditional rule of withholding
patronage from area games if a recognized member were not
invited or if an unrecognized member were invited. The IOC was in
no position to argue, lest it risk alienating members of the Olympic
movement whom it had been so assiduously courting.

The IOC decision was followed by the admittance of the PRC

into more federations. In May the weightlifting federation provisionally admitted the PRC, expelling the Taiwanese.[85] With membership in the weightlifting federation, the PRC's total membership in international federations had reached five. The others were ice hockey, skating, rowing, and volleyball. Later that month the fencing federation joined the ranks of those federations recognizing the PRC, and they also turned down Taiwan's application for membership. The International Amateur Athletic Federation (IAAF) announced that it had agreed to meet with representatives of both Taiwan and China in July.[86] At the July meeting the IAAF council (the executive organ) proposed altering the rules to allow a non-affiliated country to take part in a meet staged by an affiliated member.[87] With the IAAF ruling, the PRC position in international sport was considerably strengthened and Taiwan's became less tenable.

By 1975 the PRC was a member of nine federations. Although still not affiliated with the IAAF, the PRC had participated in track and field meets in Pakistan, Tanzania, and Jamaica and was scheduled to compete against Italy, Rumania, Spain, Japan, and the United States. It had taken part in the volleyball championships the previous year, and planned to attend the rowing championships later in 1975. By April 1975, the PRC had formed an Olympic committee and had applied for IOC membership, stipulating that Taiwan should be expelled.[88] Now it was up to the IOC to decide if the PRC could participate at the 1976 Games.

The IOC was reluctant to make a decision. The PRC claimed jurisdiction over all of China including Taiwan, but would not accept dual membership. On the other hand, the Taiwan committee had been a member for more than twenty years and now claimed jurisdiction only over Taiwan. In addition Taiwan was not opposed to dual membership. In May, at an IOC meeting with the national committees, forty-two committees spoke on the Chinese issue. Twenty-five favored dual membership and seventeen favored the expulsion of Taiwan.[89] The PRC was still not affiliated with the IAAF or FINA, two major federations, but its membership in international federations had been on the rise while Taiwan's was declining. There was a clear trend toward the integration of the PRC into international sport, but although the IOC favored bringing 800 million people into the Olympic movement, it could not very well simply exclude 15 million.

The PRC continued its vitriolic attacks on the IOC and the late

(April 1975) Avery Brundage, which did not augur well for PRC membership. Because little was known of China's recently established Olympic committee, Killanin decided to pay a personal visit to both Taiwan and Peking. His trip was ostensibly to inquire if the committee had met all the rules and regulations of the IOC, but by making a point of going to both Taiwan and Peking, Killanin's proposed visit would obviously attempt a negotiated settlement.

By October 1975 Killanin had not made his fact-finding trip. He was stalling for time, hoping the situation would blow over. At the IOC general session prior to the Innsbruck Winter Games, the issue of China was not even on the agenda. It was clear the IOC hoped the issue would abate. It would not. As the Montreal Games drew near, the Canadian government voiced concern to the IOC over the possibility that the athletes from the Republic of China (Taiwan) might come to the Games competing under the designation of the "Republic of China." Canada, having instituted a one-China policy in 1970, recognized the PRC as the only legitimate representative for all of China. Canada felt it would compromise that policy if it allowed the athletes from Taiwan to compete as representatives of the Republic of China. Peking had formally requested the Canadian government to bar unconditionally the entry of the Taiwanese delegation. Canada refused to do this, requesting only that the Taiwanese delegation compete without reference to the word "China." Lord Killanin replied on June 8 that the Canadian position was in "complete conflict" with Olympic principles. Taiwan was a full fledged member of the IOC and had competed in the Winter Games and the last World University Games as the Republic of China.[90] The IOC considered the Canadian action to be a breach of its promise made in 1970, when Montreal was chosen, that no recognized member country would be denied entrance.

Both parties were adamant in their positions, causing considerable concern that the Games might be canceled if Canada did not relent. Nothing was done until July 9, however, just eight days before the opening ceremonies, when several Taiwanese team members were refused entry. Negotiations began between the IOC and Canada. Canada proclaimed its one-China policy. The IOC insisted that the PRC was not a member of the IOC, that the Republic of China was a member, and that under the agreement given by Canada it should be allowed entry as the Republic of China.[91]

Canada had taken a very unpopular position. The United States government opposed the Canadian stand, and the press unleashed scathing attacks on the Trudeau government. The Canadian Olympic Committee was opposed to the government stand. The issue was noted in the United States presidential race. Ronald Reagan, a Republican candidate, called the Canadian action "an affront" to Taiwan.[92] The IOC submitted a compromise plan to Canada—that Taiwan would march as "Taiwan-ROC" behind a flag bearing the Olympic rings.[93] The Taiwanese delegation was opposed, demanding to march and compete under its own flag and name, the Republic of China.[94]

On July 11 the IOC executive board capitulated and announced that it would submit a resolution to the full session of the IOC that Taiwan should compete as Taiwan under the Olympic banner.[95] Killanin called the Canadian action a dangerous precedent for the future, emphasizing that the IOC had not been forewarned until May 28, 1976, that Canada had any intention of barring Taiwan's entrance. Killanin and the IOC maintained, quite accurately, that Canada's action was totally unexpected and completely political. A member of the Canadian Olympic Commission referred to the IOC capitulation as the "blackest day in Canada's history" and went on to lament that a nonmember country of the Olympic movement was dictating Canadian policy. President Ford urged United States Olympic officials to persuade the IOC board to change its mind. In turn, Ford was accused by the Canadian External Affairs Minister of "external interference" in Canada's affairs.[96]

The Canadian Parliament was not unanimous on the government's stand. In defense of his position, Trudeau retorted to John Diefenbaker of the opposition party and former prime minister, "The world has moved on since the right honorable member was a prime minister." Joe Clark, Diefenbaker's successor as conservative party leader, shouted back, "Yes, it has. In his day commitments were honored." Nevertheless, the government's position was firm.[97] At the IOC general session the executive board resolution was approved by the full body in a vote totaling fifty-eight in favor, two against, with six abstentions.[98]

The Canadian stand and the IOC capitulation created such an uproar in the United States that many called for cancellation of the Games, or United States withdrawal, or both. Within a few days before the Games were to open, the Taiwan question was still undecided, the United States Olympic Committee was still debating whether to participate in the Games, and the PRC was still maintaining pressure on Canada, attacking the IOC, Taiwan, and anyone in favor of Taiwan. Bringing to the forefront the Sino-Soviet dispute, the PRC accused the Soviets of backing Taiwan's bid to enter the Games, charging that Moscow and Taipeh were working in collusion.[99] Finally, on the day before the Games were to begin, July 16, the Taiwanese delegation refused the compromise solution and did not participate. The United States government was so incensed over the decision and Taiwan's nonparticipation that Henry Kissinger refused to attend the Games.[100]

The IOC asserted that Canada had given a guarantee in 1970 and had not lived up to it, that Canada was mixing politics with sport and was threatening the very foundations of the Olympic movement. The IOC contended that absolutely no forewarning had been given. Lord Killanin stated that the May 1976 letter gave the first indication to him of Canada's possible refusal of Taiwan's entry. He said that in April 1975, at an informal lunch with Canadian officials, he had indicated that he could foresee no change in the status of Taiwan, and that no concern had been expressed to him by Canadian officials. Taiwan competed at Innsbruck in February 1976 and nothing was said to him. In April 1976, the Canadian Ministry of Immigration sent out identity cards as travel documents without exception. Killanin said that in the letter of November 1969 to the IOC, guaranteeing free entry of all recognized Olympic committees, the Canadian qualification "pursuant to the normal regulations" was not interpreted by the IOC or by Mayor Drapeau of Montreal as political, pertaining to Canada. The president of the organizing committee, also an official in the Canadian Department of External Affairs, was not notified of the Canadian position and was issuing accreditations to the ROC through June 22, 1976.[101]

The Canadian side of the story was almost totally opposite. The qualification "pursuant to normal regulations" had applied to Canada. At the April 1975 meeting with Killanin, Canadian officials had advised him of a possible problem if the ROC athletes tried to represent themselves as such. The matter had been raised at Innsbruck in February 1976. Taiwan could represent itself as in 1960, under the Rome formula, but since 1970 the consistent Canadian position had been that while people from Taiwan were free to come on an individual basis, they could not publicly proclaim themselves as representatives of the government of China. In 1974, at the World Bicycle Championships held in Montreal and again at the pre-Olympic boxing matches in Montreal, the Taiwanese team had not been allowed to compete. In both cases Taiwan had tried to represent itself as the Republic of China.[102]

The true situation will probably remain a mystery. It was charged the PRC had pressured Canada to keep Taiwan out by threatening to go elsewhere for its wheat. This was flatly denied; that such a mercenary motive could possibly have been a consideration was out of the question. The amount of Canada's exports to the PRC amounted to only one-and-a-half percent of total Canadian exports, so Canada was not vulnerable to economic pressure from the PRC. The PRC had urged that Canada bar Taiwan unconditionally, but this Canada had not been willing to do. Taiwan could compete, but as Taiwan, not as the Republic of China.[103]

The IOC position was politically naive and was also at cross-purposes with the concerns of the individual athletes. Obviously, with all the clamor for PRC participation over several years, to ignore this trend was to court disaster. To be unaware of Canada's consistent policies, or to believe that the IOC was somehow invincible and supranational showed a serious lack of political acumen. In practice this inability to keep up with the times made the IOC vulnerable to political stresses to the ultimate detriment of the Olympics, of sport, and of the athlete.

The Canadian position may have been politically consistent, but it had set a dangerous precedent, not only for future Olympics but for sport in general. The relative merits of Canada's policy were not the issue. Its policy was not generally known, and its action appeared arbitrary and politically expedient. The central ideal of the Olympics was peaceful competition, and the central protagonist was the athlete. A last minute refusal of entry over something so trivial as a name was diametrically opposed to the central value of the Games. It destroyed all that the athlete had worked for and it lacked humanitarian concern.

In this sense, the Olympics have been at fault for perpetuating and structuring themselves along nationalistic lines. The importance of the individual has become lost in the process. Alas, until nationalism is taken out of the Games—until the IOC restructures itself—politics will remain a part of the Olympics. With precedents such as that set by Canada, the propensity for future political machinations will increase. Unless the IOC should decide to restructure itself along less nationalistic lines, it must conduct itself with greater political acumen in order to minimize the episodes of political intrigue and byplay that seriously detract from the sport.

Another major issue that plagued the XX Olympiad involved South African and Rhodesian participation, but this did not become an overriding cause until just prior to the 1976 Games. South Africa had been banned from the Olympic movement for some time but still participated in sporting exchanges with various countries. Rhodesia was still recognized by the IOC, although it had been denied participation at Munich at the last moment, ostensibly because of a passport violation but really because of a boycott threat.

The African countries, the Soviet Union, and the Eastern European countries continued to press for worldwide severance of sporting links with South Africa and Rhodesia. In 1973, the USSR, GDR, and Czechoslovakia asked for the suspension of South Africa from the gymnastics federation.[104] Their request was granted. Because of claims by the African states that the Rhodesian Olympic committee practiced racial discrimination, the IOC decided in February 1974 to send a fact-finding commission to Rhodesia.[105] In late 1974 the United Nations issued another appeal to the international sport organizations to "cut off all contacts with racist sports bodies in South Africa."[106] That same year the IAAF upheld its suspension of South African national teams from international competition for two years, but the suspension did not apply to individual athletes competing on their own.[107] South Africa still remained a member of the Davis Cup tournament, but was moved to the North American Zone to control the possibility of a boycott. South Africa did well in competition, and went all the way to the finals where it was to meet India. India boycotted, preferring to default rather than to play South Africa.[108] Similar problems arose in the 1975 Davis Cup competition, this time extending to Mexico, Colombia, and Rumania. In fact, the only country promising to compete against South Africa in South Africa was the post-Allende Chile. Not even the United States would compete against South Africa within South Africa in Davis Cup play, insisting instead that the competition take place in the United States.[109] Even New Zealand, a country having a long history of close sporting ties with South Africa, balked at competing. A South African rugby team was to tour New Zealand, but the outcry was so strong against the proposed tour the New Zealand government called off the tour, citing the very real threat of violence as justification. The government said, "When it has been clearly demonstrated that all South Africans have equal opportunity to be selected through mixed trials, the government would have no objection to a visit by such a team." The decision was made by the new labor government. The previous government would not have called off the tour, saying it preferred "building bridges to erecting walls."[110]

By May 1975, because of the IOC decision to expel Rhodesia from the Olympic movement,[111] it appeared the Olympic Games would be free of a boycott threat for the first time in three Olympics. In May 1976, that hope was dispelled. New Zealand, which in 1973 had stopped a rugby tour by South Africa, was now planning a rugby tour in South Africa itself. The threat of a boycott was once again raised, not only by the African countries but by the Eastern European and Caribbean countries as well.[112] The threat was confirmed when the SCSA threatened to boycott the Olympic Games or, at least, those events in which New Zealand was involved. The SCSA cited violations of United Nations resolutions condemning South African racial policies, and the establishment of sporting exchanges—softball championships earlier in the year and the proposed rugby tour—as the reasons for the boycott.[113]

The boycott threat was particularly galling to track and field fans because it involved a classic confrontation between the two top milers in the world—Tanzania's Filbert Bayi and New Zealand's John Walker. Tanzania for a year, however, had not allowed Bayi to compete against Walker for the very reasons cited by the SCSA. With all the concern over the Taiwan affair, the New Zealand issue was relegated to a lesser position, but its impact on the 1976 Games was devastating. By the time the IOC had capitulated to Canada over Taiwan, it was deep in the throes of the New Zealand controversy. On July 9 Tanzania said it would not compete if New Zealand competed.[114] The OAU said its member states would not compete unless New Zealand were banned.[115] Before the Games, the United Nations anti-apartheid seminar in Havana urged a boycott if the rugby tour took place.[116] Forty-eight hours before the opening of the Games fifteen African countries sent Killanin an ultimatum—send New Zealand packing or they would boycott.[117]

The IOC was stunned by the African threat. Even the African members of the committee were opposed to the boycott. The IOC protested that it had nothing to do with the question of a rugby tour. New Zealand did not practice apartheid; rugby was not an Olympic sport; the New Zealand Rugby Federation was not affiliated with the New Zealand Olympic Committee; and the IOC had expelled both Rhodesia and South Africa from the movement.[118] The IOC did not give in to the African demands and thirty countries boycotted.

The choices of New Zealand and rugby as targets were blatantly arbitrary. Why not attack the twenty-six other states that continued to have sport relations with South Africa?[119] In fact, in the midst of the controversy a United States gymnastics tour of South Africa was planned.[120] The 1976 boycott made it clear, as had the 1972 Rhodesian affair and the 1968 threatened boycott, that the question of sport or violations of Olympic rules had nothing to do with the position of the African countries. Sport and the Olympics provided a convenient forum for the exposition of a social and political cause, which went far beyond sport.

During the XX Olympiad, in addition to the major issues of PRC participation and the New Zealand affair, other incidents or events reflected global political controversies or trends. As was the case during the XIX Olympiad, the United States and the Soviet Union were vying for selection as the site for future Olympic Games. This time Los Angeles and Moscow were the only bidders for the 1980 Summer Games. Moscow had come in second for the 1976 Games and was the favorite for the 1980 Games, but recent events at the World University Games held in Moscow had sent a torrent of protest against Moscow as the choice for the 1980 Games.

At the University Games the Israeli athletes were jeered and harassed by Russians, though the Russian Jews helped to create disharmony by displaying Israeli flags and by being overtly antagonistic. It was reported that Soviet officials did little to restrain the mobs that harassed the Israelis and attacked the Russian Jews.[121] The Soviet government was in a dilemma. On the one hand they wanted to show they could handle major international events, with their bid for the 1980 Games in mind. on the other hand they felt they could not tolerate such open support of the Israeli presence by the Russian Jews. As a result, they invited Yassir Arafat to the Games, the leader of the Palestine Liberation Organization, and his presence was widely publicized. The Soviets tolerated an initial fraternization between the Israeli athletes and the Soviet Jews, but then they isolated the Israeli team, citing security measures as justification to prevent another Munich affair. Yigal Allon, the Israeli foreign minister, called the Soviet action "racism and anti-Semitism" and said the Soviet Union should not host the 1980 Games.[122]

Similar remarks and statements were made in the United States. Forty Congressmen sent a letter to the IOC protesting a proposed designation of Moscow for 1980.[123] The United States Olympic Committee publicly opposed Moscow on the basis of the University Games experience.[124] Of course it had its own candidacy and could not very well support the opposition. The Los Angeles Organizing Committee submitted its bid to the IOC, playing up the aspect of freedom of movement and of the press without reservations, and promising to protect all athletes, officials, and spectators from harm or harassment by political demonstrations.[125] All was to no avail. Moscow was chosen. The IOC was not impressed with the Los Angeles inducements. Events at the Asian Games and at other past venues had shown the IOC that if there were to be political demonstrations little could be done to stop them. The overriding consideration for the IOC was an efficient running of the Games, which Moscow promised. Perhaps most important was that the Games would go for the first time to a Socialist state. The IOC always sought to open up the Games and to expand the Olympic movement around the world. Thus it had given the Games to Mexico in 1968, the first Latin American and underdeveloped country, to Japan in 1964, the first Asian country, and to Melbourne in 1956. It is perhaps significant that Moscow was awarded the 1980 Games in an era of detente. As the Moscow mayor said, "We learned from our mistakes in 1970, and the world's atmosphere has relaxed since then."[126]

The atmosphere had not relaxed in the Middle East. The 1973 war had only heightened tensions and this was reflected in sport. At the Asian Games in September 1974, Taiwan was ousted. The PRC, Pakistan, North Korea, Kuwait and others refused to compete against Israel, and the Asian Soccer Federation, which Israel had helped to form in 1956, voted seventeen to thirteen with six abstentions to oust Israel from the federation.[127] Most of those voting against Israel were Moslem or Middle Eastern countries.

Similar incidents elsewhere reflected world tensions. At the world wrestling championships, in October 1974, Albanian wrestlers refused to compete against Russian wrestlers.[128] At the Asian

Games, the North Koreans refused to compete against the South Koreans in basketball, but agreed to compete in volleyball because a net separated the two teams.[129] At the Pan-American Games in Mexico in October 1975, the American athletes and President Echeverria of Mexico were jeered while the Cuban athletes were cheered.[130] At the 1976 Winter Games in Innsbruck, in response to objections by the Soviet-bloc, the IOC withdrew accreditation of Radio Free Europe to cover the Games. In a message to Lord Killanin, Secretary of State Henry Kissinger of the United States, called the action a "craven capitulation to the Communist countries" and said the exclusion was contrary to the intent and spirit of the Helsinki Accord.[131] Through it all the IOC and the federations stood helplessly by, deploring the actions and issuing threats of disqualification or suspension.[132] No action was ever taken by the sport organizations for the infractions.

By the XX Olympiad, not only had politics and nationalism become a prominent feature in sport and the Olympic Games, but commercialism threatened the very existence of the Games and of international sport. The Montreal Games, originally budgeted for $310 million, ended up a $1.5 billion disaster.[133] In his attempt to make the Games self-financing, before the costs escalated beyond comprehension, Mayor Drapeau stated, "The Montreal Olympics can no more have a deficit than a man can have a baby."[134] Drapeau's Games finally had to be bailed out and taken over by the Quebec provincial government. To finance the Games, Drapeau had relied on all the commercial interests providing his bankroll. By selling the rights as "official supplier," the organizing committee had hoped to finance the bulk of the expenditures. For example, such firms as Coca-Cola paid $1.3 million plus all the free coke the athletes could drink to be an "official supplier," Pitney-Bowes paid $350,000, and Adidas shoes paid $500,000.[135] The list was endless. Beyond the commercial contributions, the organizing committee had planned to sell commemorative coins and stamps, to hold lotteries, and to gain revenue through the sale of television rights. The United States television company, ABC, was to pay the most ($25 million) and the world rights would total $40 million.[136] For the 1980 Games the Soviet Union planned to spend nearly $2 billion[137] to stage the Games, and sought Western business firms to donate equipment and to pay for the rights as "official suppliers." Such firms included IBM, Kodak, Omega, and Longines.[138] The

Moscow organizing committee for the 1980 Games sold the American television rights to NBC for $85 million.[139]

The presence of commercial firms in the financial picture of the Games and international sport is not necessarily detrimental, particularly in the context of a capitalistic system, but the tremendous expenditure for the Games, the enormous sums paid by commercial firms, and the intense interest in the Games by commercial interests, all tend to take the Games out of the realm of sport. They become primarily an advertising, profit, and loss venture. Admittedly, much of the expenditure goes for the erection of permanent facilities such as stadiums, housing, communication systems, and transportation networks. In this light Japan's $3 billion expenditure in 1964 can be viewed more positively. Had it not been for the Olympic Games, needed facilities in the cities and at the sites of the Games might not have been erected. Indeed, a major consideration of the IOC when it designates the site is whether the Games will contribute to the improvement of the city. But the improvement of a city and the sporting purpose of the Games play a secondary role to the Games as a forum for commercial and political exploitation. The expensive extravaganza necessitates putting financial considerations above those of sport, merely to ensure continuation of the Games. Television and other commercial interests take precedence, dictating in large measure the conduct of sport.

Certain kinds of commercial involvement, such as the exhibition of products by the athletes, force the athlete to compete not simply for himself but for the product that he is advertising. If enough athletes are involved, the regulating sport organization is faced either with condoning the commercialism, making rule changes accordingly, or with courting the possibility of losing its athletes to another organization whose rules are more flexible in this regard. If the organization loses its athletes for failure to accommodate, it loses its central reason for existence. Without the athlete, the organization ceases to be. The Alpine skiing and the tennis organizations are classic examples of this.

The presence of television similarly affects the conduct of sport. In large measure television has helped to make the Games the spectacle they are today by opening the Games to a mass audience, playing in particular on the nationalistic rivalry inherent in the Games. Tremendous interest has been focused on the Games, creating a worldwide spectacle and enlarging the concept of the Games.

Because of this expanded interest, the television media has been willing to pay tremendous sums to televise the Games. These large sums finance the Games as well as the activities of the sport organizations—the very activities that have been increased due to the expanded interest in sport. The television revenues become a vital source of income, increasingly necessary to meet the heavy demands of operating the organizations and financing the Games. Within this vicious circle the television interests, along with the other commercial interests that increasingly help to finance the Games and organizations, can begin to demand certain concessions from the organizations. The sport organizations have no choice but to consent. Were the sport organizations to refuse such demands, the whole framework would collapse, for the media and commercial interests would refuse to "finance" the sport organizations. The commercial interests could then form their own sport organizations and Games, more commercially oriented. The sport organizations can best fend off this possibility not by totally rejecting the commercial interests, but rather by tempering their demands. The conduct of sport is affected, to say the least. Time schedules are changed for television, rule changes are made in sport to increase fan interest, and advertising becomes prevalent.

When politics and nationalism are brought into the equation, the commercial interests will exploit these as means of advertisement and product promotion. What results is not a forum for athletic competition, but an extravaganza that reflects and enhances the competitive and divisive interests in the world.

6

Conclusion

THE OLYMPIC GAMES BEGAN as a forum for the youth of the world to unite in peaceful competition through sport. The Games were to benefit the athletes, to expose them to people from other parts of the world, to broaden their horizons. Sport was seen as an ideal vehicle to revive and instill spirit and social values in the individual. The Olympic Games were envisioned as a focal point for the testing of national sporting programs and for the testing and enlarging of national spirit and values. The Olympics did not intend competition between countries; rather, they were to provide a setting where countries could meet peacefully—at worst a surrogate battlefield without the bloodshed. The individuals, the athletes, the youth of the world were to provide the central purpose of the Games.

By 1976 the individual, the athlete, the youth of the world played a role of secondary importance in the Olympic Games. The Olympics had become a vehicle for the achievement of ulterior interests. What had happened in eighty years? Did the Games ever live up to the ideal?

The structure of the Olympic Games from the outset prevented the ideal from becoming a reality. By identifying the athletes with their respective states, each athlete was subordinated to the state as its contestant. The athletes were not adjudged as individuals. Inevitably they were identified as representatives of their states. The propaganda value became readily apparent when the prowess of an athletic feat was rewarded under a national banner while a national anthem played, but the states did not originate the idea of such national identification. The Olympic officials were responsible.

[*163*]

Whether or not the Olympic officials intended such an emphasis, they structured their Games and organizations along nationalistic lines, thereby enhancing the inherent potential for nationalism. States merely capitalized on and supported an idea that was to their benefit.

Throughout modern Olympic history officials have labored under the contradiction inherent in their ideal, forever protesting the intrusion of politics into the Games and sport. Given the organizational structure of the Games, however, politics is not really an intrusion but is very much a part of the Games and of sport itself. This realization is essential to an understanding of how and why the Olympics and international sport are forums for international competition and are utilized as tools of national foreign policy.

The world can be viewed as a system of organizations that are constantly tending to evolve into higher forms. In this sense, a nation-state is but another organization having basically the same characteristics as other organizations, though its purpose may be different. The IOC and other international sport organizations comprise a set of organizations with specific purposes and goals. All organizations reflect a collective consciousness of specific combinations of individuals. Each organization has certain facets to its personality that are utilized for the achievement of its goals, just as an individual uses his personal characteristics to meet his purposes. In this sense, organizations are individual units on the world scene. When an organization structures itself in terms of other organizational entities (e.g., international sport in terms of nation-states), the facets of other organizations (the nation-state) become a part of the first organization (international sport). Since politics is a facet of nation-states, politics becomes a part of international sport. The only way to divorce politics from international sport is to alter the organizational structure of sport.

Politics then is inherent in the Olympic system, and the international sport organizations and the Olympic Games are variant arenas of world politics. The political issues that the Olympic system has confronted underscore this concept. The majority of these issues have involved the question of recognition. At the end of World War II, Germany and Japan were not recognized or allowed to participate in the Games until such time as the occupation authorities gave their consent. In the case of Germany, the issue then became no longer a question of the recognition of Germany per se, but of East or West Germany. The estrangement that erupted between the occupation authorities became an important part of the United States-Soviet, East-West conflict and carried over into the question of German recognition. That same estrangement was exhibited in the later questions of Soviet and Chinese recognition. In the latter case, the issue was similar to that of Germany.

As time went on and relations eased between the East and the West, the question of German recognition became less of an issue. By 1968 it was resolved to the satisfaction of both sides. Conversely, the problem of Chinese recognition remained because of the deepening Sino-Soviet dispute and the Chinese cultural revolution of the late 1960s. Even in the mid-1970s the issue had not been resolved, and considerable trouble ensued at the 1976 Games as a result of changing world politics and the emergence of the PRC onto the world political scene.

On other fronts the problem of Olympic recognition was again raised, this time concerning South Africa and Rhodesia. In both cases the issues reflected the African political situation and the protest against white-ruled, racist regimes. The African dissent was in part supported by other Third World areas and by the Soviet bloc countries. The Third World support represented anticolonial nationalistic sentiment; the Soviet bloc support manifested the continuing East-West conflict and the drive for solidarity with the underdeveloped, nonaligned areas. The increasing success of a boycott threat of the Olympic Games over the issue of South Africa and Rhodesia throughout the period 1956-1976 demonstrated the rise of the Third World as an alternative power source. Area Games were another source of political confrontation, dramatizing regional controversies that had spill-over effects into the Olympic Games and the world at large. The GANEFO episode of 1963 is a good case in point, as is that of the Asian Games of 1974.

Within the ranks of the Olympic system there was increasing controversy between the respective organizations, basically the product of nationalism and commercialism. The former elicited demands by national committees for expanded participation in the Olympic system. The latter had its major effect on the international sport federations and their increasing difficulty, under the influence of financial inducements, in conducting their sports in an amateur context. Here the sport federations were increasingly at odds with the IOC. For all three organizations—the IOC, the national committees, and the international federations—the role of television in the Olympic Games had become a bone of contention, especially as the Olympic and international sporting system expanded throughout the world, raising the expenditures necessary for the staging of sporting contests and the maintenance and perpetuation of the sport organizations. Earlier sources of revenue, primarily private donations, no longer were adequate to meet the expanded tasks of the sport organizations. The sale of television rights for enormous sums was seen as a panacea for this revenue deficit. The only problem was determining the distribution of the revenue. The distribution problem combined with increasing division between the three organizations produced a struggle for control within the Olympic system. It also subjected that system to external control as financial considerations became paramount, for in order to maintain financial solvency, the organizations developed a dependency on outside commercial and television interests.

These political and economic interests represented a vast, organizational nexus evolving throughout the world. Following the Second World War a nucleus of nation-states in Europe, Asia, and the American continents formed the bulwark of the prewar state system. This nucleus, primarily composed of the Soviet Union, Europe, and North America (and peripherally including South America) took the lead in establishing the predominant postwar relationships. The relationships among the nation-states in the nucleus created the conditions for the East-West estrangement that continues to dominate the world political scene. That estrangement in turn helped to forge regional integration movements, political, economic, and military, which formed organizational structures beyond the nation-state (i.e., beyond a purely national perspective).

The nucleus sought to consolidate its position once again and to establish a system of relations among states, bilateral or multilateral, which included both regional and world organizations, such as the United Nations. The colonial areas, imbued with nationalistic fervor, sought to break away from their colonial status and to establish their own separate nation-states. By the mid-1960s this process was nearly complete, expanding the nation-state system around the world and in turn propelling nationalism to its zenith. At the same time, the nationalism that had spawned the separation movements from the colonial powers brought the new states together, forming a nonaligned force in counterpoint to the East-

West controversy. This unification was expressed by declarations of nonalignment or by establishment of regional arrangements (e.g., the OAU, LAFTA) for mutual political and economic protection from more powerful states. As nationalism began to reach its zenith, the catalytic effect of environmental conditions (economic, military and political) caused nationalism itself to evolve worldwide into a higher form, producing a more international or integrated organizational framework.

There was a further organizational evolution, that of the transnational organization. These organizations had existed for some time, but following World War II their increase was phenomenal. As the economies in the nucleus states prospered, technology grew by leaps and bounds. The necessity for the protective umbrella of the nation-state became less important as the sense of security became more controlled. The primary transnational operator was the multinational business firm, but other transnational actors increased in number and importance (e.g., sport organizations) as the nation-state system expanded, spreading nationalism worldwide and creating conditions conducive to the orientation of the individual beyond his own state boundaries.

These organizational forces and trends were apparent in the Olympic system. The East-West conflict was most strongly exhibited in the question of German recognition and in the competition between the Soviet Union and the United States. As an indicator of the evolving and expanding nation-state system, the German question became less of an issue over time, and the tension between the Soviet Union and the United States became less keen. Instead, attention was shifted to the South African controversy, reflecting the changing power structure and the expanded nation-state system. In the midst of that controversy, the OAU and the United Nations were primary actors in pressuring for IOC and international action.

The Olympic system and international sport further reflected growing internationalism. As the nation-state system expanded so did the Olympic movement and international sport, growing in interest and prestige. In 1975 the IOC, having reached an international stature comparable to other international organizations and having encountered more and more problems commensurate with that stature, decided to register with the United Nations as a recognized international organization having legal status.[1]

The Olympic system is unique in that not only does it qualify as an international organization by virtue of its national identification, it also qualifies as a transnational organization in that it comprises a set of private organizations. The growth in prestige and interest acquired in its capacity as an international organization applies equally in its role as transnational actor. The corollary growth of commercial and media influence in the Olympics and sport further indicates their own increasing impact on the world at large, illustrating the mutualism existing between transnational actors on the world scene today.

The Olympics has provided a forum for international competition and confrontation and also has been an actor in that process. The IOC and the other sport organizations have sought to carry out their tasks within the amateur sport system, but in the context of the nation-state system. At the same time, they have been forced to respond to external stimuli in order to maintain control over the amateur sport system.

The original emphasis of the Olympic Games was on the athlete, but the structure of the Games and the sport organizations caused the emphasis, for reasons of efficiency, to be on the organizations. The division of labor was made easier but at the expense of the importance of the athlete. This was illustrated time and again, most poignantly during the boycott threats and the successful boycott of the 1976 Games.

Olympic officials could have dealt with the problem in an organizational context had they simply recognized that politics, within this organizational framework, was an integral part of sport. Killanin did recognize this. Once he had ascended to the helm of the IOC in 1972, he acknowledged a view contrary to that of his predecessor, stating that sport and politics did mix. The difficulty lay in trying to minimize the politics.[2] This Killanin could not do because he failed to recognize the athlete as the cardinal focus of the Olympics, choosing instead to deal with the organizations. This was a repeat of Brundage's error, to the detriment of the athlete.

Incidents during the presidencies of Brundage and Killanin underscore this shared error. During Brundage's reign, exiles from World War II created problems stemming from postwar relationships. Many athletes had fled to the United States or elsewhere with the arrival of the Soviet forces into Eastern Europe. These athletes sought to participate in the 1952 and 1956 Games, but an IOC rule prohibited an athlete from participating in the Games for one country if he had previously participated for another country. Similarly, an athlete could not participate if he were not a citizen of that country and had not received the necessary affiliation with its sport organizations. The exiles sought special dispensation or a change in the rules. They wanted to participate as athletes, as individuals, behind the Olympic flag, or in whatever way was possible. The IOC declined to permit their entry. They submitted the question to the Council of Europe, which conversely agreed with the exiles,[3] but the IOC would not tolerate anything contrary to its rules or contrary to the established organizational pattern and persisted in its refusal. Clearly, it was not the athlete who mattered but the organization.

At the 1976 Games the boycott left many athletes unable to participate because of the actions of their governments and sport organizations. The disappointment was great after so much effort, but most of the athletes resigned themselves to their fate. A few did not. One such athlete was James Gilkes of Guyana. Spurred on by earlier declarations of the IOC that any athlete who wanted to participate could do so under the Olympic banner—an obvious ploy to sabotage the boycott—Gilkes decided to apply to compete as an individual under the Olympic banner. After much deliberation the IOC turned down his request, reaffirming the Olympic rules.[4] Under Killanin's reign, as under Brundage's, the IOC was unable to realize its ideal in the face of organizational inertia.

The IOC's inability is symptomatic of a worldwide situation. It is not primarily a question of the individual versus the organization, although this is a large factor, but more a misrepresentation of the individual in an organizational context. An individual may be a member of an organization, but if he has no input into that organization he is likely to be misrepresented. The sport organizations are not in fact organizations of athletes, which they purport to be, but rather bureaucratic administrative structures. The administrative apparatus is in each case the real organization.

When Filbert Bayi of Tanzania was refused the opportunity to compete against John Walker of New Zealand before the 1976 Games, it was not Bayi who made the decision. It was his sports organization. Bayi had absolutely no say in the matter, although he was the one to do the running. The situation is a common one. The Olympics is only an isolated example.

World society is a complex of organizations. The organizations are set up with specific purposes and goals. The achievement of these goals is paramount. In order to achieve the stated goals, the organization must be maintained. Through time the latter consideration becomes paramount, and the former goal becomes the expedient justification for the existence of the organization. Therefore, the primary goal of the organization is organizational health—the maintenance of the organization at any cost. In order to achieve this, an organization sets up specific routines and standard patterns of behavior through standard operating procedures. Through standard operating procedures an organization can control its internal and surrounding environments by coordinating and categorizing the issues and problems it faces into set patterns of operation and routine. An organization attempts to avoid uncertainty, for uncertainty—the lack of standard behavior—creates chaos, and chaos disrupts organizational patterns, then organizational structure, and finally the organization itself.

The organization is a cooptive device. It must be in order to sustain its existence. It must have adherents; it must grow; but the growth is defined in terms of bigness rather than quality. Quality, unlike bigness, is not readily measured. Bigness can be measured and used as an index of organizational health and existence. Thus growth is defined in terms of such indicators as budget, manpower, and territory. The main problem for any organization lies in the conflict between its organizational patterns of behavior and its stated purpose for existence, that is, in the maintenance of the organization as opposed to its stated ideal.[5]

In this light, the Olympic system can be analyzed in terms of its past performance to determine future considerations and potentialities. For the IOC and all the amateur sport organizations, the maintenance of the organization has been paramount, utilizing the ideals of the organizations as excuses for their existence. The IOC and the sport organizations have standardized their behavior and procedures in order to control their environment. They have set up structures of organization and procedure in terms of nation-states in order to control the athletic world. The sport organizations have been symbols of nation-states—the dominant organizational units on the world scene—and as such have been able to maintain their existence through the process of identification. Their growth along with the nation-state—and hence the identification factor—has facilitated the opportunity to coopt all the amateur sport organizations into the Olympic movement as the only legitimate sport movement. The Olympic movement has been forced to define its health in terms of the growth and size of its organizations rather than in terms of its ideals. The ideals have been made secondary but have been used as the primary justification for its existence.

The international system has been changing, however, and the Olympic organizations have found it increasingly difficult to categorize the environment into standard procedure. When the attempt has failed, as in the 1976 boycott, the credibility of the organizations have been lowered. Increasingly in the latter years of the period 1944 to 1976, as the Olympic system has retrenched its routine, the central questions of Olympic ideals and the rights of the individual athletes have become burning issues. The Olympic system has been viewed increasingly as archaic and inadequate for the performance of international sport, because it has not been perpetuating but has been hampering that performance, and because the individual has not been sufficiently considered. It remains to be determined what is in store for the future, what must be done in order to improve international sport, and, correspondingly, what the Olympic organizations can do to help this process.

Perhaps it is best to begin with the premise upon which the Olympic organizations exist—the encouragement of peace through the spirit of athletic competition. Past Olympic Games have certainly not demonstrated that athletic competition has encouraged peace. If anything, the contrary has been true. The nation-state orientation of the Games has only led to rivalry and tension, conditions hardly conducive to peace. As a first step, the premise of the Olympics should become one simply of providing a forum for world sport competition. The nineteenth-century ideal of the Games has no place in the twentieth century. There are other forums where the ideal of peace can be more adequately and efficiently carried out.

Too much evidence exists showing that sport and politics are indeed inseparable. This must be recognized and accepted if one is to deal with the numerous problems facing the Olympics. To deny the obvious is to court ruin. The Olympics were created at a time when sport was an extraneous pastime and when the structure of the international system was considerably different and much less complicated. As the nation-state system has developed its many ramifications, so has the Olympics gained in stature, size, and political and economic significance. The Games have become too large, simply providing a spectacle of nationalism and all the world's competing interests. Certainly no justification exists in the sporting world for such a huge spectacle, particularly as it is presently structured.

The IOC should seriously consider opening the Games to all sportsmen, that is, to professional and amateur alike, and it should consider a divestiture or expansion of Games sites in an Olympic year. In many events the best athletes in the world, the professionals, are not allowed to compete, although the Olympics claims to be a forum where the best compete. Having all the sports at one site has become too much of a financial and engineering problem. By splitting up the sites—for example, one country instead of one city holding the Games—the financial burden would be lessened, more sports could be contested than at present, and more areas of the world would be exposed to sport because they could more easily afford to hold the Games.

Beyond this, but certainly closely tied in with these changes, would be a complete restructuring of the Olympic system. The present association and identification with nation-states only enhances nationalism and detracts from sport. The idea would be to maximize the latter not the former. The IOC could make itself more representative of the world, but not in terms of nation-states. Perhaps regional identification would be more appropriate.[6] For example, each region would have the same number of representatives. The regions would not be determined by continents, because of the obvious population differences leading to possible conflicts over misrepresentation. Rather each region would be approximately equal in population. For example, half of the United States and all of Canada might be a region, while the other half of the United States and Mexico or all of Central America might constitute another region. The possibilities of division are endless. At the Games the athlete contingents would correspond to the IOC membership regions. There would be no national flags or anthems, merely awards for the winners as at present, with less pomp and circumstance. The central idea would be to promote sport. As a sideline, such regional arrangements would require the promotion of increased cooperation between the world's people. The encouragement of the athlete and the promotion of sport would be the primary goals.

Unless the IOC and the sport organizations seriously consider

major changes, they will succumb to the very inertia tha
ried them to their present inadequate state. The Olympics h
come a forum of organizational interaction and conflict,
organizational policies are carried out as a means of achievin
desired goal. That goal has been determined by the organization
administration, not through decisive policymaking but through
inertia.

The Olympics began as an ideal, but that ideal was swept up by
the reality of the organizational world and became in effect the
hypothetical excuse for the existence of the organization. The
Olympics can still become a valuable forum for international participation by the athlete. The Olympics must be seen for what they
are, for what they possess, rather than for what they hope to
achieve. The world exists more in the concrete than the abstract.
Once this is recognized and understood, the Olympics can be more
readily adapted to the concrete world—the organizational world—
and can provide a more efficient and valuable forum for sport competition at a worldwide, transnational level for outstanding individual athletes.

t has car-
ave be-
where
g a
al

7

Epilogue, 1976-1980

THE YEAR 1980 MAY prove pivotal in the history of the modern Olympic Games, for it was in that year the Games truly came of age: no longer were they simply a sideshow of international politics but instead were elevated to the main event. If anything is clear from what took place involving the Games in 1980, it is that the Olympic Games are here to stay, in one form or another, for a long time, until they are no longer useful or interesting for the powers that be on the world scene.

In 1980, athletes, Olympic and sport officials and Olympic enthusiasts were wringing their hands in collective worry as the fate of the Moscow Summer Olympic Games seemingly hung in the balance. Led by the United States, Western governmental leaders played a kind of "pinball" with the Games as their main response to the Soviet Union's invastion of Afghanistan in late December 1979. Unless the Soviet Union withdrew its invasion force Western leaders threatened to boycott the Moscow Summer Games. The Soviet Union called their bluff, and Western leaders were faced with having to carry out their threat. Athletes, Olympic and sport officials had to try to salvage what they could of the Games in the face of what many considered the most serious challenge yet to the Olympics, and one that might have spelled the end of the Games. The boycott did not mean the end of the Games; they took place, albeit reduced in size, but ironically stronger because of the boycott.

The boycott forced Olympic leaders to take a hard look at their Games, to attempt some reforms to salvage them, and to consider more reforms for the future. But the real impact of the boycott was to show, perhaps better than any other event could have, the popularity of the Games and the importance attached by governments, business interests and the public to participation in them. As the African countries found out in 1976 with their boycott of the Montreal Games, so United States and Western leaders realized (or should have) with the 1980 boycott, that participation in the Games is everything, non-participation is a soon-forgotten memory. The spotlight of the Games only exists for those who take part. This realization, perhaps more than any other factor, influenced the decision by the majority of African countries to refuse to support the United States in its Moscow boycott—to participate in the Games. It also has forced them to re-evaluate their previous actions and change their methods of dealing with the issues important to them.

What about future Olympic Games, what will they be like? What issues will confront them, and more importantly, how will Olympic officials deal with them? As prior Olympiads, future ones will be the product of existing international trends, pressures, conflicts and events, unresolved issues from prior Games and Olympiads and past decisions taken to deal with those issues. In this respect, what will happen in 1984 will be as much a function of what the world is like in 1984 as it was of what it was like in 1980 and what was done in 1980 to deal with the issues then confronting the Olympics. A look at what did happen in 1980 will help in trying to predict Olympic events in 1984 and beyond.

Three major issues confronted Olympic leaders during the XXI Olympiad (1976-1980). These issues, combined and separately, will have a bearing on Olympic affairs in the future; in some cases the effect could be profound. These issues also reflect trends or events at work in international politics.

As has been the case in Olympic affairs since the late '50s, South Africa—its apartheid policies and participation in international sport—was once again an issue during the XXI Olympiad. While the controversy did not boil over at the 1980 Games as it had at the two previous Games, it still went unresolved and could erupt again at Los Angeles in 1984. Significantly, that South Africa did not become an issue at Moscow could prove decisive when events unfold in 1984; the main factor is Black Africa's attitude toward the Olympic Games and what appears to be a reassessment of how to deal most effectively with the situation of white minority rule and apartheid in South Africa.

The other two major issues, which did explode at the 1980 Games, both winter and summer, were the question of Chinese participation—which one, Taiwan or the People's Republic of China (PRC)?—and the United States-led boycott of the Moscow Games. Both issues reflect the simultaneous warming and cooling of relations between the United States, the PRC and the Soviet Union. The question of Chinese recognition reflects the warming of relations between the United States and the PRC, and the efforts by both countries to counterbalance and stem the power and influence of the Soviet Union. The boycott issue over the Soviet invasion of Afghanistan reflects the deterioration in the relationship between the Soviet Union and the United States.

Following the 1976 Summer Games in Montreal, Olympic and international sport officials intended to make sure no further such boycotts would disrupt their Games. Acting on recommendations made by both the national Olympic committees and the international sport federations, the IOC decided at its June 1977 General Session in Prague, Dzechoslovakia, in the future to suspend for five years any committee or individual who withdraws from the Games for reasons other than sickness or "force majeure." Twenty of the national Olympic committees that withdrew from the '76 Summer Games were censured, but no sanctions were imposed.[1]

These measures, however, only covered the Olympics, and had no bearing on or authority over those sports not on the Olympic agenda. As in 1976, it would be the outside sports and the politics concerning them that would spill over into the Olympic arena to menace the 1980 Games. The first hint of this spill-over came with a threatened extension of the '76 Montreal boycott to the August 1978 Commonwealth Games slated for Edmonton, Canada. The SCSA demanded as a condition for African participation at the Commonwealth Games that New Zealand, the crux of the problem at Montreal, either be banned from these contests or sever its sporting links with South Africa.[2] The intention was to pressure New Zealand, and in turn other countries, either directly or indirectly, to sever sporting links with South Africa, and it was having its intended result. In January 1977, New Zealand's Prime Minister, Robert Muldoon, told African sports leaders of his government's support for their efforts,[3] and in March, the PGA, meeting in the Ivory Coast, approved a resolution to suspend any national committee maintaining sporting links with South Africa.[4]

Just prior to the June Commonwealth Conference in London, the African countries made another threat to boycott the Commonwealth Games unless the conference resolved the issue of member countries maintaining sporting ties with South Africa.[5] This last minute threat worked. As part of the conference's overall resolution, the delegates agreed unanimously to "discourage contact or competition by their nationals with sporting organizations, teams or sportsmen from South Africa or from any other country where sports are organized on the basis of race, colour or ethnic origin."[6] To discourage is a far cry from prevention, however, and the omission of this latter word from the final agreement—the Gleneagles Agreement—would have future unfortunate repercussions. For the moment, at least, the pressure was off New Zealand.

The anti-South Africa tide continued into 1978 when the 22-member Council of Europe at an April meeting in London adopted a resolution supporting the Gleneagles Agreement and opposing discrimination of any kind in international sport.[7] The Council of Europe decision was further bolstered by individual international sport federations taking action on their own to sever ties with South Africa. In July 1977, the International Chess Federation, on a motion proposed by the Soviet Union and Ghana, voted to bar South Africa from competition until 1980.[8] In April 1978, the International Lawn Tennis Federation ordered South Africa not to enter the Davis or Federation Cup competitions until it formed a multi-racial governing body.[9] And South African attempts to be readmitted into the Olympic Games proved fruitless; IOC President Lord Killanin advised South Africa not to seek readmission as it had made "no material changes" in its sporting organization; in his opinion, it was still discriminatory.[10]

While the international community was seemingly lining up in support of the Black African position against South Africa, an undercurrent of opposition to this position was developing simultaneously, a current which because of governmental indecision and unwillingness to take firm action placed the Moscow Olympic Games in jeopardy. The offending sport in the '76 boycott, rugby, was again at issue. While much of the rest of the international sporting community was breaking its ties with South Africa, the rugby unions (overseeing organizations for rugby) and players in New Zealand, France and Great Britain were trying to organize competitions with their counterparts in South Africa.

In the case of New Zealand, the South African rugby federation sent invitations to individual members of New Zealand's all-star rugby team the "All-Blacks" (the term refers to the uniform). The players would accept the invitations as individuals, then once inside South Africa would form a team with their countrymen, thus skirting the issue of New Zealand sending an official team. The New Zealand government, aware of the invitations, voiced its opposition but made no effort to prevent the individuals from going. The charade was not lost on the African countries, and Nigeria, for one, was having none of it. Just prior to the Commonwealth Games Nigeria announced it would boycott and accused New Zealand of circumventing the Gleneagles Agreement. "New Zealand has not been persuaded to review her relations with Pretoria," said Sylvanus Williams, Minister of Sport. "It would be illogical in the extreme, therefore, if Nigeria were now to participate at the Commonwealth Games."[11] Nigeria was alone in its decision, however. The other twelve African Commonwealth countries refused to go along, instead they abided by the decision of the SCSA not to boycott.

The SCSA decision not to boycott marked a fundamental change in Black Africa's method of dealing with the issue of South African apartheid. No longer was the response simply to boycott, but rather to target offending countries selectively on a bilateral basis. The SCSA decision on the Olympics the following year would make this change more clear.

In the meantime, the rugby undercurrent continued, next turning up in Great Britain and France. While the French government would bow to international pressure, the British government would not, setting the stage for an Olympic showdown. In 1978, a tour of France by the South African Springbok rugby team was announced. Despite initial pressure from international sport federations, the IOC and the Soviet Union, the French government refused to cancel the tour. Concerned about possible repercussions to the 1980 Moscow Summer Olympic Games, Soviet authorities warned that "they would not hesitate to exclude countries which have contacts with South Africa and Rhodesia. We prefer to sacrifice one country than ten from the Games," they said.[12] By May 1979 pressure was mounting on France both internationally and domestically, and the government announced it would ban the tour, but did not indicate how. By July, it looked as though the tour would take place after all. Again the Soviet Union threatened, this time the French government relented. It announced it would require South African players to obtain visas. Visas seemed to present no problem for the South Africans and they reaffirmed their intention to come. Forced to act, the French government refused to grant the visas, thus cancelling the tour.

Such was not the case in Great Britain. Following the Gleneagles Agreement, several reciprocal tours of Great Britain and South Africa by rugby teams from each country had been either cancelled or postponed. By 1979, however, a new government was in power in Great Britain, a Tory government, and while it agreed to abide by the Gleneagles Agreement, its support was not as strong as the previous Labour government's had been, paving the way for the rugby unions once again to propose competitions with South African teams. A tour of South Africa by British rugby teams was planned in 1980, and in late August 1979 an eight-match tour of Great Britain by a South African team was announced for October of the same year. With the Olympic Games just around the corner, the British Olympic Association (BOA), British sport federations that participated in the Games and the British government were uneasy, if not alarmed, at the prospect of the matches and the possible repercussions.

The Soviet Union was already on record as opposing such matches, and reiterated its concern to the British government and the BOA. BOA General Secretary Richard Palmer, after coming away from talks with the Soviets in mid-July, said there was no question in his mind that Britain would be banned from the 1980 Olympic Games.[13] By August, however, the Soviet Union was retreating. Concerned it would upset the IOC and hence damage its Moscow Games by taking unilateral action on the issue, Soviet authorities announced they would leave up to the IOC any decision to ban and would abide by that decision. Since rugby is not an Olympic sport, the IOC had no decision to make.

The British government, concerned about its country's future sporting relations and relations in general with Africa, called on the rugby unions to cancel the tours. The rugby unions refused, claiming it to be unnecessary because rugby in South Africa is now racially integrated, and countered the British government's decision to withhold financial support by agreeing to pay all police costs for the contests. Unlike in France, the government could not withhold visas as none were required. It could, under extraordinary circumstances, prevent individuals from coming into the country who were deemed not in the "public interest." This the government refused to do and decided to let the October tour proceed. Home Secretary William Whitelaw, explained that it was the rugby unions' right to hold the tours, and that the government did not consider the October tour an extraordinary circumstance.[14] Immediately following the British government's decision to allow the tour to proceed, Jean Claude Ganga, secretary general of the SCSA, declared his organization would do whatever it could to ban Britain from the Olympic Games, never dismissing the possibility of a full African boycott. The October tour took place amid massive demonstrations.

But it was not the tour of Britain by a South African team that worried British government and sport officials; it was the proposed tour of South Africa by a British rugby team that was their real concern. Well aware that the same kind of tour in 1976, involving New Zealand, set off the Montreal boycott, new Minister of Sport Hector Monro declared, "the problem is the tour of the future. It is not only the Olympics I am worried about but other world championships and other international events, which could all be affected by continued breaches of the Gleneagles Agreement."[15] Monro's concern about future international events was well founded, as it had been less than a month since Abraham Ordia, president of the SCSA, declared the proposed tour would be a major item on the organization's agenda at its December meeting. Ordia warned Britain and the IOC that the SCSA was already canvassing the Third World and socialist countries for support, and he added menacingly that those who "defy the world" have no right to play and "they have no moral right to trade with them [the world] either. They shall be confronted on all fronts."[16]

The BOA and British sport federations ran for shelter. In order to cover themselves in the event of possible international retaliation, they adopted a resolution deploring the tour and calling on the rugby unions not to make a decision which would have adverse consequences for all of British sport.[17] Taking into account the tide of opinion in Britain against the tour, the rugby unions deferred a decision on the 1980 tour until a British Sports Council commission of inquiry into South African apartheid in sport returned from its South African factfinding trip.

The item may have been deferred in Britain, but it was still an issue for the SCSA. As the December SCSA meeting approached, rumours abounded as to what the SCSA would do. Would it boycott the Olympics, call for Britain's outster from the Games or simply break ties with Britain, leaving African participation in the Games intact? Helped by intense lobbying on behalf of the head of the Moscow Olympic Organizing Committee, the SCSA voted to ban all bilateral sporting links with Britain, not to support British members in international organizations and to encourage other countries to follow suit.[18] There would be no boycott of the Olympic Games by Africans, at least not over the issue of South Africa. As Kwamena Ocran, sports minister for Ghana, explained, Britain's rugby ties with South Africa were not sufficient to warrant another Games boycott.[19]

If New Zealand's ties with South Africa had seemed pretext enough in 1976, what had no changed? Following the new decision, some argued the change was based on Black Africa's sense of loyalty to the Soviet Union and the USSR's longtime support for Black Africa in its battle against South African apartheid.[20] While this motivation was important, more than likely it was not decisive. It would play a key role later when Africa was faced with the decision about whether to join the United States' boycott of the Moscow Games. However, the major factor influencing the SCSA's decision not to boycott over ties with South Africa was the Games themselves, and the value placed on participation in them. As Nigeria's Minister of Sport Sylvanus Williams said, although in another context, "the philosophy that sport and politics should not mix is a hypocritical one. Sporting achievements today are used as a measure of our country's greatness."[21] Indeed, the important thing is to compete, to be visible in the events or competitions that count. The Olympic Games are perhaps the most important of those events. Not to be there, to make a political protest, may be a noble gesture, but it is politically foolish; the act of protest is soon overshadowed by the grandeur of the Games themselves, and is thus soon forgotten. The Games, and participation in them, are what count.

The question is, will the Africans apply the same political judgment to the Games in Los Angeles in 1984? Given the same circumstances, probably they will. The circumstances, however, will not be the same. In 1984, the United States will host the Games, not the

Soviet Union, and if relations between the two superpowers deteriorate further, African participation may amount to a test of loyalty.

When Lord Killanin became President of the IOC in 1972 one of his major goals for his eight-year term was to bring the People's Republic of China into the Olympic fold. Killanin's predecessor, Avery Brundage, had, to all intents and purposes, written off the PRC, having been lambasted personally by that country's leadership once too often. Killanin was different. He had spent the pre-World War II years in China as a journalist and had a better understanding of the country and, as a result, a deeper commitment to PRC participation in the Games.[22] He still had to contend with a world that was not quite ready to grant the PRC full recognition, and with a China which itself was not internally ready to take its place on the world stage. Therefore, overtures for PRC membership in the Olympic movement before 1976 were premature.

This did not prevent problems at the Games concerning Chinese recognition, however. The question of PRC recognition was a major issue in a number of international forums. The United Nations had conferred recognition on the PRC already, and in the process had thrown out Taiwan (the Republic of China). Major nations, like Canada, and international sport federations had also switched their recognition. But key sport federations, such as the IAAF and FINA, as well as key countries, such as the United States, had not yet acted, which made it difficult for the IOC to perform an about-face on the question.

Nevertheless, Canada pressed the issue at the Montreal Games. Because it was too late to do anything else without serious risk to the '76 Games, the IOC gave in and required the Republic of China to compete as Taiwan. Unlike 1960, when Taiwan acceded to a similar demand, in 1976 it refused; the team packed its bags and went home. Since 1960 many things had changed, not the least of which was Taiwan's diplomatic status in the world. It no longer was recognized as the official authority over China by a majority of countries, and could ill afford to jeopardize the little recognition it did have by agreeing to Canada's demands.

After the '76 Games, Killanin did not want to continue to risk the Games over the issue of Taiwan, and he set about resolving the controversy. Helpful to his efforts were three major factors: 1) the deaths of Mao Tse-tung and Chou En-lai in the PRC and the resultant change in leadership and outlook there; 2) diplomatic recognition of the PRC by the United States; 3) recognition of the PRC by the IAAF and a relaxed attitude toward PRC participation by FINA. The key to Killanin's efforts would be the United States' recognition of the PRC; he would use it to convince IOC members to make a similar change in recognition.

Following the Montreal Games, the All China Sports Federation (the Chinese Olympic Committee) began making overtures once again for IOC recognition. In September 1977, Killanin made a trip to the PRC to discuss the issue with Chinese Olympic leaders, and upon his return, Killanin noted that progress toward PRC recognition had moved "one little step forward." Still a major stumbling block was the PRC's insistence that if it joined the IOC, Taiwan could not remain a member, because in the PRC's view there is only one China. In this respect, the PRC position has not changed in nearly thirty years.[23] Nevertheless, Killanin was optimistic, noting that the sports movement in the PRC had advanced considerably, though he said he did not think it had advanced quite far enough. He did admit, however, that "we might, in the future, look back and say we had made a mistake," referring to the IOC's past reluctance to recognize the PRC.[24] This admission told more about Killanin's views than it did about anything else, but it pointed toward the path he, and consequently, the IOC would take concerning PRC recognition.

By January 1978 the situation had not changed and the IOC executive board, meeting in Tunis, Tunisia, deferred any decision on the PRC's application for admission. Killanin commented, "the Chinese question is evolving slowly."[25] But events were to move faster than he anticipated. In March, FINA amended its statutes to allow competition with non-affiliated countries, which opened the door for competition with the PRC, a non-affiliated country. With one major federation (which had been adamantly opposed to PRC competition) now leaning in favor of such competition, combined with the PRC's eagerness to join the Olympic movement, the IOC at its general session in May formed a twenty-five-member commission to "inquire generally and report" on the question of admitting the PRC.[26] This was a major step for the IOC. Even though there had been overtures for several years for PRC recognition, they were not taken very seriously by the IOC, consequently any inquiry into PRC sports had been done on a private basis by individual IOC members.

Momentum for bringing the PRC into the world of international sport began to accelerate. In October, the IAAF recognized the PRC as the only representative of China, which included the territory of Taiwan. Under the ruling, Taiwanese athletes could no longer take part in any IAAF meet unless approval was granted by the PRC. "It is worse than expulsion, it is forceful absorption," exclaimed Chi Cheng, the former women's world record holder in the 100-meter sprint, and secretary general of Taiwan's track and field federation. "This is absolutely unfair, ridiculous and absurd. We all know very well Peking (Beijing) has no jurisdiction over the athletes in Taiwan."[27] Despite Cheng's protests, the trend was clear. The International Gymnastics Federation soon followed suit, bringing the number of federations with which the PRC was affiliated to eleven, up from just four in 1974. Taiwan's affiliations had declined accordingly, down to fifteen.[28]

The real turning point occurred later in the year when President Jimmy Carter of the United States announced that beginning January 1, 1979, the PRC and the United States, after nearly thirty years, would re-establish full diplomatic relations. The United States would revoke its recognition of Taiwan and would consider Taiwan a territory of the PRC.[29] The die had been cast, and now the IOC had to act. The 1980 Winter Games were scheduled for Lake Placid, New York, with the possibility, as some members observed, of disruptions of the Games unless the IOC found an equitable resolution to the issue.

That was the problem: to find an equitable solution. Taiwan was a member in good standing; it had not transgressed IOC rules, so there was no real basis or precedent for expelling the Taiwan committee. For Killanin the choice was clear, the only real question was how to go about it. Killanin said to a reporter after the IOC executive board meeting in March 1979, "I feel that the Chinese Olympic Committee located in Taipei made a serious error when it withdrew its athletes at Montreal. Under an agreement with the Canadian government we had authorized this delegation to retain its anthem and flag, but had requested that its name be changed from 'Republic of China' to 'Taiwan.' Today, the Republic of China is no

longer recognized by international institutions and very few countries would allow a team bearing the name 'Republic of China' to
participate in a sports event.''[30]

That would turn out to be the key question as Taiwan sought to
participate at Lake Placid. Would the United States have allowed
Taiwan to participate under its name "Republic of China?" A letter from the U.S. State Department, addressed to Julian Roosevelt,
IOC member from the United States, about United States policy
toward Taiwan was ambiguous. It stated in part: "Regarding
China's participation in the Games, this is a decision for the IOC.
. . . We do not recognize as symbols of national sovereignty the flag
and anthem of the Republic of China. However, we do continue to
make visa facilities available to travelers from Taiwan. With
respect to the Lake Placid Games, we hope that the IOC will find a
solution that will avoid politicizing the Games in a way which could
cause embarrassment to the host country or the IOC itself.''[31] It
appears the Republic of China's name was of little concern to the
U.S. government, but the position of the government was unclear.
The threat at the end of the letter was unmistakable, however, and
it would be upon this that Killanin and ultimately the full IOC
membership would base their decision.

Efforts to bring the two Chinese committees together to discuss
the issue proved fruitless. In separate talks it appeared there might
be a compromise solution; Taiwan committee members said they
would not object to dual membership as long as the PRC did not
profess control over Taiwan. Based on this assurance and the
report by the IOC's special commission of inquiry, which claimed it
would be impractical for the PRC to administer sports in Taiwan
because of the geographical distance and different ways of life, the
IOC, at its April meeting in Montevideo, voted to recognize both
the PRC and Taiwan as members. Immediately, PRC authorities
called the vote "unacceptable" but agreed to abide by it as an
interim measure for the purposes of discussion. The PRC delegation objected to the name given to Taiwan's committee—Chinese
Olympic Committee located in Taipei—and, said Lo Dabaeng of
the All Sports Federation, "we would accept an interim team from
Taiwan under the name, anthem and flag agreed by the IOC, which
would not include the name of the Republic of China nor their
national flag.''[32]

Further discussions followed, but there was growing concern

among IOC members that if the situation did not move forward, the PRC would ultimately reject the decision; or, Killanin counseled, at least there could be problems at Lake Placid similar to those at Montreal. Meeting in June, the executive board decided to rerecognize the PRC committee as the "Chinese Olympic Committee" and the Taiwan committee as the "Chinese Taipei Olympic Committee" on the condition the latter adopt a new anthem and flag.[33]

In October, the executive board reaffirmed its June decision, following discussions with both Chinese committees, and agreed to send the matter out to members for a postal vote. In his memorandum to IOC members accompanying the ballots, Killanin noted that in 1958, when the PRC dropped out of the Olympics, the PRC was not recognized internationally and specifically was not recognized by the United Nations. "The reverse situation is now the case," and, he added, "I believe it should be borne in mind."[34] Also, Killanin warned of possible repercussions at Lake Placid. The vote was not even close: 62-17 in favor, with two null ballots.

Reaction was immediate. The PRC welcomed the decision; Taiwan deplored it, vowing to fight it; the two IOC members from the United States both condemned it. Julian Roosevelt claimed the "IOC has put itself into the political arena by taking orders from Peking." Douglas Roby, the other U.S. IOC member, complained: "The Taiwanese have been members for twenty-seven years and have been model members. And here we completely pull the rug from under them. I think they have the right to have the flag and anthem they want. We don't ask other people to change their flags and anthems. We let in the Chinese who resigned and turned their backs on us. Now we take them back on their terms."[35]

Taiwan did fight the decision, both in the Swiss and United States courts. Twice the Swiss courts turned down Taiwan, but in the U.S. courts the result was different, at least at first. On the eve of the Games, Taiwan's delegation tried to enter the Olympic Village, but was turned back because the Taiwan committee had not yet formally accepted the conditions for participation as stipulated by the IOC in its October decision. Claiming they were denied their constitutional rights and that the IOC had made a decision it had no authority to make, the Taiwan delegation filed suit in New York State courts to prevent the Lake Placid Organizers from keeping the team out of the Village and the IOC from barring the team's participation. Agreeing with the delegation, New York State Supreme Court Judge Norman Harvey said:

The IOC disavows and deplores any action by anyone that might tend to utilize the Games for political purposes. However, the IOC failed to show that degree of courage when it considered the two Chinas issue. In order to encourage participation of athletes from the People's Republic of China, it bargained away the rights of the athletes from Taiwan. It made the political decision that there is no Republic of China and that the athletes who swear allegiance to the Republic of China would be placed in a category different from that of all other athletes participating in the Games.[36]

Although Harvey's decision was ultimately overruled by a higher court, thus preventing Taiwan from participation, Harvey had raised a salient point. The IOC, in fact, had made a political decision, but it had had no choice. Given the Montreal precedent, and the threat by the United States, there was reason to fear the U.S. government would have made an issue of Taiwan's participation at Lake Placid as the Republic of China, much as Canada had in 1976. It was a no-win situation. Undoubtedly, the PRC would have pressured the U.S. government in the event the IOC had allowed Taiwan to compete as the Republic of China. as the PRC had pressured the Canadian government in 1976. The fact the U.S. government helped the Lake Placid Organizing Committee argue its case in the appeal of Harvey's decision is perhaps reason enough to believe the IOC made the only decision it could have made under the circumstances.[37]

Nevertheless, the IOC's political decision in the case of Taiwan did not prevent it from bringing up the tired argument of political intrusion in sport when it came to the United States-led boycott of the Moscow Olympics. As in past situations, when it served their purpose, Olympic officials turned a blind eye to their own past political maneuvers.

The IOC's selection of Moscow in 1974 as the site for the 1980 Summer Olympic Games upset many people in the United States and Western Europe—particularly in the United States, because Moscow had been chosen over Los Angeles. As relations between the two countries deteriorated in the ensuing years, because of reported human rights violations, among other things, political columnists, human rights groups and political leaders began calling for a boycott of the Moscow Games or some related action to punish the Soviets and show the West's displeasure with Soviet policies. It was, then, not surprising to hear the Carter administration and other Western leaders adopt the idea of a boycott of the Moscow Games as one response to the Soviet invasion of Afghanistan. What was surprising was that it soon became virtually the only response.

The Soviet Union invaded Afghanistan in late December 1979, and the action was immediately condemned around the world. The United Nations General Assembly in mid-January passed by a vote of 104-18 a resolution, sponsored by twenty-one non-aligned nations which condemned the Soviet Union and called for the withdrawal of its troops.[38] A seventeen-nation Muslim conference in Kuala Lumpur, Malaysia, meeting about the same time, passed a similar motion.[39] The idea of a Moscow Olympic Games boycott, however, was first mentioned in an emergency session of NATO, January 1. Though no action was taken by that group on the boycott idea suggested by the West German delegate, Rolf Pauls, U.S. President Jimmy Carter was quick to seize upon it as one of his administration's responses to the Soviet invasion. In an address to the nation on January 4, Carter warned the Soviets: "Although the United States would prefer not to withdraw from the Olympic Games . . . the Soviet Union must realize that its continued aggressive actions will endanger both the participation of athletes and the travel to Moscow by spectators who would normally wish to attend the Olympic Games."[40]

Carter's threat was part of a package of measures he announced to punish the Soviets for invading Afghanistan. Some of the other measures included cutting off grain sales of 17 million metric tons to the Soviet Union, ceasing the sale of high technology and oil drilling equipment and curtailing Soviet fishing rights in U.S. waters.[41] It was the boycott threat, however, that struck a responsive chord in the public, particularly in the United States. The San Francisco Chronicle reported that its poll showed that 75 percent of the public was in favor of not participating at Moscow,[42] and a Newsweek magazine poll showed 56 percent of the public favored boycotting the Games.[43] In an election year such poll results are hard to disregard, and Carter, facing a strong challenge from Senator Edward M. Kennedy of Massachusetts for the democratic presidential nomination, was not about to let the opportunity pass.

In Western Europe initial reaction to the idea of a boycott was cold. In both Great Britain and West Germany public opinion was against a boycott. The French were adamantly opposed, the Italians were non-commital, the Netherlands authorities were lukewarm to the idea and the West German government was opposed, in spite of the fact that it was a West German who originally suggested the boycott idea. Interior Minister Gerhart Baum said, "sports cannot be used as a means for political ends," adding that "sports cannot solve problems whose solutions can only be achieved politically."[44] Elsewhere, reaction to a boycott was more positive. Saudi Arabia immediately announced it would withdraw from the Games, though the Soviets said Saudi Arabia already had done that months before for other reasons. Canadian Prime Minister Joe Clark said he favored moving the Games, and offered Montreal as a possible site.

The news of a possible boycott sent a shudder through Olympic and international sport circles. West German IOC member, Willi Daume, exclaimed: "I must speak out once again against political pressure on international sport and the Olympics. They are not the place to resolve political disputes."[45] USOC leaders expressed shock and fear for the effect a boycott might have on the scheduled February Lake Placid Winter Games. They were concerned that a drastic move before the Games might cause the Soviet Union and Eastern Europe not to attend in retaliation. Most of all, they feared the U.S. government was trying to usurp their authority and in the process might destroy the Olympic movement.[46]

Carter was determined to boycott, and what initially appeared as a threat soon became locked into policy. On January 10, campaigning for Carter in Iowa, Vice President Walter Mondale and Carter's wife, Rosalyn, both said they were in favor of moving the Games. Five days later, Secretary of State Cyrus Vance announced a mid-February deadline for the Soviet Union to remove its troops from Afghanistan or face a U.S. boycott. Several days later the deadline was definitely set for February 20.

By giving the Soviet Union a deadline that fell after the completion of the Lake Placid Games, Carter had effectively preserved them, though it is doubtful USOC fears were justified, given the constant Soviet pronouncements that they would attend the Games. Carter also acceded to USOC wishes and pressed his case through the USOC, thereby ultimately preserving that organization's support. In a letter to Robert Kane, president of the USOC, Carter said that while he supports the principles of the Olympic movement and does not think governments should be involved, he claimed (appealing to Kane's and other USOC leaders' sense of patriotism) that "deeper issues (are) at stake," involving "the security of our nation and the peace of the world." He called on Kane to ask the IOC to move, cancel or postpone the Games; if the IOC refused to act, then he asked the USOC, as the U.S. representative, not to attend the Moscow Games.[47]

The price of USOC support came high, however, because by not taking more decisive action, Carter effectively doomed the entire boycott effort to failure. Even though Vance admitted he did not believe the Soviets would meet the February 20 deadline,[48] which they did not, thus assuring a boycott, Carter had put the appearance of a decision in the hands of the USOC, which was determined to stall on the issue as long as possible. By relying on the USOC to act, Carter sent a message to the rest of the world that it too should follow the USOC lead. This ultimately delayed and drew out the boycott decision for many governments and national Olympic committees, which allowed the Soviet Union, the IOC and international sport to counter effectively.

At the same time, Carter was sending contradictory signals to the rest of the world, further compounding his problems with the boycott. His administration did not prevent a tour of the Soviet Union by U.S. boxers, or a U.S. tour by Soviet track and field stars. If the U.S. government was not willing to cut off all sporting ties with the Soviet Union, other governmental leaders could be expected to question U.S. resolve on an Olympic Games boycott.

Carter squandered the chance of large scale African support for a boycott when he decided in January to send Muhammad Ali, former heavyweight boxing champion, to Africa on a five-nation tour to enlist African support. African leaders were insulted that Carter considered them so low on his priority list he would send a "boxer," in the words of Tanzanian President Julius Nyerere, instead of an official diplomatic envoy. Nyerere, for one, refused to meet with Ali, and his reception in the four other African capitals was equally cold.[49] The *New Nigerian,* the Nigerian government newspaper, expressed African sentiment when in an editorial it wrote: "The people of Afghanistan rightly deserve our moral support in their struggle against Soviet imperialism. But there is a distinction between our genuine sympathy for the Afghans and the pious rantings of Western leaders."[50] The only support Ali could garner was Kenya's, a major power in track, but Kenya announced its support for the boycott before Ali arrived in Nairobi.

Lack of African support for the boycott was not simply a result of Ali's visit, however. The roots to it stretch back before the Carter administration took office, to past American failures to support Black Africa in its sports boycotts of South Africa. Ali, on his visit to Africa was confronted with this issue, and while he professed his support for Black Africa's position, he could not adequately defend past U.S. policy. The most he could do was to plead for African support in order to avert a nuclear holocaust, something which seemed genuinely remote to Africans.[51]

Carter's efforts to gain African support, and in turn Third World support, were further stifled both by the counter efforts of international sport organizations and by the Soviet Union. The nineteen-member executive council of the one-hundred-forty-one-member General Assembly of National Olympic Committees, meeting in Mexico City in early February, adopted a resolution urging the IOC to resist any site change, and to resist any outside pressures against the Games.[52] The Soviet Union, however, was much more direct—and effective. Vitaly Smirnov of the Moscow Organizing Committee, an IOC member and high government official, worked out an agreement with Mario Vazquez Nava of the Mexico Olympic committee, where the Soviet Union would provide transportation to and from the Games and room and board at the Games for any national Olympic committee delegation that asked.[53] For committees having a difficult time financing their teams' participation at the Games, the offer of aid was an attractive lure.

Back in the United States the Carter administration was using a similar financial carrot to ensure USOC support, something that might have been unnecessary under the circumstances, but aht the USOC was later able to use to its advantage. In the meantime, Carter secured the backing of the House of Representatives and not long after that the Senate, and used it to pressure the USOC to go before the IOC at its Lake Placid meeting and request it move, cancel or postpone the Moscow Games. The USOC finally agreed, though Kane admitted it was just "playing for time" as the committee had until May 24 to accept the invitation to Moscow.[54]

The IOC did not intend to take any action regarding the Moscow Games. Although Lord Killanin called the Lake Placid session "one of the most important" the IOC ever held,[55] and the IOC membership was truly worried about the possible boycott, time was on their side. The Games were not to start until July, and since there was still no massive opposition developing, any action at Lake Placid would be premature. As Killanin stated it, the IOC position was that it was too late to move the Games; the Soviet Union had lived up to all its agreements with the IOC and the IOC was thus bound to live up to its end of the bargain.[56] Besides, said IOC Executive Director Monique Berlioux, it would be wrong to try to hold the Soviet Union to the ancient principle that a host nation should not be involved in military operations during an Olympic Games. "Today many countries can be considered to be involved in military operations." She reminded U.S. officials that the U.S. was involved in Vietnam in 1970 when the IOC awarded the '76 Winter Games to Denver; the U.S. was involved in Cambodia in '74 when Lake Placid was awarded the Games; and the U.S. had landed Marines in Lebanon in '58 while it was preparing for the '60 Squaw Valley Winter Games.[57]

The IOC voted unanimously to reject the USOC request. Now there was no turning back—only the February 20 deadline remained to make the boycott definite. Expressing disappointment with the IOC decision, Carter urged the USOC to come to a prompt decision. The USOC was in no hurry, however, and postponed any final decision until its regular April meeting. This interlude was to prove disastrous. While many governments had come out in favor of a boycott, their national Olympic committees had not. For many governments, however, with each passing day the urgency to respond to the Soviet invasion became less paramount and enthusiasm for a boycott waned. An indication of this occurred at a ninety-two-nation conference of the non-aligned movement in mid-March. Although the conference approved a resolution that called for the withdrawal of troops from Afghanistan, the Soviet Union was not named directly. As one diplomat commented: "Time has softened perceptions of the invasion and relaxed the degree of concern."[58]

It was several days later that the Carter boycott was dealt its worst setback yet. The British Olympic Association, against the wishes of the British government, but in conformity with British public opinion, voted to go to the Games. "This idea of a boycott was an absolute non-starter from the beginning," said BOA Chairman, Sir Denis Follows, and he added that the BOA decision would no doubt "be listened to with interest in America."[59]

Three days later, Carter cut off all exports to the Soviet Union of sporting goods and Olympics-related products. Carter's ban affected 501 companies with products ranging from chewing gum and soft drinks to athletic equipment, a total of $20-$30 million in exports.[60] Most notably affected was the National Broadcasting Company (NBC), which had the most at stake. As it could no longer send broadcasting equipment or make further payments on the television rights to the Soviet Union, its coverage of the Games was in effect cancelled, though that decision was not actually announced until May. Even though NBC was insured for 90 percent, it still expected to lose $20 million, plus it would lose the advantage of using the Olympics to propel it to the top of the television ratings in the U.S., which it had been counting on.

Carter might have been able to control events in the United States, but developments took a turn for the worse internationally following the BOA decision. The Canadian and Norwegian Olympic committees voted to go to the Games in spite of their governments' opposition. France was wavering, and though the German government had come out in favor of a boycott, it had not yet pressed its national Olympic committee to commit itself. Carter began to press the USOC to act, calling on Congressional leaders to pressure USOC officials, threatening to change the USOC's charter, threatening to withhold federal funds, and pressuring corporate sponsors to withhold payments unless the USOC boycotted. All of these tactics USOC officials resented and considered counterproductive, but it was the question of federal funds upon which the committee's decision ultimately depended.

Athletes had complained from the very outset of the boycott drive that they were being used by a government which in the past had not acknowledged their existence; now when it needed their support, the government ought at least to be willing to pay for it. As Jane Frederick, a pentathlon star, remarked bitterly, "I grudgingly [accept the boycott] because the government has never helped us in amateur sports. They have always denied our international importance in the political arena and now when they need us, they're going to use us because they have the clout. . . . I appreciate the fact that they now find us important enough to bring us into the political arena, but I don't appreciate the fact that they continue to not fund and help amateur sports in this country."[61]

That situation was to change. In 1979, the USOC had asked Congress for $30 million. It was allocated $16 million, but Carter cut that to $4 million, and threatened to cut even that if cooperation was not forthcoming. As the USOC's April meeting drew near, negotiations began in earnest between the USOC and the Carter administration for funding in return for a USOC decision to boycott. The two finally settled on an agreement whereby the federal government would pay $1 for every $2 the committee raised, ultimately guaranteeing $10 million.[62]

On April 12, the USOC by a 2-1 margin voted to boycott, but international support never materialized. West Germany, which had been looked to as a key, did finally vote to boycott, but France did not, and while Norway and Canada reversed their earlier decisions, nearly every other Western European Olympic committee voted to go to the Games. Even the New Zealand and Australian Olympic committees voted to go, in spite of their governments' opposition. The May 24 deadline for accepting or rejecting invitations to Moscow came and went with twenty-seven Olympic committees rejecting, eighty-five accepting and twenty-nine still undecided.[63]

In an attempt to secure the participation of as many committees as possible, the IOC decreed the invitations would be left open until the opening of the Games. Ultimately, sixty-two countries boycotted, the most ever, and the number of participating countries was eighty-one, the fewest number since the '56 Melbourne Summer Games attracted only sixty-seven. Fewer than six thousand athletes participated, half the number originally expected, and only one-third of the tourists originally expected showed up—one-hundred-thousand.[64]

The boycott definitely had its impact, but was it a success? The Games still took place and thirty-six world records were broken, one more than at Montreal, and countless Olympic records also fell,[65] so from an athletic standpoint it appears the boycott was a failure. For the boycott truly to have worked, more than half the countries would have had to boycott or the Games would have had to have been moved, canceled or postponed. The boycott did not punish the Soviet Union, and any hoped-for internal ramifications, such as a massive uprising against the Soviet leadership, never materialized. How could it? The Soviet people were never told why the United States and other countries were boycotting, so they were mystified, not motivated to protest.

The Carter administration touted the boycott as the "strongest single step we (the United States) could take to persuade them (the Soviet Union) to withdraw their troops from Afghanistan,"[66] prompting Julian Roosevelt to retort, "if that's the strongest thing we can do, we have no Washington." Senator Kennedy characterized it as "basically a symbol, and symbols," he added, "are no substitute for an effective policy."[67]

While it may have been a symbol, it also could have been an effective tool had it been pursued correctly, but there was too much time between the invasion and the Games, and too many interests were involved for such a symbol really to work properly. Even those measures which did receive a great deal of support, such as the grain embargo, failed because one or two countries would not embargo their grain exports, or because the Soviet Union was able to acquire the necessary grain through indirect channels.[68] So what was to have been the symbol of the world's resolve became but a symbol of the world's weakness, and the ultimate losers were the athletes—once again.

The boycott did have some positive aspects. It forced reforms, or attempts at them, and made the IOC begin to re-evaluate its Games in light of modern circumstances. Most notable is the IOC's decision seriously to consider establishing a permanent home for the Summer Games in Greece on land to be donated by the Greek government and to be set aside as a "neutral zone" to be run by the IOC.[69] Such a site would eliminate the kinds of problems Moscow presented, but general international conflict would still present difficulties.

The IOC experimented with denationalizing the Games, something to which it had paid lip-service for years. Proposed by eighteen European national Olympic committees, the IOC adopted several reforms for the Moscow Games, allowing among them, any team to use the Olympic flag and anthem instead of its national flag and anthem, and not to march as a full team in the opening ceremonies, but only to have a standard bearer.[70]

While several European contingents did practice these reforms, they were greeted with derision by spectator and participant alike. British, French, Dutch and Italian Olympic officials, toward the end of the Games, expressed the hope that national flags and anthems would be reinstated in 1984. When the Olympic flag and anthem were displayed at the Games spectators hooted and whistled their contempt—not only Soviet and Eastern Europeans, but Western spectators as well. Competitors, such as Britain's Alan Wells, who won the 100-meter sprint, expressed disappointment that his country's flag was not raised and its anthem not played. When British middle distance man Steve Ovett won the 800-meter run, while the Olympic flag was raised and anthem played, several hundred of his countrymen in the crowd at Lenin Stadium broke out little national flags and sang the national anthem.[71]

As shown by these demonstrations and those at past Games, the Olympic Games are simply too popular a nationalistic forum to eliminate such symbols of national honor. Competitors are proud to compete for their countries, and spectators do not simply identify with individual winners or competitors, but the countries they represent. As Sylvanus Williams, the Nigerian sports minister asserted, participation and subsequent awards are viewed as a measure of a country's greatness. The Soviet Union has always made a point of this, and viewed the hosting of the Moscow Games as "convincing testimony to the general recognition of the historic importance and correctness of the foreign policy course of our country, of the enormous services of the Soviet Union in the struggle for peace."[72]

Perhaps it was the Carter administration's failure to understand this attitude, held by the world and its leaders, toward participation in the Games as a measure of a country's greatness that doomed the boycott to failure. The Carter administration approached the Games as if they were just another sports event, and as such not terribly important to anyone but the Soviets. On the assumption that few but the Soviet Union took participation in the Games seriously, it was felt that it would be easy to acquire support for a boycott, thus delivering a severe blow to the Soviet Union. Nothing could have been farther from the truth. The Games have become perhaps the most popular forum of international participation and recognition. A country may be willing to do something in the United Nations, such as condemn the Soviet Union, but it is quite a different matter to do the same at the Olympic Games.

What is important about the Games is their visibility. The Games are seen by the whole world. For each spectator, whether at the

Games or watching them on television, it is his country that is competing—and, possibly, winning. One hears about the United Nations or similar forums only indirectly, and there are rarely clear-cut winners or losers. Consequently, what happens in such forums is at best soon forgotten, often completely overlooked.

The key quality of the Games, the visual identification combined with the competition, is certainly not lost on commercial interests. Even possible boycotts do not seem to dampen their enthusiasm for the Games. The American Broadcasting Company has agreed to pay $225 million to televise the Los Angeles Summer Games in 1984, and $91.5 million for the 1984 Sarajevo Winter Games.[73] The Los Angeles Olympic Organizing Committee is already lining up commercial sponsors who have committed themselves to pay millions of dollars for the right to have their names associated with the 1984 Games. In fact, commercial sponsors will pay for all major aspects of the 1984 Games, from construction to administration.

Following the 1980 boycott, the question is no longer whether the Games will continue, but rather, in what form? Will they become simply a commercial extravaganza? Will they be hostage to the political conflicts that are paramount on the international scene? There will always be politics in the Games, but given the 1980 experience, the international politics which have so buffeted the Olympics in the last decade may become less of a factor as the world of international sport finally seeks some workable solutions. What is cloudy in the Olympic future is the role that commercialism will play, a question the IOC and international sport in general have failed fully to confront but which they will eventually have to face if these sport organizations intend to retain the autonomy they now possess.

Appendix

The Structure of the IOC and the Olympic System

THE IOC IS COMPOSED OF two bodies: the Executive Board or the Executive Commission as it was called in previous times, and the General Assembly. From out of the General Assembly the members of the Executive Board are elected. The Executive Board is composed of: (1) a president, elected for 8 years and reeligible for periods of 4 years, (2) three vice-presidents, elected for 4 years, (3) five members, elected for 4 years. As of 1976 the IOC had 76 members.*

Handling administrative matters is the General Secretariat, located in Lausanne. At the head of the General Secretariat is a director, assisted by a technical manager, and a staff. In the past the director has been called by a variety of names. For a long period of time the position went under the rubric of Chancellor.

In order to divide up the tasks of the IOC, special commissions have been set up to deal with the particular problems the IOC encounters. The following are presently in existence: Commission for the International Olympic Academy,** Eligibility Commission,

---

The Olympic Directory, 1976.

**The Olympic Academy is an institution set up by the IOC for the study of Olympism and the Olympic Games. Founded in 1961, its residence is in Athens, Greece, the birthplace of the Olympic concept. Each year scholars of sport go to the Academy to study numerous aspects of sport, be they historical, technical, juridical, or artistic. The purpose of the Academy is to acquaint people with and hopefully to instill in them the Olympic ideals, thereby furthering the cause of the Olympic movement.

Culture Commission, Emblems Commission, Finance Commission, Juridical Commission, Medical Commission, Press Commission, Publications Commission, Commission for the Olympic Programme, Rules Editing Commission, Rules Reviewing Commission, Commission for Olympic Solidarity, Television Commission, Tripartite Commission, and the Council of the Olympic Order. The Medical, Olympic Solidarity, Tripartite and Olympic Programme Commissions are not strictly composed of IOC members but have joint membership of either technicians, specialists, doctors, or members of international federations or national Olympic committees.

The Olympic system comprises 4 bodies—the IOC, the international federations, the national Olympic committees and the organizing committee of the Games. The IOC is the overseeing body for the conduct of Olympic sport and any Games sanctioned by the IOC to use the Olympic name (e.g., Asian Games, Pan-American Games). The international federations rule each individual sport and within each country have national affiliates. The national Olympic committees are the representatives and overseers of Olympic sport in each individual country. Thus the USOC (United States Olympic Committee) oversees all aspects of Olympic sport in the United States, and the same holds true for other countries. For each Olympic Games and regional Games there are organizing committees that coordinate and administer the activities of the Games, according to the rules, regulations, and directives of the IOC.

All bodies are autonomous and are supposed to be private and free of any governmental or other influences. The IOC does not have directive power over the international federations except insofar as the conduct of the Games is concerned. The international federations completely rule their individual sports, even at the Olympic Games. As such the IOC had no jurisdiction over, for example, the outcome and conduct of the 1972 Soviet-US basketball game, won by the USSR, but protested (unsuccessfully) by the United States. The IOC can control the number of sports participating in the Games and the specific number of events in those sports, and can determine which individuals may take part. The actual conduct of events and regulations regarding the construction of facilities are under the purview of the international federations.

Outside of Olympic sport (Olympic sanctioned Games) the international federations have sole control. World championships come under their auspices as well as any other matters pertaining to their sports.

NOTES

Notes

PART I: SPORT AND POLITICS

1. The Role and Importance of Sport in International Relations

1. Vincent Cable, "The 'Football War' and the Central American Common Market," *International Affairs* (London) 45 (October 1969): 662.

2. James Riordan, "Soviet Sport and Soviet Foreign Policy," *Soviet Studies,* 26 (July 1974): 331.

3. *The New York Times,* 14 August 1960.

4. *Olympic Review,* 87-88 (January-February 1975): 72.

5. Baron de Coubertin, "The Re-establishment of the Olympic Games," *The Chautauquan,* 19 (6) (September 1894), 699.

6. Ibid.

7. P. Goodhart and C. Chataway, *War Without Weapons* (London: W. H. Allen, 1968), p. 13.

8. "Minutes of the Meeting of the Executive Board of the International Olympic Committee," Lausanne, 11-13 April 1965, Box 92, University of Illinois, Archives, Avery Brundage Collection, 1908-1975.

9. Comite International Olympique, *Speeches of President Avery Brundage 1952-1968* (Lausanne: Comite International Olympique, January 26, 1964, 61st Session of IOC, Innsbruck), pp. 73-74.

10. Circular, no. AB/M/487, to IOC members, 26 April 1969, Box 71, University of Illinois, Archives, Avery Brundage Collection, 1908-1975.

11. In 1948 the total United States retail sales of sporting goods was $1,127,000,000, and by 1969 it had risen to $4,077,500,000. See Richard Snyder, "Trends in the Sporting Goods Market" and "The Sporting Goods Market at the Threshold of the Seventies," in *Sport in the Socio-Cultural Process,* ed. M. Marie Hart (Dubuque, Iowa: Wm. C. Brown Co., 1972), pp. 429 and 441.

12. William Oscar Johnson, "A Contract with the Kremlin," *Sports Illustrated,* 46(9) (21 February 1977), 19.

13. Bud Greenspan, "The Olympiad: The African Athlete," Cappy Productions (New York: WNET/13, Educational Broadcasting Corporation, 1976).

2. *The World Political Structure*

1. See Morton A. Kaplan, *System and Process in International Politics* (New York: John Wiley and Sons, 1957); Hans Joachim Morgenthau, *Politics Among Nations: The Struggle for Power and Peace* (New York: Alfred A. Knopf, 1948); Kenneth N. Waltz, *Man, the State and War, a theoretical analysis* (New York: Columbia University Press, 1954).

2. John H. Herz, "The Rise and Demise of the Territorial State," in *International Politics and Foreign Plicy,* ed. James N. Rosenau (New York: The Free Press, 1961), pp. 80-86; and later John H. Herz, "The Territorial State Revisited: Reflections on the Future of the Nation-State," in *International Politics and Foreign Policy,* 1969.

3. J. David Singer, "The Global System and its Sub-system: A Developmental View," in *Linkage Politics: Essays on the Convergence of National and International Systems,* ed. James N. Rosenau (New York: The Free Press, 1969), p. 30.

4. See Kaplan, *System and Process,* and Waltz, *Man, the State, and War.*

5. George Modelski, *Principles of World Politics* (New York: The Free Press, 1972), pp. 58-73.

6. Ibid., p. 151.

7. Ibid., p. 96.

8. Peter J. Katzenstein, "The Last Old Nation: Austrian National Consciousness Since 1945," paper presented to the Annual Meeting of The American Political Science Association, San Francisco, California, September 2-5, 1975, p. 1.

9. F. H. Hinsley, *Nationalism and the International System* (Dobbs Ferry, New York: Oceana Publications, 1973), p. 34.

10. Karl W. Deutsch, *Nationalism and Social Communication: An Inquiry into the Foundations of Nationality* (New York: John Wiley and Sons, 1953), pp. 3-14.

11. The latent nationalism comes to the surface primarily as a result of the world conditions of violence and insecurity, which diversifies rather than solidifies. See Stanley Hoffmann, "Obstinate or Obsolete? The Fate of the Nation-State and the Case of Western Europe," in *International Regionalism,* ed. Joseph S. Nye, Jr. (Boston: Little Brown and Co., 1968), p. 181.

12. Coined by Indonesia for the Games of the New Emerging Forces (GANEFO) in 1962. See George Modelski, ed., *The New Emerging Forces, Documents on the Ideology of Indonesian Foreign Policy* (Canberra: Department of International Relations, The Australian National University, 1963).

13. Geoffrey Goodwin, "The Political Impact of the Developing Nations in the United Nations," in *The Evolution of the United Nations,* ed. C. R. Bunting and M. J. Lee (New York: Pergamon Press, 1964), p. 37.

14. William P. Avery and James D. Cochrane, "Subregional Integration in Latin America: The Andean Common Market," *Journal of Common Market Studies* (December 1972), 85-89.

15. See the Preamble and Article I of the United Nations Charter. 1970 Yearbook of the United Nations 1001.

16. Such activities would include common labor policies, investment and pricing policies, tariffs, industrial concentration.

17. Ernest B. Haas, *The Uniting of Europe, Political, Social and Economic Forces 1950-1957* (Stanford, California: Stanford University Press, 1958), p. 243.

18. Johan Galtung, *The European Community: A Superpower in the Making* (London: George Allen and Unwin, 1973), pp. 57-63.

19. Raymond Vernon, *Sovereignty at Bay: The Multinational Spread of U.S. Enterprises* (New York: Basic Books, 1971), p. 74.

20. J. David Singer and Michael Wallace, "Intergovernmental Organizations in the Global System 1815-1964," *International Organization* 24(2) (Spring 1970), 272.

21. Kjell Skjelsbaek, "The Growth of International Nongovernmental Organization in the Twentieth Century," in *Transnational Relations and World Politics,* ed. Robert O. Keohane and Joseph S. Nye, Jr. (Cambridge: Harvard University Press, 1971), pp. 74-75.

PART II: THE INTERNATIONAL RELATIONS OF THE OLYMPICS

3. *1944-1956*

1. R. R. Palmer and Joel Colton, *A History of the Modern World* (New York: Alfred A. Knopf, 1971), p. 907.

2. Lloyd Gardner, "From Liberation to Containment 1945-1953," in *From Colony to Empire—Essays in the History of American Foreign Relations,* ed. William Appleman Williams (New York: John Wiley and Sons, 1972), p. 339.

3. Charles L. Robertson, *International Politics Since World War II: A Short History* (New York: John Wiley and Sons, 1966), p. 42.

4. Olympism is the term used in Olympic circles to denote the ideals of the Olympic Games and concept.

5. See Appendix I for the structure of the IOC.

6. Otto Mayer, *A travers les anneaux olympiques* (Geneva: Pierre Cailler, 1960), pp. 176-177.

7. Richard N. Gardner, *Sterling-Dollar Diplomacy, Anglo-American Collaboration in the Reconstruction of Multilateral Trade* (Oxford: Clarendon Press, 1956), pp. 309-312.

8. Donald E. Fuoss, "An Analysis of the Incidents in the Olympic Games from 1924 to 1948, with Reference to the Contribution of the Games to International Goodwill and Understanding" (Ph.D. diss., Teachers College, Columbia University, 1951), p. 223.

9. Ibid., pp. 222-223.

10. Ibid., p. 226.

11. Robertson, *International Politics Since World War II,* p. 48.

12. Gardner, "From Liberation to Containment," p. 359.

13. Ibid., p. 353.

14. Palmer and Colton, *A History of the Modern World,* p. 934.

15. John W. Spanier, *American Foreign Policy Since World War II* (New York: Praeger Publishers, 1971), p. 40.

16. Truman's Congressional speech, quoted in Spanier, ibid.

17. See George F. Kennan's "X" article, "The Sources of Soviet Conduct," *Foreign Affairs Quarterly* 25(4) (July 1947), 566-582. Kennan, however, did not favor the Truman Doctrine.

18. David Benjamin Kanin, "The Role of Sport in International Relations" (Ph.D. diss., Fletcher School of Law and Diplomacy, Tufts University, April 1976), p. 117.

19. Brundage to Edström, 26 October 1946, Brundage Papers, Box 42.

20. Edström to Brundage, 4 December 1946, Brundage Papers, Box 42.

21. Brundage to Edström, 4 March 1947, Brundage Papers, Box 42.

22. Brundage to Edström, 21 January 1947, Brundage Papers, Box 42.

23. Edström to Brundage, 3 September 1947, Brundage Papers, Box 42.

24. *The New York Times,* 8 July 1948.

25. Ibid., 23 December 1947.

26. Fuoss, "An Analysis of the Incidents in the Olympic Games from 1924 to 1948," pp. 206-207.

27. *The New York Times,* 24 July 1948. Before each Summer Olympic Games, a series of ceremonies are held in Greece in commemoration of the ancient Games and their continued spirit in the modern Games.

28. Ibid., 28 July 1948.

29. Ibid.

30. Fuoss, "An Analysis of the Incidents in the Olympic Games from 1924 to 1948," p. 247.

31. "Minutes of the Meeting of the 44th General Session of the IOC,"

15-17 May 1950, Brundage Papers, Box 90.

32. Brundage to McCloy (American High Commissioner in Berlin), 14 October 1950, Brundage Papers, Box 127.

33. Mayer, *A travers les anneaux olympiques,* pp. 200-201.

34. Edström to Brundage, 9 April 1951, Brundage Papers, Box 43.

35. "Minutes of the Meeting of the 45th General Session of the IOC," 7-10 May 1951, Brundage Papers, Box 90.

36. Edström to Brundage, 17 June 1952, Brundage Papers, Box 43.

37. "Minutes of the Meeting of the Executive Commission of the IOC," Lausanne, 22 May 1951, Brundage Papers, Box 90.

38. Edström to Brundage, 14 November 1950, Brundage Papers, Box 43.

39. *The New York Times,* 9 February 1952.

40. Mayer, *A travers les anneaux olympiques,* p. 208.

41. Circular, Edström to members of the Executive Commission, 10 June 1952, and letter, Brundage to Edström, 16 June 1952, Brundage Papers, Box 43.

42. Jonathan Kolatch, *Sports, Politics and Ideology in China* (New York: Jonathan David Publications, 1972), p. 172.

43. Disabled American Veterans to Brundage, 17 July 1952, Brundage Papers, Box 120.

44. David B. Kanin, "The Role of Sport in the International System," paper presented at the Annual Convention of the International Studies Association, Toronto, Canada, February 25-29, 1976, p. 3.

45. Brundage to Edström, 21 January 1947, Brundage Papers, Box 42.

46. Minutes of the Meeting of the Executive Commission with the National Olympic Committees," Oslo, 13 February 1952, Brundage Papers, Box 90.

47. *The New York Times,* 10 November 1956.

48. Lloyd Gardner, "The Dulles Years 1953-1959," in *From Colony to Empire—Essays in the History of American Foreign Relations,* ed. William Appleman Williams (New York: John Wiley and Sons, 1972), p. 389.

49. Robertson, *International Politics Since World War II,* p. 157.

50. Ibid., p. 186.

51. Mayer to Brundage, 14 March 1953, Brundage Papers, Box 46.

52. "Minutes of the Meeting of the 50th General Session of the IOC," Paris, June 1955, Brundage Papers, Box 91.

53. "Minutes of the Meeting of the 51st General Session of the IOC," Cortina de Ampezzo, 24-25 January, 1956, Brundage Papers, Box 91.

54. "Minutes of the Meeting of the 50th General Session of the IOC," Paris, June 1955, Brundage Papers, Box 91.

55. Kolatch, *Sports, Politics and Ideology in China,* p. 174.

56. Circular, no. 125, Mayer to IOC members, NOCs, IFs, the press, 5 September 1958, Brundage Papers, Box 70.

57. *The New York Times,* 15 May 1954.

58. Mayer, *A travers les anneaux olympiques,* p. 212.

59. *The New York Times,* 11 May 1954.

60. Brundage to Gun Sun Hoh (Taiwan committee president), 16 September 1954, Brundage Papers, Box 120.

61. England, France, and the United States issued the "Tripartite Declaration" in 1950 guaranteeing borders in the Middle East, and imposed an arms blockade in order to stabilize the area. See Robertson, *International Politics Since World War II,* p. 211.

62. In 1945, 46 national committees were recognized by the IOC. By 1956 that number had nearly doubled to 83. *The Olympic Directory* (Lausanne: International Olympic Committee, 1976).

63. Circular, no. 24, 30 January 1954, Brundage Papers, Box 70.

64. "Minutes of the Meeting of the 48th General Session of the IOC," Mexico City, 17-20 April 1953, Brundage Papers, Box 90.

65. Ibid.

66. Circular response, Bolanaki to Brundage regarding circular no. 167, 1960, Brundage Papers, Box 73.

67. Circular, Belgian Olympic Committee to NOCs, June 1952, Brundage Papers, Box 70.

68. Circular, Brundage to IOC members, NOCs, IFs, 24 June 1953, Brundage Papers, Box 70.

69. *The New York Times,* 13 September 1953.

70. Circular, no. 28, Brundage to IOC members, 12 April 1954, Brundage Papers, Box 70.

71. *The New York Times,* 17 February 1956.

72. Burghley (Exeter) to Brundage, 20 July 1956, Brundage Papers, Box 54.

73. "Minutes of the Meeting of the Executive Board of the IOC with delegates from the NOCs and IFs," Paris, 11 June 1955, Brundage Papers, Box 91.

74. "Minutes of the Meeting of the Executive Board of the IOC with delegates of the IFs," Lausanne, 4-5 May 1954, Brundage Papers, Box 91.

75. "Minutes of the Meeting of the Executive Board of the IOC with delegates of the NOCs and IFs," Paris, 11 June 1955, Brundage Papers, Box 91.

76. "Minutes of the Meeting of the Executive Board of the IOC," Melbourne, 17 November 1956, Brundage Papers, Box 91.

77. *The New York Times,* 30 October 1956.

78. Ibid., 17 August 1956 and 31 August 1956.

79. Ibid., 7 November 1956.

80. Mayer to Brundage, 28 October 1956, Brundage Papers, Box 47; "Minutes of the Meeting of the Executive Board of the IOC," Melbourne, 17 November 1956, Brundage Papers, Box 91.

81. *The New York Times,* 9 November 1956.

82. John Kieran and Arthur Daley, *The Story of the Olympic Games, 776 B.C.-1960 A.D.* (New York: J. B. Lippincott Co., 1961), pp. 316-317.

83. *The New York Times,* 17 November 1956.

84. Kieran and Daley, *The Story of the Olympic Games,* p. 318.

85. *The New York Times,* 3 April 1957.

86. Kieran and Daley, *The Story of the Olympic Games,* pp. 318-319.

4. *1956-1968*

1. The multinational corporation is not just a post-World War II phenomenon. It has been on the world scene since at least the beginning of the twentieth century. It has come into its own, however, only since World War II.

2. *The New York Times,* 13 July 1957.

3. Ibid., 6 September 1957.

4. Ibid., 18 September 1957.

5. Kolatch, *Sports, Politics, and Ideology in China,* p. 183.

6. Ibid., p. 186.

7. Robert C. North, *The Foreign Relations of China* (Encino, Calif: Dickenson Publishing Co., 1974), p. 90.

8. "Minutes of the Meeting of the 55th General Session of the IOC," Munich, 25-28 May 1959, Brundage Papers, Box 91.

9. Circular, no. 136, Brundage to IOC members, NOCs, IFs, 3 June 1959, Brundage Papers, Box 70.

10. *The New York Times,* 10 June 1959.

11. Circular, no. 138, Brundage to IOC members, 23 June 1959, Brundage Papers, Box 70.

12. *The New York Times,* 4 June 1959.

13. Copy of letter from Wilfred Kent Hughes to Otto Mayer, circa 1957-58, Brundage Papers, Box 120.

14. Exeter to Brundage, 30 July 1959, Brundage Papers, Box 54.

15. "Minutes of the Meeting of the Executive Board of the IOC," Paris, 2 October 1959, Brundage Papers, Box 91.

16. Kieran and Daley, *The Story of the Olympic Games,* p. 335.

17. "Minutes of the Meeting of the Executive Board of the IOC," Paris, 2 October 1959, Brundage Papers, Box 91.

18. Andrianov to Mayer, 18 January 1958, Brundage Papers, Box 50.

19. *The New York Times,* 23 November 1959.

20. "Minutes of the Meeting of the 56th General Session of the IOC," San Francisco, 15-16 February 1960, Annex 3, Brundage Papers, Box 91.

21. *The New York Times,* 19 February 1960.

22. Bruce M. Russett, *Trends in World Politics* (New York: The MacMillan Co., 1965), p. 77.

23. Robertson, *International Politics Since World War II,* p. 269.

24. Ibid., p. 261.

25. "Minutes of the Meeting of the Executive Board of the IOC with the NOCs," Rome, 19 May 1959, Brundage Papers, Box 91.

26. Richard Edward Lapchick, *The Politics of Race and International Sport* (Westport, Conn: Greenwood Press, 1975), p. 26.

27. "Minutes of the Meeting of the 55th General Session of the IOC," Munich, 25-28 May 1959, Brundage Papers, Box 91.

28. International Olympic Committee, *Speeches of President Avery Brundage 1952-1968* (Lausanne: International Olympic Committee, speech for the opening session of the 55th General Session of the IOC held in Munich, 23 May 1959, p. 43.

29. Circular, Brundage to IOC members, 25 April 1958, Brundage Papers, Box 70.

30. Copy of Brundage statement on the proposed tax, Exeter to Brundage, 10 October 1957, Brundage Papers, Box 54.

31. Circular, Brundage to IOC members, 25 April 1958, Brundage Papers, Box 70.

32. Exeter to Brundage, 10 August 1957, Brundage Papers, Box 54.

33. Exeter to Brundage, 10 August 1957, Brundage Papers, Box 54.

34. *The New York Times,* 13 September 1953.

35. In 1912, £ = about $5. Circular, no. 120, Brundage and Mayer to IFs, 8 May 1958, Brundage Papers, Box 70.

36. Extrapolated from the share received by the IOC—5% or $60,000. "Minutes of the Meeting of the Executive Board of the IOC," Rome, 19 August 1960, Brundage Papers, Box 91.

37. Rome Organizing Committee, *Official Report of the Rome Organizing Committee 1960* (Rome: Rome Committee, 1961), pp. 661-663.

38. "Minutes of the Meeting of the 55th General Session of the IOC," Munich, 25-28 May 1959, Annex, Brundage Papers, Box 91.

39. "Minutes of the Meeting of the Executive Board of the IOC with the delegates of the NOCs," Rome, 19 May 1959, Brundage Papers, Box 91.

40. Exeter to Brundage, 11 January 1960, Brundage Papers, Box 54.

41. Exeter to Mayer, 26 April 1962, Brundage Papers, Box 54.

42. Circular response to circular no. 167, Erik Von Frenchell of Finland, 1960, Brundage Papers, Box 73.

43. Dryssen (president of the Pentathalon Federation) to Brundage, 10 September 1959, Brundage Papers, Box 54.

44. Robert Legvold, *Soviet Policy in West Africa* (Cambridge: Harvard University Press, 1970), pp. 29-31.

45. Tokyo Organizing Committee, *Official Report of the Organizing Committee for the '64 Summer Games* (Tokyo: Tokyo Organizing Committee, 1965), vol. 1, p. 66.

46. Spanier, *American Foreign Policy Since World War II,* p. 169.

47. Ibid., p. 170.

48. *The New York Times,* 5 March 1962.

49. Circular, statement of IOC to all NOCs, IFs, IOC members, the press, 26 March 1962, Brundage Papers, Box 70.

50. Circular, to Allied Travel Office, 17 April 1962, Brundage Papers, Box 70.

51. Circular reply, 31 May 1962, Brundage Papers, Box 70.

52. Circular, no. 266, to IFs, NOCs, and IOC members, 9 July 1964, Brundage Papers, Box 70.

53. Ibid.

54. "Minutes of the Meeting of the 62nd General Session of the IOC," Tokyo, 6-8 October 1964, Brundage Papers, Box 92.

55. Schoebel (GDR committee president) to IOC members, Brundage Papers, Box 129.

56. Exeter to Mayer, 25 November 1963, Brundage Papers, Box 54.

57. The Asian Games are regional Games begun after World War II. They operate under IOC auspices, are allowed to use the Olympic name and insignia, and are conducted through national committees. Similar regional games are carried out under the same conditions all over the world between Olympic years. They are essentially regional Olympics, but not in an Olympic year.

58. Circular, no. 268, to IFs, 9 July 1964, Brundage Papers, Box 70.

59. *The New York Times,* 15 February 1963.

60. Kolatch, *Sports, Politics and Ideology in China,* p. 191.

61. Ibid., p. 190.

62. Ibid., pp. 195-196.

63. Ibid., p. 191.

64. Modelski, *The New Emerging Forces,* p. 90.

65. "Minutes of the Meeting of the 60th General Session of the IOC," Baden-Baden, 16-20 October 1963, Brundage Papers, Box 92.

66. "Minutes of the Meeting of the Executive Board of the IOC with delegates of the NOCs," Tokyo, 3 October 1964, Brundage Papers, Box 92.

67. Brundage to Exeter, 28 November 1964, Brundage Papers, Box 55.

68. Lapchick, *The Politics of Race and International Sport,* p. 44.

69. "Minutes of the Meeting of the Executive Board of the IOC with the Amateur Commission of the IOC," 2-3 March 1962, Brundage Papers, Box 92.

70. Lapchick, *The Politics of Race and International Sport,* p. 45.

71. "Minutes of the Meeting of the 59th General Session of the IOC," Moscow, 5-8 June 1962, Brundage Papers, Box 92.

72. Alexander to Mayer, 23 May 1961, Brundage Papers, Box 50.

73. Alexander to Brundage, 16 July 1963, Brundage Papers, Box 50.

74. Alexander to Executive Board members of IOC, 31 July 1963, Brundage Papers, Box 50.

75. Alexander to Brundage, 22 August 1963, Brundage Papers, Box 50.

76. Lapchick, *The Politics of Race and International Sport,* p. 52.

77. Ibid., p. 53.

78. "Minutes of the Meeting of the Executive Board of the IOC," Innsbruck, 25-26 January 1964, Brundage Papers, Box 92.

79. Ibid.

80. Lapchick, *The Politics of Race and International Sport,* p. 65.

81. Ibid., p. 66.

82. Circular, no. 214, Beaumont to IOC members, 18 January 1963, Brundage Papers, Box 70.

83. "Minutes of the Meeting of the Executive Board of the IOC with the IFs," 6 June 1963, Brundage Papers, Box 92.

84. Beaumont to Brundage, 28 August 1963, Brundage Papers, Box 51.

85. Exeter to Mayer, 26 April 1962, Brundage Papers, Boz 54.

86. "Minutes of the Meeting of the Executive Board of the IOC," Athens, 15 June 1961, Brundage Papers, Box 92.

87. Mayer to Chinese NOC (Taiwan), 16 April 1964, Brundage Papers, Box 120.

88. *The New York Times,* 9 February 1964.

89. Ibid., 31 August 1964.

90. "Minutes of the Meeting of the IFs," Lausanne, 5 June 1963, Brundage Papers, Box 92.

91. *The New York Times,* 24 April 1964.

92. Ibid., 23 July 1964.

93. Ibid., 11 October 1964.

94. "Minutes of the Meeting of the Executive Board of the IOC with the delegates of the NOCs," 4 October, 1965, Annex 11, Brundage Papers, Box 92.

95. "Minutes of the Meeting of the Executive Board of the IOC," 5-8 October 1965, Brundage Papers, Box 92.

96. "Minutes of the Meeting of the 64th General Session of the IOC," Rome, 25-28 April 1966, Brundage Papers, Box 93.

97. Ibid.

98. "Minutes of the Meeting of the Executive Board of the IOC," Mexico City, 22 October 1966, Brundage Papers, Box 93.

99. Andrianov to Brundage, 22 November 1966, Brundage Papers, Box 50.

100. Brundage to Andrianov, 5 December 1966, Brundage Papers, Box 50.

101. Lapchick, *The Politics of Race and International Sport,* pp. 75-77.

102. "Minutes of the Meeting of the Executive Board of the IOC with delegates of the IFs," 6 June 1963, Brundage Papers, Box 92.

103. Andrianov to IOC Chancellory, 1 March 1966, Brundage Papers, Box 50.

104. "Minutes of the Meeting of the Executive Board of the IOC," Mexico City, 22 October 1966, Brundage Papers, Box 93.

105. Circular, no. 312, from All African Subcommittee of the IOC to IOC members, Report, 23 April 1966, Brundage Papers, Box 71.

106. Lapchick, *The Politics of Race and International Sport,* p. 80.

107. Ibid., p. 84.

108. Ibid.

109. Ibid., p. 86.

110. *The New York Times,* 12 April 1967.

111. Lapchick, *The Politics of Race and International Sport,* pp. 86-88.

112. "Minutes of the Meeting of the Executive Board of the IOC with delegates of the NOCs," Teheran, 3 May 1967, Brundage Papers, Box 93.

113. "Minutes of the Meeting of the Executive Board of the IOC," 11-13 April 1965, Brundage Papers, Box 92.

114. Lapchick, *The Politics of Race and International Sport,* p. 97.

115. Ibid., p. 96.

116. *The New York Times,* 24 July 1967.

117. Ibid., 15 December 1967.

118. Lapchick, *The Politics of Race and International Sport,* p. 96.

119. Ibid., p. 104.

120. Ibid., p. 108.

121. Ibid., p. 109.

122. "Minutes of the Meeting of the 66th General Session of the IOC," Grenoble, 1-5 February 1968, Annex 6, Brundage Papers, Box 93.

123. Ibid.

124. *The New York Times,* 16 February 1968.

125. Lapchick, *The Politics of Race and International Sport,* p. 112.

126. Ibid., p. 113.

127. *The New York Times,* 25 February 1968.

128. Ibid., 27 February 1968.

129. Ibid., 28 February 1968.

130. Ibid., 7 March 1968.

131. Lapchick, *The Politics of Race and International Sport,* p. 104.

132. *The New York Times,* 10 March 1968.

133. Lapchick, *The Politics of Race and International Sport,* p. 119.

134. "Minutes of the Meeting of the Executive Board of the IOC," 21 April 1968, Brundage Papers, Box 93.

135. *The New York Times,* 22 April 1968.

136. Ibid.

137. Ibid., 8 June 1968.

138. Ibid.

139. Circular Response, Burghley to Brundage, regarding circular no. 16 on Rule 25 of IOC Charter, 9 September 1953, Brundage Papers, Box 73. Emphasis is mine.

140. "Minutes of the Meeting of the Executive Board of the IOC with the delegates of the NOCs," Mexico City, 3-5 October 1968, Brundage Papers, Box 93.

141. *The New York Times,* 6 February 1968.

142. Ibid., Editorial, Lloyd Garrison, "African Shock Waves," 28 February 1968, p. 57.

143. Peter H. Merkl, *German Foreign Policies, West and East: On the Threshold of a New European Era* (Santa Barbara, Calif: CLIO Press, 1974), p. 121.

144. Andrianov to Brundage, 31 May 1965, Brundage Papers, Box 50.

145. Comment by Exeter on German question in *The Observer,* 25 April 1965, Brundage Papers, Box 129.

146. "Minutes of the Meeting of the 63rd General Session of IOC," Madrid, 7-9 October 1965, Brundage Papers, Box 92.

147. *The New York Times,* 7 October 1965.

148. "Minutes of the Meeting of the 63rd General Session of the IOC," Madrid, 7-9 October 1965, Brundage Papers, Box 92.

149. "Minutes of the Meeting of the 67th General Session of the IOC," Mexico City, 7-11 October 1968, Brundage Papers, Box 93.

150. Statement of the Olympic committee of the DPRK, 12 October 1968, circular, no. 457, 12 December 1968, Brundage Papers, Box 71.

151. "Minutes of the Meeting of the 67th General Session of the IOC," Mexico City, 7-11 October 1968, Brundage Papers, Box 93.

152. Ibid.

153. Those present included: Albania, Arab Palestine, Bulgaria, Cambodia, Ceylon, China, Cuba, Czechoslovakia, the Dominican Republic, Finland, the German Democratic Republic, Guinea, Hungary, Indonesia, Iraq, Italy, the Democratic People's Republic of Korea, Laos, Mongolia, Pakistan, Poland, Syria, Somali, the USSR, the UAR, the Democratic Republic of Vietnam, Yemen, Lebanon, the South African Non-Racial Olympic Committee; observers were: Afghanistan, Algeria, the Central African Republic, Congo (Brazzaville), France, Mali, Mauritania, Nepal, Rumania, Sudan, Tanzania, Uganda, and Morocco. See Kolatch, *Sports, Politics and Ideology in China,* p. 197.

154. Ibid., p. 198.

155. Circular, no. 322, to IFs and NOCs, 17 June 1966, Brundage Papers, Box 71.

156. "Minutes of the Meeting of the Executive Board of the IOC," Mexico City, 30 September-6 October 1968, Brundage Papers, Box 93.

157. Kanin, *The Role of Sport in International Relations,* p. 212.

158. Ibid.

159. "Minutes of the Meeting of the Executive Board of the IOC," Mexico City, 22 October 1966, Brundage Papers, Box 93.

160. Kanin, *The Role of Sport in International Relations,* p. 212.

161. Exeter to Brundage, 7 December 1964, Brundage Papers, Box 55.

162. "Minutes of the Meeting of the 63rd General Session of the IOC," Madrid, 7-9 October 1965, Brundage Papers, Box 92.

163. *The New York Times,* 2 March 1968.

164. Circular, no. 314, Jones (Secretary of ICSPE and FIBA, the international basketball federation, to IOC, 23 April 1966, Brundage Papers, Box 71.

165. "Minutes of the Meeting of the 63rd General Session of the IOC," Madrid, 7-9 October 1965, Brundage Papers, Box 92.

166. "Minutes of the Meeting of the Executive Board of the IOC," Mexico City, 22 October 1966, Brundage Papers, Box 93.

167. "Minutes of the Meeting of the Executive Board of the IOC with delegates of the IFs," 23 April 1966, Annex 2, Brundage Papers, Box 93.

168. "Minutes of the Meeting of the Executive Board of the IOC with delegates of the IFs," 12 April 1965, Brundage Papers, Box 92.

169. Ibid.

170. Circular, no. FML/404, to IFs and NOCs, 29 February 1968, Brundage Papers, Box 71.

171. Exeter to Brundage, 2 September 1968, Brundage Papers, Box 55.

172. Circular, no. FML/404, to IFs and NOCs, 29 February 1968, Brundage Papers, Box 71.

173. "Minutes of the Meeting of the Executive Board of the IOC," 23 April 1966, Brundage Papers, Box 93.

174. "Minutes of the Meeting of the Executive Board of the IOC," 21-24, April 1966, Brundage Papers, Box 93.

175. "Minutes of the Meeting of the Executive Board of the IOC," Mexico City, 22 October 1966, Brundage Papers, Box 93.

176. Brundage to Exeter, 11 April 1967.

177. "Minutes of the Meeting of the 66th General Session of the IOC," Grenoble, 1-5 February 1968, Brundage Papers, Box 93.

178. Brundage to Andrianov, 5 December 1966, Brundage Papers, Box 50.

179. "Minutes of the Meeting of the Executive Board of the IOC with the delegates of the NOCs," 3-5 October 1968, Brundage Papers, Box 93.

180. "Minutes of the Meeting of the Executive Board of the IOC," Mexico City, 30 September-6 October 1968, Brundage Papers, Box 93.

181. Circular, no. M/357, 17 April 1967, Brundage Papers, Box 71.

182. "Minutes of the Meeting of the Executive Board of the IOC," Teheran, 2-8 May 1967, Brundage Papers, Box 93.

183. Circular, no. M/357, 17 April 1967, Brundage Papers, Box 71.

184. Exeter to Brundage, 10 June 1965, Brundage Papers, Box 55.

185. *The New York Times,* 15 April 1966.

186. "Minutes of the Meeting of the Executive Board of the IOC," 16-17 December 1967, Brundage Papers, Box 93.

187. "Minutes of the Meeting of the Executive Board of the IOC," Grenoble, 29-31 January 1968, Brundage Papers, Box 93.

188. *The New York Times,* 4 February 1968.

189. Circular, no. AB/M/487, Brundage to IOC members, 26 April 1969, Brundage Papers, Box 71.

190. John Underwood, "No Goody Two-Shoes," *Sports Illustrated* 30(10) (10 March 1969), 14-23.

191. Ibid.

192. Jack Scott, *The Athletic Revolution* (New York: The Free Press, 1971), p. 87.

193. *The New York Times,* 18 October 1968.

194. Scott, *The Athletic Revolution,* p. 87.

195. Ibid.

196. Brundage to Exeter, 22 August 1968, Brundage Papers, Box 55.

197. *The New York Times,* 25 August 1968.

198. Ibid., 15 September 1968.

199. Markl, *German Foreign Policies, West and East,* p. 127.

5. *1968-1976*

1. Max Silberschmidt, *The United States and Europe, Rivals and Partners* (New York: Harcourt Brace Jovanovich, 1972), p. 179.

2. A primary reason for the United States' going off the gold standard was the excessive amount of dollar reserves held in countries throughout the world, notably in Europe, Japan, and the Middle East. The idea that every dollar was backed by an equal amount of gold was recognized as a mere fiction that weakened the dollar in the world money markets, produced unfavorable exchange rates for the dollar, and helped to boost the domestic inflation rate.

3. See Richard D. Mandell, *The Nazi Olympics* (New York: The Macmillan Co., 1971).

4. Lapchick, *The Politics of Race and International Sport,* p. 185.

5. Ibid., p. 140.

6. Ibid.

7. Ibid., pp. 138-142.

8. Ibid., p. 143.

9. *The New York Times,* 8 June 1969.

10. Lapchick, *The Politics of Race and International Sport,* p. 145.

11. *The New York Times,* 24 October 1969.

12. Lapchick, *The Politics of Race and International Sport,* p. 148.

13. *The New York Times,* 24 October 1969.

14. "Minutes of the Meeting of the Executive Board of the IOC with the delegates of the NOCs," 25-26 October 1969, Brundage Papers, Box 94.

15. *The New York Times,* 16 May 1970.

16. Lapchick, *The Politics of Race and International Sport,* pp. 155-178.

17. Ibid., p. 194.

18. *The New York Times,* 16 May 1970.

19. Statement, Exeter, 21 July 1972, Brundage Papers, Box 55.

20. *The New York Times,* 10 August 1972.

21. Exeter to Brundage (statement on Rhodesia by the IAAF, 5 April 1971), 3 September 1971, Brundage Papers, Box 55.

22. *The New York Times,* 17 August 1972.

23. Ibid., 19 August 1972.

24. Ibid., 21 August 1972.

25. Ibid., 22 August 1972.

26. Ibid., 23 August 1972.

27. Ibid., 8 April 1970.

28. Ibid., 26 April 1970.

29. Ibid., 27 April 1966.

30. Ibid., 8 April 1970.

31. Ibid., 9 May 1970.

32. Ibid.

33. Ibid., 13 May 1970.

34. Ibid.

35. Ibid., 24 May 1970.

36. Ibid., 13 May 1970.

37. Ibid., 28 November 1964.

38. Ibid., 13 September 1972.

39. Ibid.

40. Ibid., 20 September 1972.

41. *The Times* (London), 14 April 1973.

42. Circular response to circular no. 167, Erik Von Frenchell of Finland, 1960, Brundage Papers, Box 73.

43. The IOC had been trying for years to get states to enact laws to protect the Olympic name and symbols and to get an international convention on the subject. Some states had responded and did have laws against the illegal use of the Olympic name and symbols, but most did not. France was one of the latter.

44. Circular, no. AB/M/487, 26 April 1969, Brundage Papers, Box 71.

45. Ibid.

46. "Minutes of the Meeting of the Executive Board of the IOC, Report on Amateurism and Eligibility," 22-23 March 1969, Brundage Papers, Box 94.

47. Baron Pierre de Coubertin, "Why I revived the Olympic Games," *Fortnightly Review* 84 (1908), 112.

48. Circular, no. PS/614, to international press, 26 March 1971, Brundage Papers, Box 71.

49. *The New York Times,* 2 May 1971.

50. Ibid., 20 July 1971.

51. Ibid., 9 May 1971.

52. Circular, no. M/687/b, to IOC members, 10 February 1972, Brundage Papers, Box 71.

53. *The New York Times,* 31 January 1972.

54. Ibid., 9 February 1972.

55. Text of a speech delivered by the Malaysian delegate at the Executive Board meeting with the national Olympic committees on 24 October 1969, Dubrovnik, enclosed in a letter to Brundage from Khaw Kai-Bow, the Malaysian delegate, 2 April 1970, in response to circular, no. 544, Brundage Papers, Box 73.

56. Ibid.

57. Exeter to Brundage, 20 July 1970, Brundage Papers, Box 55.

58. Exeter to Brundage, 7 April 1969, Brundage Papers, Box 55.

59. Circular, no. C/M/544, 15 March 1970, Brundage Papers, Box 71.

60. "Minutes of the Meeting of the Executive Board of the IOC with the delegates of the NOCs," Dubrovnik, 25-26 October 1969, Brundage Papers, Box 94.

61. Circular response to no. 544, Khaw Kai-Bow to Brundage, 2 April 1970, Brundage Papers, Box 73.

62. *The New York Times,* 22 October 1972.

63. Circular, no. C/800, to NOCs, OC, IOC members, IFs, 16 May 1973, Brundage Papers, Box 72.

64. *Olympic Review,* no. 72-73 (November-December 1973), p. 475.

65. *The Times* (London), 2 October 1973.

66. Ibid., 5 October 1973.

67. Ibid., 4 October 1973.

68. *The New York Times,* 7 October 1973.

69. Rich Telander, "A Voice for those long silent," *Sports Illustrated* 42(26) (30 June 1975), 60.

70. *The New York Times,* 23 May 1973.

71. Ibid., 6 February 1973.

72. *The Times* (London), 3 October 1973.

73. Kanin, *The Role of Sport in International Relations,* p. 196.

74. *The Times* (London), 13 February 1973.

75. *The New York Times,* 22 March 1973.

76. *The Times* (London), 3 April 1973.

77. *The New York Times,* 23 May 1973.

78. *The Times* (London), 19 September 1973.

79. Ibid., 5 October 1973.

80. *The New York Times,* 4 October 1973.

81. *Olympic Review,* no. 72-73 (November-December 1973), p. 473.

82. *The New York Times,* 6 October 1973.

83. *The Times* (London), 11 February 1974.

84. *Olympic Review,* no. 76-77 (March-April 1974), p. 103.

85. Ibid., no. 80-81 (July-August 1974), p. 374.

86. *The Times* (London), 17 May 1974.

87. *The New York Times,* 19 July 1974.

88. Ibid., 18 April 1975.

89. *The Times* (London), 17 May 1975.

90. *Los Angeles Times,* 2 July 1976.

91. Frank Deford, "More Dark Clouds Over Montreal," *Sports Illustrated* 45(3) (19 July 1976), 33.

92. *Los Angeles Times,* 8 July 1976.

93. Ibid., 11 July 1976.

94. Ibid.

95. Ibid., 12 July 1976.

96. Ibid., 13 July 1976.

97. Deford, "More Dark Clouds Over Montreal," p. 34.

98. Canadian Embassy, Public Affairs Division, "Olympics and Taiwan," *Canada Report,* no. 4 (22 July 1976), p. 2.

99. *Los Angeles Times,* 15 July 1976.

100. WNET/WETA, "The Olympics and Politics," *The Robert MacNeil Report,* 16 July 1976, Show no. 1140, Library no. 209.

101. *Olympic Review,* no. 107-108 (September-October 1976), p. 460.

102. WNET/WETA, "The Olympics and Politics."

103. Ibid.

104. *Olympic Review,* no. 72-73 (November-December 1973), p. 543.

105. Ibid., no. 76-77 (March-April 1974), p. 94.

106. *The New York Times,* 7 December 1974.

107. *Olympic Review,* no. 87-88 (January-February 1975), p. 63.

108. Kanin, *The Role of Sport in International Relations,* p. 264.

109. Ibid., p. 265.

110. *The New York Times,* 11 April 1973.

111. Ibid., 23 May 1975.

112. *The Times* (London), 4 May 1976.

113. *The New York Times,* 23 May 1976.

114. *Los Angeles Times,* 10 July 1976.

115. *Sports Illustrated* 45(2) (12 July 1976), 8.

116. *The Times* (London), 29 May 1976.

117. *Sports Illustrated* 45(4) (26 July 1976), 17.

118. *Olympic Review,* statement of vice-president Mohamed Mzali, no. 107-108 (September-October 1976), pp. 463-464.

119. Ibid.

120. *Los Angeles Times,* 21 July 1976.

121. *The New York Times,* 23 August 1973.

122. Ibid., 27 August 1973.

123. Ibid., 12 September 1973.

124. Ibid., 13 September 1973.

125. Ibid., 24 October 1974.

126. Ibid.

127. Ibid., 15 September 1974.

128. *The Times* (London), 25 October 1974.

129. *Olympic Review,* no. 89-90 (March-April 1975), p. 79.

130. Kenny Moore, "Not on the Up and Up," *Sports Illustrated* 43(17) (27 October 1975), 17-19.

131. *The New York Times,* 14 February 1976.

132. *The Times* (London), 25 October 1974.

133. *Sports Illustrated* 45(3) (19 July 1976), 34.

134. *The New York Times,* 15 October 1974.

135. Ibid.

136. Ibid., 4 January 1973.

137. *The Times* (London), 20 May 1976.

138. *Moscow News,* no. 38, 1976.

139. William Oscar Johnson, "A Contract with the Kremlin," *Sports Illustrated* 45(9) (21 February 1977), 19.

Conclusion

1. *Olympic Review,* no. 76-77 (March-April 1974), p. 92.

2. Ibid., no. 85-86 (November-December 1974), pp. 572-574.

3. Mayer, *A travers les anneaux olympiques,* pp. 212-220.

4. *Los Angeles Times,* 23 July 1976.

5. See Graham T. Allison, *Essence of Decision, Explaining the Cuban Missile Crisis* (Boston: Little, Brown and Co., 1971), chapter 3, for a discussion of organizational theory and procedures.

6. Witness the first World Cup track and field competition held in Dusseldorf in 1977. Sponsored by the IAAF, this was the first world championship in track and field to be held in other than an Olympic year. The World Cup was structured along regional lines rather than by nation-states. Thus there were the contingents of Europe, East Germany, West Germany, Africa, the United States, America (comprising Canada and South America).

Epilogue, 1976-1980

1. *The Times* (London), 24 June 1977.
2. *The New York Times,* 28 August 1976.
3. *The Times* (London), 27 January 1977.
4. Ibid., 30 March 1977.
5. Ibid., 9 June 1977.
6. Ibid., 16 June 1977.
7. *Olympic Review,* no. 125-126 (March-April 1978), p. 189.
8. *The Times* (London), 25 July 1977.
9. Ibid., 27 April 1978.
10. Ibid., 23 March 1978.
11. Ibid., 27 July 1978.
12. *The Daily Telegraph,* 15 April 1979.
13. Ibid., 28 July 1979.
14. Ibid., 27 September 1979.
15. *The Times* (London), 15 November 1979.
16. *The Daily Telegraph,* 23 October 1979.
17. *The Times* (London), 17 November 1979.
18. Ibid., 19 December 1979.
19. Ibid., 24 December 1979.
20. Ibid., 14 December 1979.
21. Ibid., 27 July 1978.
22. Ibid., 21 September 1977.
23. *The New York Times,* 21 September 1977.
24. *The Times* (London), 21 September 1977.
25. Ibid., 27 January 1978.
26. *The New York Times,* 21 May 1978.
27. Ibid., 1 December 1978.
28. *The Times* (London), 28 October 1978.
29. *Hearings Before the House Committee on Foreign Affairs,* 96th Congress, First Session, 7-8 February 1979, p. 12.
30. *Olympic Review,* no. 137 (March 1979), p. 139.
31. *The Times* (London), 26 November 1979.
32. *The New York Times,* 8 April 1979.
33. *Olympic Review,* no. 141-142 (July-August 1979), p. 403.
34. Ibid., no. 145 (November 1979), p. 628.
35. *The New York Times,* 27 November 1979.
36. Ibid., 10 February 1980.
37. Ibid., 12 February 1980.
38. *Los Angeles Times,* 15 January 1980.
39. Ibid., 12 January 1980.
40. *The New York Times,* 5 January 1980.
41. *U.S. News and World Report,* 88 (21 January 1980), p. 18.

42. *The New York Times,* 12 January 1980.

43. *Newsweek,* XCV(4) (28 January 1980), p. 21.

44. *The New York Times,* 7 January 1980.

45. Ibid., 4 January 1980.

46. Ibid., 21 January 1980.

47. Ibid.

48. Ibid., 16 January 1980.

49. Ibid., 5 February 1980.

50. Ibid., 8 February 1980.

51. Ibid., 5 February 1980.

52. Ibid., 6 February 1980. The members of the executive council included members from the national Olympic committees of Mexico, Sweden, Nigeria, Kuwait, New Zealand, Bahamas, Dutch Antilles, Puerto Rico, Bulgaria, Great Britain, Lichtenstein, Sudan, Cameroon, Ethiopia, India, Malaysia, Japan, Australia and Fiji.

53. *Los Angeles Times,* 6 February 1980.

54. *The New York Times,* 27 January 1980.

55. *Olympic Review,* no. 149 (March 1980), p. 106.

56. Ibid., no. 147-148 (January-February 1980), p. 37.

57. *Los Angeles Times,* 11 February 1980.

58. *The New York Times,* 19 March 1980.

59. Ibid., 26 March 1980.

60. Ibid., 29 March 1980.

61. *Los Angeles Times,* 23 March 1980.

62. Ibid., 29 July 1980.

63. *Olympic Review,* no. 151 (May 1980).

64. *Los Angeles Times,* 20 July 1980.

65. *The Times* (London), 5 August 1980.

66. *The New York Times,* 26 January 1980.

67. Ibid., 21 January 1980.

68. *Los Angeles Times,* 12 May 1980.

69. *The New York Times,* 18 February 1980.

70. *Olympic Review,* no. 151 (May 1980), p. 273.

71. *Los Angeles Times,* 28 July 1980.

72. *The New York Times,* 21 January 1980.

73. *Olympic Review,* no. 152-153 (June-July 1980), p. 318.

BIBLIOGRAPHY

Bibliography

BOOKS

Allison, Graham T. *Essence of Decision: Explaining the Cuban Missile Crisis*. Boston: Little, Brown and Co., 1971.

Bunting, G. R., and Lee, M. J., eds. *The Evolution of the United Nations*. New York: Pergamon Press, 1964.

Deutsch, Karl W. *Nationalism and Social Communication: An Inquiry into the Foundations of Nationality*. New York: John Wiley and Sons, 1953.

Galtung, Johan. *The European Community: A Superpower in the Making*. London: George Allen and Unwin, 1973.

Gardner, Richard N. *Sterling-Dollar Diplomacy: Anglo-American Collaboration in the Reconstruction of Multilateral Trade*. Oxford: Clarendon Press, 1956.

Goodhart, P., and Chataway, C. *War Without Weapons*. London: W. H. Allen, 1968.

Haas, Ernest B. *The Uniting of Europe: Political, Social and Economic Forces 1950-1957*. Stanford, Calif.: Stanford University Press, 1958.

Hart, M. Marie, ed. *Sport in the Socio-Cultural Process*. Dubuque, Iowa: Wm. C. Brown Co., 1972.

Henry, Bill. *An Approved History of the Olympic Games*. New York: G. P. Putnam's Sons, 1948.

Hinsley, F. H. *Nationalism and the International System*. Dobbs Ferry, New York: Oceana Publications, 1973.

Kaplan, Morton A. *System and Process in International Politics*. New York: John Wiley and Sons, 1957.

Keohane, Robert O., and Nye, Joseph S. Jr., eds. *Transnational Relations and World Politics*. Cambridge: Harvard University Press, 1971.

Kieran, John, and Daley, Arthur. *The Story of the Olympic Games: 776 B.C.-1960 A.D.* New York: J. B. Lippincott Co., 1961.

Kolatch, Jonathan. *Sports, Politics and Ideology in China.* New York: Jonathan David Publications, 1972.

Lapchick, Richard Edward. *The Politics of Race and International Sport.* Westport, Conn.: Greenwood Press, 1975.

Legvold, Robert. *Soviet Policy in West Africa.* Cambridge: Harvard University Press, 1970.

Mandell, Richard D. *The Nazi Olympics.* New York: The Macmillan Co., 1971.

Mayer, Otto. *A travers les anneaux Olympiques.* Geneva: Pierre Cailler, 1960.

Merkl, Peter H. *German Foreign Policies, West and East: On the Threshold of a New European Era.* Santa Barbara, Calif.: CLIO Press, 1974.

Modelski, George. *Principles of World Politics.* New York: The Free Press, 1972.

————, ed. *The New Emerging Forces: Documents on the Ideology of Indonesian Foreign Policy.* Canberra: Department of International Relations, The Australian National University, 1963.

Morgenthau, Hans Joachim. *Politics Among Nations: The Struggle for Power and Peace.* New York: Alfred A. Knopf, 1948.

North, Robert C. *The Foreign Relations of China.* Encino, Calif.: Dickenson Publishing Co., 1974.

Nye, Joseph S. Jr., ed. *International Regionalism.* Boston: Little, Brown and Co., 1968.

Palmer, R. R., and Colton, Joel. *A History of the Modern World.* New York: Alfred A. Knopf, 1971.

Robertson, Charles L. *International Politics Since World War II: A Short History.* New York: John Wiley and Sons, 1966.

Rosenau, James N., ed. *International Politics and Foreign Policy.* New York: The Free Press, 1961, 1969.

————, ed. *Linkage Politics: Essays on the Convergence of National and International Systems.* New York: The Free Press, 1969.

Russett, Bruce M. *Trends in World Politics.* New York: The Macmillan Co., 1965.

Scott, Jack. *The Athletic Revolution.* New York: The Free Press, 1971.

Silberschmidt, Max. *The United States and Europe: Rivals and Partners.* New York: Harcourt Brace Jovanovich, 1972.

Spanier, John W. *American Foreign Policy Since World War II.* New York: Praeger Publishers, 1971.

Vernon, Raymond. *Sovereignty at Bay: The Multinational Spread of U.S. Enterprises.* New York: Basic Books, 1971.

Waltz, Kenneth N. *Man, the State, and War: A Theoretical Analysis.* New York: Columbia University Press, 1954.

Williams, William Appleman, ed. *From Colony to Empire: Essays in the History of American Foreign Relations.* New York: John Wiley and Sons, 1972.

MAGAZINES, NEWSPAPERS, AND JOURNALS

Avery, William P., and Cochrane, James D. "Subregional Integration in Latin America: The Andean Common Market." *Journal of Common Market Studies* 11(2) (December 1972), 85-102.

Cable, Vincent. "The 'Football War' and the Central American Common Market." *International Affairs* (London) 45 (October 1969), 658-671.

Coubertin, Baron Pierre de. "The Re-establishment of the Olympic Games." *The Chautauquan* 19(6) (September 1894), 696-700.

———. "Why I Revived the Olympic Games." *Fortnightly Review* 84 (1908), 110-115.

Daily Telegraph, 1979.

Los Angeles Times, 1976-1980.

Moscow News 38, 1976.

New York Times, 1945-1980.

Newsweek, 1980.

Riordan, James. "Soviet Sport and Soviet Foreign Policy." *Soviet Studies* 26 (July 1974), 322-343.

Singer, J. David, and Wallace, Michael. "Intergovernmental Organization in the Global System 1815-1964." *International Organization* 24(2) (Spring 1970), 239-288.

Sports Illustrated, 1954-1977.

The Times (London), 1973-1980.

U.S. News and World Report, 1980.

"X" (Kennan, George F.). "The Sources of Soviet Conduct." *Foreign Affairs Quarterly* 25(4) (July 1947), 566-582.

OLYMPIC MATERIALS

Comite International Olympique. *Speeches of President Avery Brundage: 1952-1968.* Lausanne: Comite International Olympique, 1968.

———. *The Olympic Directory.* Lausanne: Comite International Olympique, 1976.

The Olympic Review, 1972-1980.

Rome Organizing Committee. *Official Report of the Rome Organizing Committee, 1960.* Rome: Rome Organizing Committee, 1961.

Tokyo Organizing Committee. *Official Report of the Tokyo Organizing*

Committee, 1964. Tokyo: Tokyo Organizing Committee, vol. 1 and 2, 1965.

Urbana, Illinois. University of Illinois. Avery Brundage Papers.

OTHER SOURCES

Canadian Embassy, Public Affairs Division, "Olympics and Taiwan." *Canada Report* 4 (22 July 1976): 1-4.

Fuoss, Donald E. "An Analysis of the Invidents in the Olympic Games from 1924 to 1948, with Reference to the Contribution of the Games to International Goodwill and Understanding." Ph.D. diss., Teachers College, Columbia University, 1951.

Greenspan, Bud. "The Olympiad: The African Athlete." Cappy Productions. New York: WNET/13, Educational Broadcasting Corporation, 1976.

Hearings Before the House Committee on Foreign Affairs, 96th Congress, First Session, 7-8 February 1979.

Kanin, David Benjamin. "The Role of Sport in International Relations." Ph.D. diss., Fletcher School of Law and Diplomacy, Tufts University, 1976.

———. "The Role of Sport in the International System." Paper presented at the Annual Convention of the International Studies Association, Toronto, Canada, 25-29 February 1976.

Katzenstein, Peter J. "The Last Old Nation: Austrian National Consciousness since 1945." Paper presented to the Annual Meeting of The American Political Science Association, San Francisco, California, 2-5 September 1975.

WNET/WETA. "The Olympics and Politics." *The Robert MacNeil Report.* Show no. 1140, Library no. 209, 16 July 1976.

INDEX

Index